This map is based on the information taken from © Her Majesty the Queen in Right of Canada with permission of Energy Mines and Resources Canada.

D1052821

The Guiding Spirit

Frontispiece: Ernest Feuz on Asulkan Ridge
E.C. Porter photograph.

The Guiding Spirit

Andrew J. Kauffman
William L. Putnam

FOOTPRINT

©Andrew J. Kauffman
   William L. Putnam   1986

All rights reserved.
This book or any part thereof may not be reproduced in any form whatsoever,
whether by graphic, visual, electronic, film or micro-film, tape recording or
any other means except in the case of brief passages embodied in critical
reviews and articles, without the express written consent of the publisher.

ISBN 0-9691621-2-X

Kauffman, Andrew J. (Andrew John)
The Guiding Spirit

Includes index.
Bibliography: p.
ISBN 0-9691621-2-X

1. Mountaineering — Rocky Mountains, Canadian — History.
2. Rocky Mountains, Canadian — Description and travel. I. Putnam, William L.
(William Lowell) II. Title.

FC219.K39 1986   917.11   C86-090244-7
F1090.K39 1986

Printed in Canada by D.W. Friesen and Sons Ltd., Altona, Manitoba.

Typesetting by Walford & Foy, Calgary, Alberta.

Design by Catherine Garden.

Published by Footprint Publishing
            Box 1830
            Revelstoke, British Columbia V0E 2S0

CONTENTS

PREFACE AND ACKNOWLEDGEMENTS

This narrative is drawn from many sources: numerous personal conversations with Edward Feuz, Jr. around whose words and life this entire fabric is built; interviews with his brother, Walter, and sisters-in-law, Elise and Joanna; Ed's daughters, Gertie and Hedye, his niece, Alice, and with our old friend, Ed's nephew, Sydney, and his industrious wife, Beda. The notes and memories of these conversations have been refreshed and greatly enhanced by taped interviews loaned by the Archives of the Canadian Rockies, and others made by Syd's daughter, Karen, who initiated this project independently, and whose groundwork has been indispensable.

Much information on early family history was given to us by Ed's sisters, Ida (who still lives, at this writing, in her father's house) and Clara, both of whom we interviewed at Interlaken; and a number of useful insights were provided by Otto Staeger, proprietor of the Hotel Staubbach at Lauterbrunnen. Ken Jones and Norman Brewster went over the whole manuscript, fleshing out important points and eliminating error. Hans and Margaret Gmoser, Polly Prescott, Louis Bergmann, Bill Field, Henry Hall and Lillian Gest have answered questions, corrected pages, recalled facts, supplied photographs and given us much of their time. They have all joined in a labor of love for a man whose vigorous life was an era in which they shared, and from whose keen memory and spirit we have all gained so much.

As with the predecessor volume to this, "THE GREAT GLACIER AND ITS HOUSE", there seems to be no end of the kind cooperation of Ted Hart and his associates at the Whyte Foundation in Banff, and Jim Shields and Dave Jones of the Corporate Archives of the Canadian Pacific Railway in Montreal. Our friend, Roger Laurilla, has once again helped immensely with the photographic chores.

Ed was a lovable egotist, a delightful storyteller, and gifted with a remarkable memory. Upon occasion, though, even his recollections were at slight variance with authoritative records. This narrative has been adjusted to conform with the facts in every significant aspect, although we have included a discussion on certain discrepancies as Appendix "E".

We have used the words of Edward, himself, to tell as much of this story as possible. In certain instances, though, his grammar and syntax have been altered to conform better with modern English usage. Ed's words had told us about his father and his early years, his good days, and his difficulties. Insofar as is consonant with a logical verifiable thread we have kept those words intact and in order.

Portions of this story can be glimpsed in the pages of an enormous variety of published material in alpine and other journals. We do not attest to the completeness of them all, nor to their accuracy as primary sources; in fact, some are notable for the opposite. But, for better or for worse, a judgement we leave to the reader, where pertinent, they are listed at the end of each chapter. A fuller bibliography of related material is given as Appendix "D".

Rather than burden the text with lengthy introductions of all the peripheral figures in this story, we have included further biographical data on all the "dramatis personae" as Appendix "A".

To have written this book in strict chronological order would have been tedious for the reader. Chronology has been preserved at the beginning and the conclusion. Much of the material, however, revolves around particular individuals, each with special merits, most of whose activities with Edward Feuz, Jr. span several decades. The authors decided, therefore, to present this material in episodic and anecdotal form in an effort to describe what life was like for a Swiss guide and settler in western Canada in the early 20th Century, rather than as a consecutive narrative. We have provided, in Appendix 'F' a strict chronology of alpine accomplishment in Canada for those who wish to examine him in that manner.

INTRODUCTION

This history has a very precise end point; April 13, 1981, in Golden, British Columbia, the day that closed the ninety-six year life of Edward Feuz, Jr. — our Uncle Ed.

The narrative should start at some point in the Twelfth Century when the high passes of the Alps were largely free of snow, and migrations from one major valley to another were more easily done by the herdsman ancestors of the present Swiss nation. Various families were involved in migrations from the Valais region, in the shadow of the Matterhorn and the drainage of the Rhone River, across the passes west of the Jungfrau and into the Lutschine valley, which drains though the Thunersee into the Rhine. The names of those families making the move into the high valleys of the Oberland are still to be found on both gravestones and storefronts, as well as throughout the literature of alpinism, for these were mountain people, first and foremost.

Though some of the sidelights are intriguing, they are not the subject of this book. Thus we pass over the centuries of adaptation in a cooling climate, to the economic realities of life in the high north-facing valleys. Before the profession of bergfuhrer came into being, these were the generations of farmers, wood cutters and dairymen in the uplands; while in the larger settlements men became shoemakers, wood carvers, and entered other trades and professions.

We pick up our thread in the mid-Nineteenth Century when Johannes Feuz married a girl from across the lake, Marianna Soltermann. Johannes and his brothers owned land above Interlaken, near the settlement of Gsteigwiler, just south of the Rutigrabe, and reaching down to the rushing Lutschine River. Above this home, beyond the fields and forests, rises the Schynige Platte, where younger sons still spend their summers tending the families' herds on the slate dotted alps below the big hotels. Johannes and his brothers were industrious folk, and like others, their barn had its share of cattle, but his father had given the family another claim to fame. They were specialized stone masons. Not for them was the prosaic of pavement or wall. Painstakingly with mallet and chisel, they carved out the combination fountain and horse troughs that presently abound in the area.

Their monuments are ubiquitous. In Gsteigwiler alone three of them still adorn public places. Others have withstood the test of time in Lauterbrunnen, Unterseen, Grindelwald and elsewhere in the Oberland. Sturdy, practical and artistic, the typical model contains two chambers through which the water flows. At one end is an upright from which projects a pipe fed from a nearby spring or rivulet. In summer geraniums grace the upright and hang down the sides. The troughs were carved from a single block of granite weighing ten to twelve tons in the raw state, requiring great effort merely to move. This mass was then shaped out by hand over a period of weeks, sometimes months. Such a task required much care and skill; a single misplaced blow could destroy a month's labor. Once finished, with side walls about fifteen centimeters thick, the trough segment, separate from the headpiece, has a residual weight of four to five tons. While considerably more portable, it is now more delicate, and thus needed careful handling from the quarry site, near the river, by sledge and wagon, to the spot where public demand had called for its placement. Johannes and his wife, Marianna, raised their family, including daughter, Suzanna, born in 1857, in a household of stone carvers whose work was known and sought throughout the district.

Meanwhile, up the wilder, white-water branch of the Lutschine (which means "valley of springs") in the settlement of Lauterbrunnen ("noisy stream"), a distant cousin, also named Johannes, gave the name, Edward, to the youngest child in his household, born in 1859. (See Appendix "B" for genealogical background)

The practice of guiding was now becoming respectable; to the point that it was inscribed on gravestones, entered into the Zivilstatsamt, and its practicioners licensed by the government. Tourism was big business in Switzerland, and growing, with Lauterbrunnen an early Oberland center, having been popularized a generation earlier by no less than Johann Goethe. Economically speaking, however, the magnificence of the local waterfalls was eclipsed in the Twentieth Century by the vaster view obtainable at Grindelwald.

However, to survive at the calling of bergfuhrer often meant going to where the customers were, rather than awaiting their arrival in the higher valleys. Thus it was that in the 1880's, before the railroad made for readier access to Lauterbrunnen and Grindelwald, Edward was in the habit of going down to Interlaken, the big city between the lakes of Brienz and Thun, where visitors came from all over the world to glimpse in luxury the famous mountains of the Oberland.

Watering trough at Lauterbrunnen in 1981, a product of the Gsteigwiler Feuz family. E. Broman photograph.

The old hotels in Interlaken where Edward Feuz, Senior solicited clients. E. Broman photograph.

Bergfuhrer — if good — were now highly respected, often sought after, even becoming world travellers in the employ of gentleman alpinists from several nations. Mostly, though, the more adventurous of these spoke English and found their favorite avocation enlarged by newly accessible areas in the Caucasus, Andes, New Zealand, Himalaya and North America.

The first professional mountain guides to be employed in North America were all Italians: Guiseppe Petigax and Lorenzo Croux of Courmayeur, Antonio Maguinaz and Andrea Pellissier of Valtournanche and Erminio Botta of Biella, all in the retinue of Luigi Amadeo of Savoia, Duke of the Abruzzi, whose successful expedition to Mount Saint Elias in 1896 became an Alaskan and mountaineering legend. The next summer, Professor H. B. Dixon followed his example and engaged Peter Sarbach to accompany him on several weeks of climbing in the "Canadian Alps". It was the obvious success of this particular act which prompted the Vaux brothers, distinguished amateur scientists of Philadelphia, to suggest again in 1898, that the Canadian Pacific Railway should engage some Swiss guides to be available for their patrons in the mountain regions the company was seeking to exploit.

This is the story of those men, who prided themselves not merely on being guides, but on being *Swiss guides*. These men carved out an unique niche in the loyalties they both earned and gave. Their words often indicated conflict, hardship and unhappiness; but their actions were those of persons engaged in a rewarding vocation, who had found an emotional satisfaction in life that few of us are privileged to enjoy.

Journals cited in the chapter references are abbreviated as follows:

AJ — *Alpine Journal* by the Alpine Club, London.

AAJ — *American Alpine Journal* by the American Alpine Club, New York.

App — *Appalachia* by the Appalachian Mountain Club, Boston.

Beaver — *Quarterly* of the Hudsons Bay Company, Winnipeg.

CAJ — *Canadian Alpine Journal* by the Alpine Club of Canada, Banff.

GJ — *Geographical Journal* by the Royal Geographical Society, London.

HM — *Harvard Mountaineering* by the Harvard Mountaineering Club, Cambridge.

LAJ — *Ladies Alpine Journal* by the Ladies Alpine Club, London.

AJ XV-74, Intercourse Between the Valais and Grindelwald in the 16th and 17th Centuries

AJ XIX-97, Mt Lefroy and Other Climbs in the Rockies

AAJ VII-455, Fuhrerbuch of Edward Feuz

CHAPTER
I

YOU'RE GOING TO CANADA SOON

"There's a land where the mountains are nameless
And the rivers all run God knows where
There are lives that are erring and aimless
And deaths that just hang by a hair
There are hardships that nobody reckons
There are valleys unpeopled and still
There's a land — Oh, it beckons and beckons
And I want to go back; and I will."
Robert Service, "The Spell of the Yukon"

The little man with the weather-beaten face, the sparkling blue eyes and the loud voice paused to refill his pipe. As he did so our eyes travelled around the living room. Everywhere we looked, on tables, desks, over the walls, interspersed as in an alpine museum with relics of ancient climbing equipment, were pictures of remote Canadian mountains and photographs of the famous men and women who had been the old fellow's clients in earlier days. Then inevitably, our eyes turned to something else, something huge, over the fireplace, surveying the surroundings. It was an enormous moosehead, by far the largest we'd ever seen, with antlers so wide they nearly spanned the room. We could hardly believe such a colossus, no doubt the relic of a vanished breed, could ever have browsed the mires and swamps of Western Canada. It was, indeed, as though we had been brought face to face with the ghost of Teddy Roosevelt's Wendigo. We would have loved to have asked about it, but we didn't dare.

Besides, the moose was not our concern, not yet, anyway. We were here in Golden, British Columbia, to interview our old friend, Edward Feuz, Jr., affectionately known as Uncle Ed, master of this house and, as we also knew, master of all the mountains, visible and invisible, within two hundred fifty kilometers of where we sat.

"My father was a summer guide. By trade he was a carpenter,

and most of the year he built houses with a broad axe from logs he cut in the forest. But he loved those Swiss Oberland mountains where he was born. He wanted to be in them as much as possible. Yet he had to earn a living — and he had no time for long vacations, So as soon as the snow melted and the mountain flowers began to bloom, he'd hire himself out as a mountain guide to take the tourists up to the summits and over the passes, and show them how beautiful and peaceful it was up there."

"I loved my father. I guess in a way I owe it to him for most of the wonderful life I've had these ninety-odd years, ever since I climbed my first mountain. He was a great person, my father — and the best of the guides."

Ed relit his pipe. "I'm ninety-five years old, you know," he started out; "and in that time I've forgotten more things than I remember. But I've got a pretty good picture of the important ones, especially about the mountains I've climbed and the people I've known — those I liked who were my friends, and a few no-good ones I'll never forget, either."

Ninety-five years old! He didn't look it, didn't act it, didn't sound it. The voice was clear, the words peppery, the memories opinionated. More like sixty, we thought.

"Yes, my father was a summer guide, the best. He had lots of clients, and he not only knew how to climb all the mountains, he also knew how to make friends who could find him more business; you know, public relations."

"What he'd do was buddy up to the concierge — that's the fellow who fixes everything up at hotels — arranges trips, boat rides, train tickets, gets you guides and porters, even a girl friend if you need one. Father knew every concierge in that line of hotels a mile long across Interlaken in the Oberland. That's how all the guides got their clients in the early days."

"The climbing season started when the cows were sent to the alps above timber to fatten up for the summer. It was quite a show, those cows. They all had bells that rang every time they lifted a hoof, and the young people always put flowers on the lead cow; then they were led to the high pastures where they stayed until the first snow fell up there. The cow boys and shepherds would sleep on straw in little huts high on the alplands. In the beginning that's where the tourists and the guides also stayed before a big climb. Everyone slept in the straw. But there was always plenty of good wholesome food — wonderful milk fresh from the cows, and cream, butter and cheese. All you had to bring was bread and wine, and maybe some chocolate or sausage for snacks. Those huts, they were the only shelters; the Alpine Club cabins came much later."

"Before my time, when my father was a boy, the tourists didn't even walk up to the alps. They'd ride in a chair which was carried on poles between two porters. Other people would haul the gear.

Ernest   Emil   Suzanna   E. Feuz   Ed Jr.   Ida Emma   Frieda
    Walter   Werner   Clara

Feuz family of 1903. Collection of E. Broman.

That way tourists could spend a week or more high in the mountains without working for it. Prices were very low in those days, too, so it was cheap."

"My father was from Lauterbrunnen, where they kept his family's records. I never saw them. He was not a rich man, and so were his people; mostly they'd been woodsmen, poachers, hunters, that sort of thing. My father's father, he'd been kind of a guide, but I never knew him. He was killed in an accident long before I was born. He'd gone to cut wood on a hillside, up on some bluffs and a branch of the tree he was chopping hit him when the tree fell and everything went over the cliff. His wife had to look after my father and uncle who were very small. In time they grew up and married. My parents had eight children; I was the oldest and that made me the boss. My uncle had only two, a daughter and my other cousin, Gottfried, who was about ten years older than me. He came to Canada with us in 1906 as a guide."

"My mother? She was a tiny woman — but strong. At the start we lived in her father's house (my other grandfather) in Gsteigwiler, out beyond the Rutigrabe, and that's where I was born. You had your babies at home in those days, not in the hospital."

"My grandfather was quite wealthy. He was a stone-mason, one

The home of Johannes Feuz, father of Suzanna, where Edward, Jr., was born in 1884. The view from these windows looks straight out to the Jungfrau. E. Broman photograph.

of the best. In those days stone-masons were the top of the building trades; they looked down on all the others, carpenters, plasterers, window-framers and all of them. To be a fine stone-mason took a lot of training, and you had to have a good eye, too, because this was more of an art than a craft. My grandfather was sort of born into the business. His people had been stone-masons as far back as anyone could trace. His four brothers, strong fellows like him, were stone-masons, too. They made those big beautiful stone horse troughs and fountains, all over the Oberland. They'd carve them out of a single slab of rock with their chisels, a very tricky job — one mistake and you have to start all over. You can still see their work in all the village squares, today. Those stone-masons were well paid — almost always they were the richest men in every mountain village, and even in some towns."

"Later on, my father moved to Aarmuehle — that's an old name for Interlaken — so he could be nearer to hotels and the clients; he could also be a carpenter there. You don't get rich as a carpenter or a guide, so father was always poor. I guess he should have been a stone-mason instead. But at least once in a while he'd give me a couple of francs pocket money. Besides, when I was growing up, I'd cut wood, sell leather and carry food for some of the neighbors and pick up a few extra cents that way. I was always careful about

Feuz family home in Interlaken. E. Broman photograph.

money; it isn't everything, but it can be precious — especially if you're hungry. That's why I always saved all the silver pieces I could until I could exchange them for a yellow piece that I'd hide under the mattress for a rainy day or a special celebration."

"My mother used to send me back to Gsteigwiler to my grandfather's place as soon as I was old enough to push a cart up the hill. He had a farm with cows, goats, milk, eggs and all kinds of vegetables. So I'd come back down to Mother with everything I could get into the cart."

"I remember my father's wine cellar — everyone else had one, too — with the bottles, mostly dry Swiss white wine, turned down so the corks wouldn't dry out. Whenever we wanted wine, we'd just pour it into a glass, right from an opened bottle in the cellar. If we had an important guest, father would pick out a special bottle or two, bring them upstairs, and there would be quite a party."

"I loved animals. I still do, mostly when I'm out hunting them. For a while I raised weasels in a root cellar back of the house — big white things, almost as large as a cat. But then they got into the potatoes and turnips and my parents made me get rid of them. I cried."

"We had a large family. I was a poor boy with a new brother or sister coming along almost every year for a while, and my mother

17

counted on me because my father was away a lot. I shopped and cleaned, scrubbed and polished. The only time I got away was in the summer when I'd go into the high pastures with another boy and we'd spend six weeks tending a herd of eighty goats. We'd bring the goats to the huts every evening where other boys from below would milk them and carry that milk down for the village people. In time, as they grew up, my brothers came to help; Emil, Ernest, Werner and Walter."

"Our house in Aarmuehle was pretty, but very simple. No modern frills like plumbing or electricity. I had to fetch the water from the community fountain, two pails at a time, every morning, which sometimes made me late for school. That was half a mile away, and we'd come home for lunch and I'd have to fetch another two buckets — every day, every month, every year."

"In summer I'd collect wood for the stove. It wasn't made of iron, just flagstones, and no cement, no binder. There were two holes on top where you cooked, and it had a pipe that led into the living room under the flags and then upstairs to keep the place warm in the winter."

"You want to know what started me climbing? My father, and that's why I'm so grateful to him. He opened my eyes to a wonderful life. One day he had a client for an easy climb, so he asked me to come along even though I was only a little boy. We went up to the Mutthornhutte, over the Tschingeltritt; it was late October, very cold and there were big icefields all around. The hut was above the glacier, so tiny you could hardly get in. Father cooked up powdered soup, packed like a sausage — Maggi, he called it, a German company. Then we put on warm slippers and slept in the hay." [NOTE — E-1]

"Next morning we crossed the glacier and climbed a small mountain, the Tschingelhorn; and went down the other side to a place called Kandersteg where we took the train back to Interlaken. It was my very first climb."

"When I was thirteen, my father took me up the Jungfrau, the most famous peak in the Oberland, over four thousand meters. We went up by Lauterbrunnen to the Rottalhutte, where we spent the night. We started for the summit at two in the morning, pitch dark. We roped up and Father went ahead, slowly up the glacier with the lantern, then the two clients, and I came last. I felt I was in a dream. At daybreak I could see the rocks ahead. They were shiny, like diamonds. 'It looks like little nails were here,' I said. 'Yes' Father replied, 'that's from nails in the shoes. Many people come here — it's like a trail.' "

"The sun rose and everything sparkled. We reached the cliffs, the toughest part, and I loved it, even the tricky places where they'd put in iron spikes so you could hang on. When I looked down I could see all the houses in Interlaken — just like little toys, they seemed."

"We went back on the snow, and just below the top came to a huge crevasse, blue ice, straight down and no bottom. Father went to the side, where it narrowed, but it was still wide. He took a great running leap and jumped over. Then he stuck his ice-axe deep into the snow, wrapped the rope around it and made the other fellows jump while he hauled in the slack around the axe handle. Then it was my turn, and I was scared. I hesitated and began to cry. Father got angry and gave a big pull on the rope and I had to go. I made it, but barely — I landed just on the edge, and I was so frightened I let go of my climbing stick. It went into the crevasse and I never found it. Father growled at me and told me I should never, never, NEVER drop my stick or my ice-axe, or anything else. And I never did — in all the years I guided for the Canadian Pacific."

" 'LITTLE BOY CLIMBS JUNGFRAU', that's what the paper said. My school teacher got hold of it; that's how she found out what I'd been up to for two days. She scolded me for climbing mountains and getting bad grades in school. I hated that teacher. My buddy, Rudolph, and I used to throw spitballs at her when she wasn't looking and stick out our tongues when her back was turned. But I hated that newspaper, too, for tattling on me. I never really liked publicity after that."

"It took years, but I finally got back at that teacher. When I got married in 1909 she came to the party with the manager of the hotel where we were celebrating. It turned out she was a friend of my wife's. I was a famous guide by then; I'd spent years in Canada and could speak good English. She thanked me for a beautiful evening. Then she asked; 'How are you getting along?' 'Madam,' I replied, 'I never did well in your school because you thought I was a numbskull and held me back. But since I left you, I've done alright in the world; but no thanks to you.' She never said a word; just stared."

"I'd had my fill of school from that teacher and my start at climbing thanks to my father; but I was a long way from being a guide, and an even longer way from Canada, which I'd hardly heard of except in class. It was my father who got me to Canada, but I was the one who decided I wanted to be a guide."

"Things had begun to happen with the Canadian Pacific. In 1886 they'd completed the first railroad across Canada. As you know, it went right through some of the most beautiful mountain country in the world. The management wanted customers and figured this was a great place for tourism, so they built a string of hotels; Glacier House, Field, Lake Louise. People heard about the mountains, but nobody'd been up any of them, which was an added attraction. They came from all over, mostly the United States, then England, some Canadians, too, to climb there. But there were no guides, nobody who'd been trained to go up mountains in a professional manner and look after others. Then one day in 1896, when a group of amateurs was trying to climb Mount Lefroy, near Lake Louise, for the first time, one of them fell off and was killed. His name was

Abbot and he'd had quite a lot of experience, even in the Alps, but he wasn't good enough; he was no guide. The accident caused a lot of talk and the Canadian Pacific worried it might get a bad name as a result." [Note — E-2]

"Then the next year two English chaps, Professor Dixon and Norman Collie, came over from Europe and brought a real guide with them, Peter Sarbach, from Saint Niklaus near Zermatt. Sarbach had no trouble on Lefroy or anywhere else. He showed everybody there was no substitute for trained guides. But he went home at the end of the season and never came back."

"It was Sarbach, though, who gave the push. The Canadian Pacific figured it might be good business to have a few real Swiss guides at its hotels in the summer season, people who could show others how to climb mountains and take care of themselves so as not to have accidents. But the Company didn't know how to go about finding the right guides, so they inquired through the Cook Agency, the big English travel outfit, which had offices all over the continent, even one in Interlaken."

"My father knew a rich English doctor who had retired to live in Interlaken and owned a big house on Alpenstrasse, even a boat on the lake. His name was Clarke and he knew all the big shots but never really learned the language, but he had a son, Charlie, who spoke good Swiss (in Ed's view, the language of his forbears was a distinct national tongue, though all linguists define it more properly as Swiss-German) and who loved the mountains. The Clarkes knew the people at the Cook Agency and since my father was now the chief guide in this part of the Oberland, when the request came to Cook, they went to Clarke and Charlie, who was always the interpreter, came to my father. Everyone got together in the fall of 1898 and they hammered out an agreement." [Note — E-3]

"In the Oberland in those days you never did anything important before you consulted your family. So before signing anything, my father got us all together, ten of us, and talked it all over with my mother. It would mean a separation of several months in summer, but it sounded like a good deal with steady pay, free travel back and forth, lodging and a chance to see a lot of new country and make first ascents. When he came back he'd be famous, so Father signed on. So did his friend, Christian Haesler. And the younger Clarke, Charlie, who was much nearer my age, he went along with them partly to help with the climbing, but also because he could speak English."

"I remember when they left. We all went over to the station and kissed our father goodbye. Mother cried a lot; she was worried about the long ocean crossing and all the distance, but she never said anything, just cried a lot for the first days."

"Haesler and my father went to Field, in the Rockies, then up to Glacier in the Selkirks. They were the first CPR guides, a real novelty. That summer they didn't have many climbing parties, but there weren't any more accidents, either. So the Company liked the idea and asked my father and Haesler back the next year, and then every year. Business picked up, so my father had to find more guides to come over, but he was always the boss. He made all the arrangements and if there was a fellow he didn't like, or who got out of hand, he'd tell the CPR and they would fire him."

"My father wanted me to be in the hotel business. 'That's where the money is,' he'd say, 'no one can ever make a decent living as a guide.' He wanted me to learn good French because it was important in the hotel business in those days. So, in 1900, between trips to Canada, and after I'd got my papers saying I'd spent nine years in school, father sent me to work for a Swiss farmer in a small town near Lausanne, in the Canton of Vaud where everyone spoke French. There were no real mountains, just hills and lots of farmland."

"I was barely out of school, but I had new pants, new shoes, and my mother cut a twig off a tree to make a cross on my new hat. 'Mother,' I said, 'What's that for? Can't you give me a flower instead?' 'Never mind,' she replied, 'Lausanne's a big city, and your new boss, the farmer, will be waiting at the station, and we've written him that's how he'll recognize you.' I got on the train — I'd never taken a long train ride alone before, just short ones around the Oberland. I was all alone, very excited and a little scared; this was my first time away from home and my parents. I was fifteen years old."

"The farmer, a tall, strong, large man, met me with his wife at the station. He spoke to me in Swiss-German. It was market day in Lausanne, very crowded. They took me to a tiny restaurant where we had rich split-pea soup. Don't ask me why, but I'll never forget that soup. After a while we loaded my stuff in their democrat, the farmer cracked his whip and the horses pulled us up through the hills to his place at a village called Bettens. They had four kids in their stone house, and a great big farm spread all over the hillside."

"I thought I'd have a room in the house; but no. The farmer took me to an outbuilding where they kept pigs; we climbed some stairs and went into a room with two beds. It was clean, a lot cleaner than you'd expect just above the pigs. The farmer pointed to one bed and said; 'That's yours. The other is for my wife's brother. He's German, and he sleeps there.' Then he left."

"I unpacked and looked around. Right over my bed was a huge cowbell with a wire attached which went out the window. 'Wonder what's that for?' I thought. Then the farmer came back and took me to the stable to show me my job. 'Did you see that big bell over your bed?' he asked. 'That's to wake you up in the morning. There's a wire across to my room, and when I wake up, you will, too.' "

"Well, every morning after that, rain or shine, that bell would ring me out of bed; it made a terrible racket. Things got so I dreamed

Farmhouse with courtyard in Bettens, 1983. D. Bidwell photograph.

of bells every night, and I've never liked the sound of a bell since."

"Those people, for over a year they worked me like a slave. Real martinets, they were. They had six or eight cows and some calves, and I had to tend the stables, clean everything with a hose, pile the manure just right, harness the horses and plow the fields, clear willow brush with an ox, pull up roots with a pick and shovel. I had to pile wheat in sheaves, criss-cross them on my back, and if I ever made a mistake and dropped them, that farmer gave me Hell. Every day I also had to carry the milk in a big aluminum tank and leave it at the store in town. I worked from dawn to dark, sometimes till ten or eleven at night, seven days a week, even Sundays; and then I had to sleep over all those pigs in the same room with that lousy Boche. They never gave me a day off."

"That farmer, he had two girls and a boy, kind of young; but they just fooled around and never did any work. There was another girl, older, from somewhere else, who had no father or mother. Those people raised her, but she wasn't related, so she had to work as hard as I did and go to school at the same time. I don't know how she did it. The boss was always watching us spread manure, and he'd yell whenever we slowed down. The only time we got away was when we two went to the far end of the fields to spread manure. That girl liked to be in the fields with me where we could talk. She was the one who taught me all the French I ever knew. She was as strong as a man and very helpful; I really liked her."

"We all ate together in the kitchen, but we might as well have fed with the pigs; except for lots of rancid bacon, it was all swill. I never ate such bad food in my life. My mother would send me a few pennies from time to time, so at least I could buy a bit of chocolate and some decent cheese at the creamery where I carried the milk in the village."

"My parents came to visit me that year in October. They saw the situation and wanted to take me home; but I had signed papers for a full year, and the farmer wouldn't let me go. Besides, I believed in honoring my contract, even though I hated those people and would never do it again. That's the way it is with us Oberlanders, you keep your word. But it would have been the same on any farm in French-speaking Switzerland. All those French-Swiss are like that, real hypocrites and misers, all of them. That's how they get rich, eventually sell the farm and buy a bank."

"Do you know what they paid me for working eighteen hours a day for a year? One hundred and twenty francs! That was $30 in those days — less than $30 a month in today's purchasing power. 'Never again', I said."

After his son was issued a porter's license, a special insert page was issued to Edward Feuz "Vater" thirty years after his first certification. E. Broman photograph.

"I finally got home in the spring and headed straight up for the mountains. I climbed everything in sight, and decided to become a guide, even if my father wasn't really happy about it. I took out a porter's license and began my apprenticeship. When Father came back from Canada in the fall of 1902 he found out what I had been up to. He still disapproved — officially, anyhow — but there was a twinkle in his eye, and I know he was very proud of me. 'Would you like to come to Canada with me next summer, as a porter?' he asked. 'I think I can arrange it. You've done great things here in the Oberland; but there's lots of new mountains in Canada nobody's ever been up, just waiting for you to climb them. How about it?' "

"I was overjoyed."

App VII-108, "An Ascent of the Weisshorn"
App VII-212, "Three Days on the Zinal Grat"

CHAPTER
II
A VERY SPECIAL KIND OF GUIDE

My name is Tell — *tel que je suis, je suis*
An old Swiss family known very well;
My sisters keep the Rigi Kulm hotel;
My nieces sing the Ranz des Vaches when called
Up to the table d'hote in Grindelwald;
My nephews carve in wood, and make those things
Which every tourist back to England brings,
And gives as souvenirs to those relations
From whom he thinks he's any expectations.
My uncles are all guides — ne'er at a loss
To climb the Jungfrau or the Grimsel cross.

> From "William Tell", or the "Strike of the Cantons" —
> a burlesque, performed June 2, 1856 by the Fielding
> Club at the Royal Italian Opera (Lyceum).

Guides have existed ever since humans, in search of something they wanted or needed, left their normal hunting grounds and wandered into the unknown. Later, when man went to war and became civilized, guides helped direct invading armies to victory or sometimes into ambush. The Pharaohs hired guides to help Egyptians find slaves in the Sudan. One of the first true mountain guides was Ephialtes, a renegade Spartan, who took the Persians through Thessaly's hidden trails and defiles so they could defeat Leonidas at Thermopylae. Hannibal used alpine tribesmen to show his elephants and Iberian horsemen the way into Italy. Pyrenean shepherds guided Charlemagne's palladin, Roland, against the Saracens. Marco Polo hired pathfinders to assist him in crossing Persian and Tibetan deserts and mountains on the road to Cathay; and Massena retained Swiss peasants, including perhaps one or more of Uncle Ed's forebears, to help French revolutionary armies track Souvarov across the Alps

Among North Americans who among us has not read about wilderness scouts, first in the eastern forest, then on the western prairie; Marquette, Joliet, Verendrye, Ogden, Carson and how many others? Wherever man has trod or settled, there has always evolved a need for guides.

Noah Webster defines a guide as "one who leads or directs another in his way or course, as in strange country or through difficult terrain." Like all occupations, guiding has always had its share of charlatans who claim skills or knowledge they do not possess. Such persons have often been the cause of dramatic tragedies. The Donner Party was in large measure the victim of bad guides. So, too, may have been the men who first scaled the Matterhorn.

A good guide knows his territory, life in the outdoors, local climate, and must quickly and correctly assess the competence and limitations of those in his charge and be able to tend to their needs. No book-learning is necessary, but good judgment and common sense are essential. At the least his is a skilled trade, more realistically a responsible profession. If and when the chips are down, he must sacrifice himself for those in his care. In the forty-four years he served as a licensed guide, from 1905 to 1949, Uncle Ed never once deviated from that tradition. Neither did any of his Swiss-born fellow professionals in Canada.

Mountain-guiding is no ordinary business. It can appeal only to persons who have a strong physique, a love of the outdoors, a preference for the aesthetic over the pecuniary. Mountain-guides, without exception, never manage to get rich by their occupation which nevertheless requires a balanced knowledge of many skills. And as time has passed, it has become ever more intricate.

The roots of modern mountain guiding began after the Napoleonic Wars, and were fed by the growth of tourism which came with the Industrial Revolution, the veneration of nature and a revived thirst for travel and adventure that started in the late eighteenth century through the teachings of philosophers like Jean Jacques Rousseau and later the charismatic appeal of traveller-poets like Lord Byron.

The first serious tourists were British. This was to be expected, for after generations of recurrent warfare, Britain had emerged as the world's richest and most powerful nation, and, through its merchant fleet, the most mobile. Britons had been denied access to the continent for a generation and were eager to return.

There were plenty of affluent English men and women who wanted to travel away from their rainy island in search of adventure and diversion. For nature-lovers the closest and best vacation land was the Swiss Confederation. It offered gorgeous scenery, reasonably good transport, and increasingly comfortable accommodations. The people were friendly: there were no xenophobic and irreconcilable Frenchmen, dour Teutons or unpredictable Italians.

Thus, along with sightseer compatriots, English sportsmen went to Switzerland with its high mountains, mostly unclimbed. The French and Genevese had already scaled Mont Blanc, but the British decided to go them one better. Britons, more than a few of them, became true mountaineers.

What the British had in money and incentive they lacked in knowledge of local topography and conditions, nor did they have alpine know-how. So the visitors looked for help from native peasants, most of whom had never been on high peaks, but who did know their surroundings. They had herded cows, goats and sheep above timberline, and some even hunted chamois. Hired by the English, these peasants became the first modern mountain guides.

The habits, mores and customs of nineteenth century Swiss villagers were to have a fundamental impact on the behavior of their descendants, such as Uncle Ed and his fellows who emigrated to Canada. The life was hard and the land unyielding. This created hard and unyielding people who seldom learned much of life outside their native valleys except when called up for military service. More often, but still rarely, the young, unmarried village women might sojourn in Geneva, Bern or Zurich to work for virtual slave wages as domestic servants in bourgeois families and, more often than not, to become pregnant by the man of the house — a practice which continued almost until World War II. But for most, the native villages and valleys remained the world; and everything on the other side of the encompassing mountains or in the plains below, was largely unknown, possibly hostile, and certainly foreign.

Life was a question of survival, and this made for hard working, parsimonious and tough people. The isolation bred parochialism and promoted clannish attitudes and native pride. The greatest virtues were loyalty and reliability; the worst sins, breach of promise or the slur of a stranger, things that were rarely forgiven and never forgotten.

No one starved, but neither was there much real wealth in the high valleys. To own a half-dozen cows was to be rich. Swiss money was as hard as its mountains' granite and correspondingly difficult to extract. This was a principal reason why free-spending Englishmen were welcomed as visitors, although otherwise kept at a distance.

Everywhere, too, were the twin prides of Swiss citizenship and the centuries-old traditions of liberty and independence. It was the tribesmen of Uri, Schwytz and Unterwald who had first rebelled against the Hapsburg tyrants; later it was the mountain-warriors of Bern who three times crushed the proud armies of Charles the Rash and drove him to perish miserably in a swamp; and, finally, it was the immediate parents and grand-parents of the first guiding families who had fought for Napoleon, somewhat grudgingly but, generally victoriously. Even if not always precisely victorious, as in Russia, Swiss soldiers attached to the Grande Armee had always been the best of the best and the bravest of the brave.

It was all obviously true, because everyone had learned it in school, even at the expense of more immediately useful subjects. School consisted of no more than primary education; reading, writing, arithmetic, and, of course, a bit of French so you could converse with compatriots from the western cantons whose co-citizenship you acknowledged, although in all other ways you despised them.

But it was history that really counted, the history that taught you how the Swiss had fought through the ages to become invulnerable. The bit of geography that went with it would some day be useful, because, sure as fate, if you were a boy you would do your military service and then spend years in the active reserve. If you didn't know how to sneak around the mountainside to catch the enemy from behind, then Switzerland might not be so invulnerable any more.

Boys spent the summer herding livestock on high pastures. But in winter they tried to learn a trade, because that was the only way one could hope to make a decent living. In time most became carpenters, cabinet-makers, others specialized tradesmen, some even reaching the exalted status of a master stone mason. The good ones prospered. The money thus saved — which was most of it — was squirreled away in a savings account in a Swiss bank in Zurich or Bern, or, sometimes (and with misgivings), in Geneva or Lausanne, where it was safe, safe, safe, protected by the building's iron vaults and the overwhelming might of the Swiss Army, to which all men belonged.

The health of people in the high valleys was pretty good, for the times. The twin curses were goiter and endemic cretinism, both the result of iodine deficiency. Accidents also took a toll. But the isolation and clean mountain air provided protection against the common infectious diseases such as scarlet fever, diptheria, smallpox and tuberculosis that plagued most urban areas.

It takes a tough man to make a tough guide. British sportsmen were happy to find an ample supply of tough, knowledgeable and semi-literate peasants. From the outset guiding also appealed to Swiss natives. As a summer occupation, it provided an outlet from the drudgery of winter trade and the chores of caring for livestock. There was a bit of glamor attendant on going where no one had been before, even if some of your neighbors called you a damn fool for taking chances. There was an opportunity to exchange a few words with foreigners who were interesting even though not to be trusted. The pay was good, and it was reliable, provided you had both customers and fine weather. In a season you might sock away a half dozen or so gold Vrenelis in your impenetrable Swiss savings account.

In a very few years mountain guiding in Switzerland evolved into a recognized trade. The authorities conferred their blessings by according it a status similar to that of the medieval guilds. Long apprenticeship as a porter was followed by strict examinations by one's seniors and, obviously, betters (who, if you were lucky, might eventually be your peers). If you passed, your subsequent career was governed by standards of excellence, rules of conduct and a code of ethics. A day of guiding was well paid, but the seasonal nature of the task and weather uncertainties meant a low overall annual income, although there was job security of sorts. Outsiders need not apply. Each native village and valley maintained pretty much a monopoly on guiding in its environs.

Most guides rarely left, or wanted to leave, the familiar grounds of their birth and training; it was, after all, the only world they and their ancestors had ever known. They never were quite sure how they would be received elsewhere, but they had an indication from the way they themselves often treated the rare guide from distant valleys who dared to practice his trade in their home territory. The guides of Zermatt, the Engadine, of Saas Fee, Martigny, the Val d'Anniviers and Uncle Ed's Oberland worked out of their respective valleys and rarely went anywhere else. To a large extent, this is still true.

Swiss guides thus became specialists in their immediate territory. Some became super-specialists because they concentrated on a particular mountain or even particular routes on one mountain. Local ridges and summits were good enough for them. More to the point, centuries of prejudice convinced them that theirs were the finest possible mountains in the finest of possible mountain worlds.

Such, in the last decades of the nineteenth century and first years of the twentieth, was the school and mentality of guiding into which Ed Feuz and his colleagues were initiated.

In all times most alpine guides have known their jobs and territory well. But, like all of us, they often lacked the ability to adapt to new and unfamiliar surroundings. Even today guides from Zermatt and Grindelwald sometimes have difficulty adjusting to the Chamonix complex or to the limestone pinnacles behind Cortina d'Ampezzo, and vice versa. Ingenuity and adaptability have usually been the province of the amateur mountaineer.

Of course there have been exceptions: Carrell, Petigax and Croux; Guido Rey, Joseph Knubel and Alexander Graven; Comici, Solda, and Gervasutti; Lachenal and Terray, and the indefatigable Genevese, Raymond Lambert, to name a few. However, these exceptions in most cases have turned out to be not just the best guides, but also the best climbers of their time. Edward Feuz, Jr. proved to be most adaptable even though, while an excellent climber, he was by no means the best alpinist of his generation. But in both his ability and eagerness to adjust to new territory, he was one of the most brilliant exceptions.

Today there are so many first-class climbers it is hardly possible to distinguish between professionals and amateurs. Yet critical differences separate the two. No guide need be a super-mountaineer, but a super-mountaineer often is a very bad guide. Attitude and training are the sources of these differences.

The guide's paramount duty is toward his clients, who are his sacred trust. His presence represents an assurance, as much as possible an absolute guarantee, of safety. Everything the guide does from the moment of departure to that of return is focused on the comfort of his employers and, above all, on their security. To hire a guide is to minimize the danger. On the other hand, if amateurs climb with amateurs, they all share the risks and responsibilities.

The amateur super-climber can climb with whomever he pleases. Not so the guide. He goes with the people who hire him. This means he will deal with a very small percentage of good to excellent climbers and a vast number of semi-competents. He knows he can expect no help in tight spots. On the contrary, he must consider his clients to be capable of imperilling everything. The guide's attitude is that of a solo climber with the added burden that he must constantly keep an eye on his companions' behavior. His only trump card is that he is the autocrat of the excursion.

Amateurs usually have considerable prior knowledge of the people with whom they climb. The guide, however, must test out a new client before embarking on any serious project. Thus a guide must learn to assess the climbing ability of others, quickly.

Another line separates expert amateurs and guides. Amateurs are judged by their exploits, first ascents of new peaks or routes. It is they who push the limits of the possible. In a dangerous sport like mountaineering, novelty involves risk, and risk invariably leads to accidents. Guides, on the other hand, are measured by their safety record and devotion to clients. One of the greatest mountaineers of his generation, an Italian alpinist who also made a career of guiding, was deemed by his peers to be a poor professional because he repeatedly took clients on ascents that exceeded their abilities and imperilled their lives. But the super-amateur whose less experienced companion gets killed is rarely disparaged.

A guide needs one final, further quality that distinguishes him from at least some amateurs. He is married to his environment and must forever love it. It is the source of his uncertain livelihood, it is where he must spend his life, often repeating monotonous and run-of-the-mill ascents. The amateur, by contrast, comes and goes at his pleasure. After a few exploits that bring him fame, he may choose to persevere, or like all too many, he may divorce the sport and go elsewhere.

There is one more thing to remember about professional guides, and most especially about those who went to Canada. They were and remained ordinary working people, no better and no worse than the common laboring men of all nations; and they never tried to be anything else. They lived to be remembered only by those whom they served — and they were loved by many.

Uncle Ed, though neither super-guide nor super-climber, truly loved his mountains. When Hans Gmoser took him, at the age of eighty-two and on a splendid day, to the head of Bugaboo Glacier to contemplate once again some of the magnificent alpine scenery where he had struggled to earn his bread for almost half a century, Uncle Ed could only stand there with tears in his eyes. Unremitting love of the mountains is the sine qua non of a true alpine guide.

Guides worked with very limited resources. The business had

Hans Gmoser talks with Edward, Jr., at Banff Centre during the 1971 visit of Tenzing Norgay. Nephew Sidney is in center background. W. McCusker photograph.

started informally as a simple trade. All you needed were a strong back and legs, a sense of balance, a knowledge of terrain and climate, an ability to look after others, and sound judgment. With the development of equipment and improved standards of ability, things began to get more complicated — even in Uncle Ed's earlier days. Yet at the time of his formal retirement, climbing equipment remained primitive by today's standards. Nailed boots, wool clothing, a rucksack, sun goggles, an ice-axe and a rope — the last being also a guide's badge of authority — were all you needed. Until 1949, things evolved slowly. Boots were poorly insulated, with leather soles and soft iron edge-nails to grip into rock, and steel tricounis for hard snow. So long as nails held on rock, all was well and good, but one slip converted both tricounis and edge-nails into skates. Nails tended to loosen, cut into leather and eventually ruin footwear.

Because all nails were unsatisfactory on ice, guides often had to chop innumerable steps. Early crampons failed to eliminate step-cutting for they were clumsy affairs and their proper use was poorly understood. On ice there was, practically speaking, no protection. The few ice-pitons in existence were merely glorified ice picks, heavy and badly designed. Most of the time they merely chipped ice away and at best, provided psychological comfort. In very cold weather one sometimes did manage to get some security by urinating on them after they had been driven and then waiting for the urine to freeze. Guides led only the most reliable clients on steep ice, and urinated often.

On rock there were rock pitons, but they were introduced only gradually. Mostly they were of forged soft iron, and of uncertain strength. Carabiners, made of steel, rusted easily and weighed a lot. The guides of Ed's day usually scorned both pitons and carabiners. Besides, most of the routes they used did not require them.

A few ropes were made of silk, which was the closest thing to today's nylon, most were of Italian hemp and some climbed with manilla — a shorter fibred hemp — and less trustworthy. In dry weather these ropes were pleasant to handle, but their fracture point was about 800 kilograms for an 11 millimeter line compared with 1,800 kilograms or more for modern nylon. Moreover, all hemp waterlogged easily, became completely unmanageable when frozen (which was often) and, while in storage, deteriorated rapidly under attack by fungi.

Ice-axes evolved from primitive alpenstocks, themselves an outgrowth of the shepherd's staff; they were weighty, long handled and crude. They served well for cutting steps, glissading and self-arrests on snow. On rock, whether carried by hand or in rucksacks, they almost invariably got in the climber's way.

Clothes were heavy, at best water-repellent, and eiderdown

Edward Feuz, Jr., Swiss Mountain Guide, circa 1915. Byron Harmon photograph, Archives of the Canadian Rockies.

garments were unknown. For those going far afield, expedition gear was even heavier, cumbersome and ill-adapted to mountain terrain. This included everything from tents, sleeping bags and air-mattresses to packboards and cooking gear. There was no such thing as freeze-dried food, nutrition was yet to become a science, and diets were often poorly considered.

Communications, other than by voice, were in their infancy, medical knowledge was limited and many rescue techniques yet to be developed. There were no radios to summon helicopters with paramedics in case of accident. When things went wrong, you were on your own until help arrived, if it arrived at all.

Today's guides with modern resources and techniques can afford to go on far more ambitious projects than could those of a century ago. The miracle is not what today's guides can do, but rather the achievements of men like Uncle Ed who had little more than rope, ice-axe, nailed boots, and sheer determination.

The societal status of guides in Ed's time differed radically from what it is today. To be sure, on climbs the guide was a respected and absolute dictator. Elsewhere he had little rank. But the client, wherever he went, invariably got gentleman's treatment whether, like Professor Fay, he deserved it, or, like Edward Whymper, he did not. By contrast, a guide had about as much social status as a locomotive engineer; that is, envied by a few for his place at the top of the blue-collar class.

The early records of Chateau Lake Louise are revealing on this subject; invariably the guides are referred to by their first names. Clients, however, are designated Mr., Mrs., or Miss unless meriting higher titles yet. Except on a climb, guides and clients did not mingle. Maybe it was just as well. After all, Uncle Ed was more often than not spared the need to associate, other than in a professional way, with a multitude of socially prominent employers who had far less of the real gentleman in them than he.

Things have changed since Uncle Ed closed his fuhrerbuch in 1949. Today we are all children of the egalitarian revolution. In addition, guides are academically better educated, they use intricate tools, their trade has become a respected profession, usually in conjunction with the more lucrative and equally prestigious occupation of ski instructor. The guide's social status is on a par with that of the commercial airline pilot. For some reason, the locomotive engineer never made the transition, even though flying a plane and driving a train have much in common. But the guides have crossed what was once considered an unbridgeable abyss.

The competent, handsome ski instructor-mountain guide today has a touch of glamor and mingles everywhere. He has his pick of rich, attractive, socially prominent young women as bedmates if not as wives, this to such a degree that he often wastes much of his time sitting at bars and jeopardizing his career in the process.

Those with more serious interests become personal friends of their clients and clients' families, marry well, develop new talents and may even in time become successful entrepreneurs in some business related to mountain tourism. No such opportunities existed for guides during Uncle Ed's working years. Life did, however, hold other rewards. Those who emigrated to Canada did so at what was to be a most propitious time, and the decision to expatriate themselves when they did gave those guides advantages over the colleagues left behind.

At the turn of the century much of Western Canada and almost all its mountains were wilderness. They remained that way for another fifty years, parts of it even longer. Only a few of the highest, easiest and most prominent peaks nearest rail lines had been scaled. Behind them, as far as the eye could see, and beyond, rose myriads of unclimbed, unnamed, snow and rock mountains. For anyone who loved high places and adventure, this was Paradise.

There were restraints, however — some of them imported from Europe. The guides ended up not much richer than in Switzerland, had little free time, and had to earn their livings. This resulted in routine ascents of prominent summits near tourist hotels and only rare opportunities to venture afield. In a twenty-five year period, Ed Feuz made two dozen ascents apiece on Mounts Victoria, Temple, and Whyte, not including hundreds of other common itineraries. These were the bread-and-butter mountains. Ed always enjoyed them, too; but he loved the unknown more.

Luckily for him and his colleagues there existed a nucleus of competent, adventuresome visitors eager to leave the beaten path, to make first ascents on new ground, and who needed the help of guides. Thanks in large measure to these, Uncle Ed, when he retired, had to his credit over one hundred first ascents on peaks exceeding 10,000 feet, of which at least fifteen were over eleven thousand. Few if any guides in Europe of his generation could claim such a distinction. It was no surprise that, in his declining years, Ed's memories always focussed on his first ascents.

Ed Feuz had the added distinction that by age forty he had become the patriarch of the Swiss guides in Canada. His story, therefore, is also that of his brothers Ernest and Walter, of the handsome ladies-man and would-be movie star, Rudolph Aemmer, and of the tragic Christian Haesler, Jr. All five had personalities of their own, and differed greatly in temperament, but throughout their lives it was always clear that they sprang from the identical Oberland soil.

Much in them that was Swiss mountain peasant survived, and the rest adapted to the new land's imperatives. To his dying day, Uncle Ed believed that because it was hard to acquire a few Canadian pennies, they were to be expended as frugally as Swiss francs and treated like treasure; that a man's finest virtues were loyalty and reliability; and, of course, that the Swiss guides were not only the best guides, but also the best mountaineers. And behind Ed's benign appearance there could, at times, be glimpsed dark clouds when he evoked old injuries and quarrels. This, after all, was the essence of the Oberland peasant. What matters, however, is that to those (like these authors) who liked and respected him, he remained a true friend in good times and bad.

All guides are special people; mountain guides are special guides; those few mountain guides who expand their workplace beyond their native valleys are even more special; the Swiss guides in Canada, because they had the vision and courage to move their roots from one continent to another, were still more special; and Uncle Ed, because he became their patriarch and acted as their counselor in times of trouble, was the most special and unusual of all.

Edward Feuz, Junior, raised in the Bernese Oberland and trained at an early age to be a mountain guide, came to Canada with his father while still a young man. Aside from a few trips home in the early years, he lived in modest circumstances for the rest of his days in British Columbia near a narrow stretch of steel track that was to remain, almost throughout his life, the only important mark of man's presence in a world of peaks and forests that seemed to stretch endlessly on all sides. As much as the hunter, the trapper, the woodsman, and the prospector, Uncle Ed, certified Swiss guide, became a part of that wilderness.

AJ V-87, The Comparative Skill of Travellers and Guides
AJ XIII-170, Regulations as to Guides
AJ XIII-271, Lectures to Guides
AJ XIII-422, Regulations as to Guides
AJ XIII-471, Regulations as to Guides
AJ XV-500, The Payment of Guides

CHAPTER
III
THE NEW LAND

". . . Built my barns and strung my fences in the little
border station tucked away below the foothills where
the trails run out and stop." (Kipling)

It was real wilderness on that warm spring day in 1903 when
Uncle Ed first crossed the Continental Divide. Until a few years
before he retired in 1949, hardly anyone had driven a motor car
completely across Canada. Three lonely ribbons of steel, all single
track, separated one from another by one hundred and fifty miles
of wild forest and wilder mountains, were the only links between
the prairie provinces and the Pacific. The southernmost of them,
a frail branch line of the Canadian Pacific, hugged the United States
border as if for protection. The main line cut through the ranges
over two high passes where traffic was often paralyzed for weeks
during winter months by an unending cataract of avalanches. The
third, formerly the Grand Trunk Pacific, today the Canadian
National, had similar problems. Beyond this northernmost track
there was nothing until you had passed over the Pole into the
Russian Empire and encountered the Trans-Siberian Railway. But
nobody, not even a guide, was known to have made that journey.

It was a land of peaks, glaciers, canyons, roaring torrents,
impenetrable forests and much eternal snow. Nobody lived there;
nobody ever had. True, the Indians on occasion ventured briefly
into the Rockies to hunt or hold inter-tribal pow-wows, but they
never frequented the Interior Ranges where game was scarce and
movement difficult.

By contrast at least some parts of Switzerland had been
populated since long before Roman times, and by the mid-
nineteenth century a network of roads and rail lines connected all
but the remotest valleys. In effect, Ed Feuz and his colleagues
transmigrated from the fringes of a cosmopolitan, sophisticated
civilization to an untamed wilderness of isolation.

The lonely track through the mountain wilderness. CPR Archives.

Near the hotels and tiny outposts created by the railroad there were occasional trails to timberline, as in Switzerland, but beyond a limited periphery, there were no paths except such as had been created by wandering wild animals. If you wanted to climb, you first had to learn how to bushwhack.

The forest had one dubious advantage not found in Switerland. Because the tree-line was the same as in the Alps, while many of the summits were lower, the actual amount of mountain exposed to the worst of the elements was less than in much of Europe. In the Rockies and Interior Ranges summer storms usually, but not always, lacked the intensity of their Swiss counterparts. But then there were nuisances, obstacles and perils unknown in the Alps.

Swiss forests were manicured, even where there were no trails. Not so in Canada. The trapper, prospector or climber who went far afield only to stumble over a fallen log or loose boulder and break a leg was in serious trouble. One poor fellow in the wilds above the Columbia River, who had fractured his femur, had to wait all summer under a tarpaulin before evacuation came. Worse, that episode cost the lives of two others. And in spite of superior skill and sense of balance, the guides were not immune from such accidents. Chris Haesler, Jr. was once laid up for weeks with a broken ankle.

The country was a paradise for mosquitos, green horse-flies, no-see-ums and other pests. They didn't kill you, of course, and it was too cold for malaria. but insects swarmed in enormous numbers and delighted in making the life of all mammals, men included, unpleasant and uncomfortable. Big game was known to have remained under water for hours on end with only nostrils above the surface in a desperate and vain attempt to avoid mosquitos. Men doused their faces with kerosene and a product called Citronella, and sometimes wore head-nets. In any one year Uncle Ed must have swatted the exposed parts of his body many thousand more times than he ever swung his ice-axe.

Mosquitos, you mashed. But it gave no satisfaction to crush them, and, besides, there was no shortage of reinforcements, endlessly filling the breach left by their deceased brethren. Killing mosquitos was a chore. With the green horse-flies, however, you could at least have some fun. For them Uncle Ed invented an amusing sport. He would capture a live horse-fly, drive a spruce needle up its rear, and then release it. ZOOM! The victim, now tail heavy, flew in an ascending spiral never to be seen again. Cruel? It was just the tortured getting even with the torturer.

There were more deadly things than bugs. For instance, untamed streams. Even where they issued from a glacier's tongue they were swift, often torrential, and always icy cold. Swollen by tributaries they rapidly became formidable rivers a few miles downstream. Sure, Swiss torrents could be equally savage, but at least in Switzerland there were frequent and convenient bridges. In Canada, there were none. You teetered across on fallen logs, or forded as best you could, or in rare cases where the stream was wide, the current reasonable, and the water deep, you built a raft and poled your way over. The guides soon acknowledged that torrents were more dangerous than mountains. To this day more people have perished in the rivers of Alberta and British Columbia than have died on the region's peaks. None of the guides ever drowned, even if, in their careers, they crossed more rivers than they climbed mountains and were more often briefly swept away in white water than they made first ascents.

In Uncle Ed's day, Western Canada was one of the world's largest menageries, and this, in addition to being fascinating, could on occasion also spell trouble. There was every manner of wild beast; wolves, cougars, lynx and coyotes, seldom seen but often heard, huge porcupines who could chew up your boots overnight and leave you barefoot and whose quills sometimes blinded your dogs; beaver, weasels, wolverines and marten which were a trapper's delight. And then there was the really big game, which on rare occasion could be extremely dangerous.

Wildlife usually kept its distance, but if surprised at close range, the larger creatures were unpredictable. Uncle Ed's young friend,

Ken Jones, a renowned hunter, excellent skier and Canada's first native-born mountain guide, more than once found himself in tight quarters with moose and wapiti, and he had a lot of respect for them. "Once, in the mating season," he would tell, "I got a bit close to a bull elk. He came for me, horns down. Those damned antlers had a nine foot spread. I'd rather have dodged a grizzly." Ken failed to add that wounded mule deer, one quarter the size and weight of an elk, have been known to trample men to death with their razor-sharp hooves.

Above timberline you could find bighorn sheep and mountain goat, often in large herds. They were distant relatives of the Corsican and Sardinian "moufflons" and the Alpine chamoix, but much larger. Some weighed hundreds of pounds; the goats were among the world's most sure-footed mammals. Uncle Ed and Chris Haesler would watch from a distance with wonder and envy as the goats scampered nimbly over steep granite boiler plates which would have taken the best alpinist hours to climb, if he could have climbed them at all.

Goats also had an uncanny way of finding the easiest route on intricate mountain terrain. "Follow the goat trails" became an almost infallible slogan for the Swiss professionals when they felt unsure of the way. There is truth to the saying that goats are the guides' guides. Chris Haesler put it even more simply: "they are my friends" he said.

Indeed, goats were Chris' friends; not so the bears.

These were of two types. Most frequently seen were the black, sometimes brown, bears who were largely parasites and moochers. One could (and still can) see them almost any day along the railroad track, and in the park campgrounds or around garbage pits. Neither friendly nor hostile, but curious and gluttonous, they could be a tourist attraction; but mostly they were pests. It was dangerous to venture too near because they were strong and could do damage without intending harm, and much of the time they acted as though tame, which was not the case. When too bold or obstreperous and gourmandizing, they had to be killed. The modern combination of tranquilizers and exile had yet to be devised.

Then there were the grizzlies. They avoided man and were therefore little known, but they had a legendary reputation for ferocity. They could be distinguished from other bears by their large size, by what appeared to be a slight hump at their shoulders, and, in some cases, by a grey streak in their hair which earned them the nickname Silvertip. Grizzlies were shy and fearful.

Shyness and fear were the roots of their alleged ferocity. Grizzlies almost always kept their distance when people had the courtesy to announce their arrival, but the beasts were quick to attack if anyone approached unexpectedly or appeared to be some threat to their tranquility.

In the forest there were six cardinal rules of protocol with regard to grizzlies. They are as valid today as in Uncle Ed's time. 1) Make plenty of noise while travelling in thick bush, with a sound unfamiliar to grizzlies which therefore will scare them away; 2) Keep a sharp lookout so as not to stumble unexpectedly into a grizzly's occupied boudoir; 3) Under no circumstances get between a female and her cubs; 4) If charged, shinny as high as possible up the nearest tree, because grizzlies, unlike other bears, don't climb; but, beware, the grizzly can reach very high if he chooses to stand on his hind feet; 5) If caught where there is no timber, try to dodge; try also if possible, to make use of the fact that while the grizzly has an acute sense of smell, he is almost blind; and be sure to remember that if his paw should hit you, he can decapitate you with a single blow, break your back, or rip out your entrails; 6) Never, never, never chase a wounded grizzly through the bush, for from being the hunter, you will become the hunted, and the grizzly is a far better hunter than you, Uncle Ed or even Ken Jones could ever hope to be.

Just about everyone in Western Canada has his favorite story about grizzly bears. Most of them are lies. There are, for instance, countless stories about men who tangled with grizzlies, stabbed the beast to death and emerged unscathed. One such story is mostly true. It happened to a CPR section foreman of Finnish ancestry named Nieminen, whose area of responsibility included the real bear country from Glacier down to Flat Creek. One day while hunting in the Gold Range west of Revelstoke, he somehow stumbled over a sleeping grizzly. In the resulting scuffle, the Finn lost his rifle after getting off one shot which severely wounded, but definitely failed to kill the bear. He was able to draw the long knife which all hunters carry and with it he finally was victorious. Somewhat better off than Kipling's Matun, he was chewed badly about the neck and lower jaw, yet managed to stumble out of the woods to collapse on the highway where he was found by a passing motorist. His hunting companion had fled the scene of the encounter, and only surfaced weeks later to see him in the hospital. In the end he largely lost the use of his voice, but was otherwise able to resume a normal life.

Remarkably, Nieminen was neither afraid nor resentful of grizzlies after his experience. One day in early summer, a few years later, Norman Brewster was sitting on a rock above the upper Cougar Valley, watching a colony of marmots migrate singly over a little snowfield to a new rock pile, when he perceived two small figures picking their way carefully down towards him. They turned out to be Nieminen and his daughter, a nurse in Vancouver, and they had come up across Cougar Mountain from Ross Peak on the railroad. This had involved some heavy bushwhacking and rock scrambling through one of the principal haunts of the grizzlies, the Cougar and

Bear Creek valleys, and the avalanche slopes lining the Illecillewaet. He and his section men were accustomed to working in the proximity of bears — or, upon occasion, not working, when the grizzlies, for their own inscrutable reasons occupied the right-of-way and could not be frightened off.

Uncle Ed, when young and rather lonely, often wandered up Cougar Valley. He saw many bears, and no doubt hunted some, as they may, too, have hunted him. There is no record of close encounters. If there were any, they were limited to peaceful differences of opinion. Not everyone has been so fortunate. A few years before Ed died, a Vancouver naturalist who was studying grizzly sociology in Cougar Valley, got a little too involved. She did not survive.

Up in the Little Yoho during the summer of 1943, the eminent English alpinist, Frank Smythe, who had been training the Lovett Scouts, retired to his bunk in the Stanley Mitchell Hut after drinking a few cups of hot cocoa. He awoke in the dark with a painful urge to relieve pressure. He groped his way through the gloom, stepped outside on the porch, leaned over the railing and let fly a heavy stream of warm fluid into the night. At once out of the darkness there came a roar of rage and terror. Both Smythe and the startled grizzly beat a retreat in opposite directions, Smythe to the safety of the hut, the bear into the depths of the forest, never to meet again.

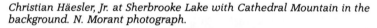

Christian Häesler, Jr. at Sherbrooke Lake with Cathedral Mountain in the background. N. Morant photograph.

A Swiss guide was, however, fated to become the principal victim of what was to be the most lethal and terrifying encounter between man and bear ever recorded in Western Canada. Ironically, the guide was Christian Haesler, Jr., Uncle Ed's partner on many climbs, related by marriage to the Feuz family, and above all, the friend of mountain goats and lover of all wildlife.

On a cool, sunny day in the fall of 1939, Chris Haesler and Nick Morant, a professional photographer, went on a hike near the Yoho Valley in the Rockies to take late season pictures. They had been following a forest path for some time when they came to a clearing through which the trail passed. The clearing lay at the foot of some bluffs and was bisected by a creek beyond which, at a short distance, the forest continued.

As they reached the clearing, Chris and Nick spotted a sow grizzly with a cub romping in the meadow. The men halted and, appropriately, made their presence known with loud noises. Immediately the she-bear showed alarm, shooed her cub into the bushes and then disappeared among the spruce. As they waited to be sure the way was safe, Nick and Chris caught repeated glimpses of the big sow high on the bluffs at ever greater distance. At last she seemed to vanish for good and, accordingly, the men proceeded into the open.

They had just crossed a stream, some five yards wide, and Chris was ahead. He turned to see whether his companion had safely forded the creek. As he turned, Nick saw a look of terror come over Chris' face such as he had never seen on any man before. That look told him precisely what was wrong.

Chris bolted and ran for the trees. Nick, paralyzed, stayed rooted where he stood. The bear, chasing the first to flee, vaulted the stream at a single bound and swept past Nick on Chris' heels. Chris somehow managed to reach a tree ahead of the bear. In an instant he was well off the ground, safe, he believed, from harm's way. Meantime, Nick cautiously worked his way to another tree and climbed it.

For a few moments, Nick watched the bear circle around Chris' tree, unable to reach her prey. As Nick later recounted, the animal's movements, far from resembling the popular stereotyped concept of ursine clumsiness, were as agile as those of a big cat. Suddenly, to Nick's horror, the bear stood on her hind legs, stretched her front paws upwards nine feet off the ground, grabbed Chris' legs and clawed him down.

The bear struck, Chris screamed, there was blood all over. Unable to stand the sight and the cries, Nick descended to the ground, picked up a log, ran over to the bear and whacked her. Nick's action, no doubt, saved Chris' life. But it nearly cost him his own. In a flash, the bear turned on him, battered him, and, finally, knocked him unconscious. Everything went black. When, some time later, Nick recovered his senses, the bear was gone, and so was Chris.

Somehow Chris, badly injured, managed to stumble back to where he could get help. Both had suffered several fractures and severe lacerations. Not only were they in physical shock, but throughout the torture of their slow journey, they were in constant mortal dread of another attack.

Chris and Nick spent the next six months in the hospital. Repeatedly at night their nurses came running to their bedsides when one or another of them awoke screaming from nightmares of grizzlies. In time Nick made a full recovery. Not so Chris. Much weakened, he was unable the following summer to devote more than a fortnight to guiding. On October 31, 1940, barely a year after the incident, he was found dead under the walls of a small house on which he had been building a chimney. His death was officially attributed to a fall from the roof. But the guides knew better; he had really been killed by that bear.

Chris was the only guide of any nationality ever to suffer such a fate. It would never have happened in the Alps, where bears are almost extinct. Even in Canada, where such incidents are given lurid publicity, attacks by grizzlies are extremely rare. Yet what happened to Chris might well have occurred to anyone in the wilderness of the Canadian Alps. It was one of the many risks of climbing in Canada; a small risk, to be sure, but a most frightening one. On his approach marches, leading clients through the forest, Uncle Ed thought almost as much about grizzlies as he did on glaciers about crevasses.

There was that steel track and, along it, in distant succession as you rolled westward, Canmore, Banff, Lake Louise, Field, Golden, Donald, Beavermouth, Glacier, Flat Creek, Albert Canyon and Revelstoke. These tiny settlements, each separated by twenty to forty miles of emptiness, remained for many years the rare ephemeral outposts of human society on the major division of the Canadian Pacific across the western mountains.

In early days neither Banff nor Lake Louise attracted much notice. Golden was a rough river settlement, principally a logging center, but where cattlemen, trappers and a few miners also brought their goods for shipment east or, more frequently, west. Riverboat captains were an interesting part of the local scene in the first years that Ed was in Canada. Beavermouth was a mere engine-switching stop, and Revelstoke was a small railroad division point and town with access to water travel on the Columbia via the Arrow Lakes.

Field and Glacier, however, were special. As early as 1886 the CPR had established eating facilities in these spots to avoid hauling dining cars over the steep grades of the Western Division. Field was situated above mud and sand flats on the Kicking Horse River and though possessed of a hotel, was relatively unattractive. It owed its name, not to the scenery, but to an attempt (unsuccessful) by

Glacier House in 1910. CPR Archives, Thompson.

CPR President Van Horne to enveigle financial support from the well heeled Chicago merchant, Marshall Field. Aside from the railroad its only economic importance was as the headquarters for the Monarch Mine, a small base metal producer, now long closed. But Glacier possessed splendid mountain beauty. A short distance from the rail stop, the shimmering Illecillewaet Glacier seemed to tumble out of the sky into the blackness of the nearby forest. So magnificent was the scenery that provision was soon made for overnight accommodations which in time expanded into a large hotel complex. It was this hotel, the Glacier House, which became the focal point of North American mountaineering during the thirty years from 1890 to 1920.

Thus Glacier was the first guides' headquarters. It retained that status until completion of the nearby Connaught Tunnel in 1916 made hauling dining cars economical. At the same time the retreat of the Illecillewaet had begun to deprive the area of its greatest scenic attraction. The hotel, therefore, was closed in 1925, railway management concentrated alpine promotion in the Rockies, and guide summer headquarters were shifted to what had become, and was to remain, the more fashionable facilities at Lake Louise.

The five Swiss guides, headed by Uncle Ed, who were to make Canada their permanent abode, thus operated, over the passage

Mt. Sir Donald was the supreme goal of the adventurous visitors to Glacier. The guides made many ascents in the course of a season mostly near the right skyline. Archives of the AAC — J.M. Thorington.

of time, out of two separate mountaineering centers. This was something few European guides had ever done. The resulting opportunity for diversification was even greater than one might expect, because the Rockies of Lake Louise differed as much from the Selkirks as did night from day. In the Rockies the valleys were wide, the forests open, the mountains massive and distant, and the rock usually of extremely poor quality. The Rockies, aside from the fact their peaks were lower and the countryside untamed, could be compared with the Alps of the Swiss Valais.

By contrast, the Selkirks soared steeply out of narrow defiles which were cluttered with slide alder, devil's club and humid rain forest. The high peaks tended to rise in small clusters. Around Glacier the rock was high quality quartzite, and in other areas of the Selkirks and their sister mountains, the Purcells, there was much granite, some of it excellent. If the Selkirks had a point of comparison in Europe, it was not the Valais Alps, but the French and Italian Maritimes with similar elevations, ranges which remained until recently among the most inaccessible of Western Europe. The Selkirks, because of colder climate and more precipitation, were far more heavily glaciated than the Maritimes. Both Selkirks and Rockies had vast expanses of snow, at least one of which, the Columbia Icefield, dwarfed the largest névés of Europe.

The Swiss guides in Canada, unlike most guides in the Alps, had the widest choice of terrain in which to improve their education. For, in addition to learning their skills in the Oberland, they were able to perfect and expand their knowledge in both the British Columbia Selkirks and the Alberta Rockies. Uncle Ed and his colleagues may not have been the world's most famous guides, but they gained as wide a variety of experience as any.

CHAPTER
IV
THE TRANSATLANTIC COMMUTER

"Adieu, adieu my native shore
Fades o'er the water blue"
Byron

Uncle Ed's first trip away from Switzerland was in 1903. It was
to be a long and eventful one. He was gone until the autumn of
1905, far off in a land where he knew neither the geography, the
customs, the people nor the idiom. There, he had to earn his living
as an apprentice in a trade he had yet to master. The only persons
with whom he could converse intelligently at the outset consisted
of a half dozen of his compatriots. Not only had he the isolation
of the Canadian wilderness to contend with, but he was separated
from most people around him by language and from the remainder,
notably hotel guests, by caste. When he first reached British
Columbia he was not yet 19 years old.

"We took the train across Germany and Belgium," Uncle Ed
reminisced, "and then the ferry to England. We'd been hired by the
Canadian Pacific, and they were paying our way. They needed Swiss
guides in Canada to make the mountains safe for those tourists
who visited the big hotels the company had built. Naturally, they
wanted to make the most of us while we waited for the boat. In
London, we had to parade around the hotels and offices and
especially Trafalgar Square where the CPR had its headquarters.
We had to dress in knickers like Swiss climbers and carry around
our rucksacks, ice-axes and ropes to give the idea we were very
brave, very loyal and very adventurous. It was all a big publicity
stunt, public relations, you know. In Switzerland we were just plain
folks. In London we were curiosities. They treated us like monkeys
in a zoo, except we weren't in cages."

"Then we took the steamer — Canadian Pacific, of course. It was
an old second-class ship, with no first-class section. They used it
mainly for the immigrants. We were very crowded because lots of

The Manitoba, a CPR one-class transatlantic steamer of the type on which the Swiss guides travelled to Canada. CPR Archives.

Mount Stephen House where Ed Feuz worked during his first season in Canada. CPR Archives.

people, mostly Scots, wanted to leave a place where there was no chance to get ahead except for lords and ladies. In Canada you could make a fortune with hard work and a little luck. We guides weren't looking for fortunes; we just wanted to make a decent living and earn a bit more than we had in Switzerland.

"In Montreal it was the London circus all over again. We had to march around in our costumes with the nailed boots, Tyrolean jackets and felt hats with a feather in them. They gave tea parties and receptions and there were reporters and photographers. Those of us who spoke English had to answer questions about how beautiful and dangerous it was to climb mountains; and the rest of us spoke through a translator or just kept quiet and tried to look friendly."

"Then we got on the train and we never got off for three nights and four days. Just like on the boat, there were immigrants going west, even some Canadians who couldn't make it in Montreal or Toronto and had gone bust."

"It was a long way across Canada. From Montreal to Winnipeg, over a thousand miles, it was all forests and marshes and lakes and no people. Just moose. And then the prairie, first big farms, then nothing." Nothing except once when Ed spotted a solitary wild Indian. He didn't even have a bow and arrow.

At last they reached the mountains. Ed began to feel at home once more even though it wasn't Switzerland and he couldn't talk with anybody. Most of the Swiss got off at Field. They were supposed to go on to Glacier, but there was construction in progress and the workers had taken over the special house reserved for the guides. There was only room enough for Ed's father. So Ed waited a month around the Mount Stephen House, doing odd jobs, and was then sent to Lake Louise to work with the old guide, Peter Kaufmann, who needed help with clients. Ed was a porter or assistant guide and only received half-pay. Of these experiences, Ed later complained: "Those fellows in the CPR, they really made me run around. Sometimes I don't think they had any idea what they were doing."

At long last Ed went to Glacier. There he met Mrs. Young, the hotel manager whose ways and abilities were to become legendary. She developed a special fondness for Ed. "Mrs. Young was like a second mother to me," he would later say.

And indeed she was. When his father and the other guides returned to Switzerland for the winter, Ed remained behind to learn English. For a long time he was desperately homesick. It was only the presence of Julia Young that eased his lonely hours and gave him companionship.

In his leisure moments, usually at night, Ed often went hunting, sometimes along the railroad track, sometimes up the Cougar Valley, which he had been told swarmed with grizzlies. Unfortunately for Ed and luckily for the wildlife, he was no worthy descendent of William Tell. He could fire off a lot of ammunition,

Julia Mary Young at Glacier, B.C., 1912. F.V. Longstaff photo — Archives of the Canadian Rockies.

but except for hitting trees and rocks, the results were unnoticed. Ed was so poor a shot that even bulky grizzly bears could have safely approached to point-blank range. Although he incessantly hunted them without success, there is no record that they ever went hunting for him.

Bears were not the only fascinating things in Cougar Valley. Geologically, it lay west of the famous Hamill Quartzite and the underlying bedrock was limestone. In most places where you find limestone, you also find caves. Ed, when first climbing above Cougar Valley, noticed that the stream down there disappeared into a hole.

A third fascinating creature, though not native to Cougar Valley, was Charles Henry Deutschman. Charlie came up from Revelstoke. He was a big fellow with a trim, little beard. He called himself a prospector, though just what kind nobody knew, and he could speak German, a language sufficently close to Ed's native dialect that they could converse easily. After meeting Uncle Ed a couple of times, the two started to talk about the Cougar Valley. Charlie had discovered some grottos up there and was exploring them. These were to become the famous Nakimu Caves, and Charlie was to be Western Canada's first and, for a time perhaps its only, speleologist.

Charlie became a good friend. Once Charlie even persuaded Ed to be lowered a hundred feet or so on a rope into a cave. His clothes got soaked and dirty. It was beautiful down there among the formations and running water, all dimly lit by his lantern, but it really wasn't Ed's cup of tea. Though he visited the caves many times, Ed never developed much enthusiasm for them; he preferred to do his climbing outdoors.

But as Ed Feuz kept climbing upwards, so Charlie Deutschman kept exploring under the earth. In time he built a shack in the valley from which he conducted his subterranean explorations. He made ladders and cut steps into the cave's main entrance. Soon the CPR got interested and built a wagon road from Glacier whereby tourists could get up the valley to the caves in a democrat. Charlie became the Nakimu caretaker and made his livelihood from a tea house and by showing people around the caverns. Years later when Glacier House closed down and the Parks Department took over, Charlie left, the ladders rotted and the caves were closed.

Uncle Ed, though a mere porter and at the bottom of the guiding totem-pole, was kept very busy on his first summer in the New World. Sometimes he went with older guides up the big peaks. The guides did the leading, and Ed came third to carry the gear and the lunch and watch that the client didn't fall off and drag everyone with him. The lunch, in some respects, was even more important than the client. It usually consisted of bread, sausages, meat slices, cheese, occasionally some delicacy like Strasbourg pate de fois gras,

The Great Glacier — 1890. Archives of the CPR.

smoked Nova Scotia salmon or even Caspian caviar, and one, or preferably, two or three bottles of wine. As important as a summit, the hearty midday meal was always considered one of the high-points of any excursion.

For an apprentice like Ed, the big source of income was the Great Glacier which came down behind the hotel almost into the trees. Lots of tourists wanted to walk out on the ice, but they needed some-one knowledgeable though not necessarily expert to show them around and keep them out of trouble. Ed was ideal for the job. Besides, he cost only half as much as a certified guide. His services were, therefore, in demand. Sometimes he made two trips a day onto the ice.

"The lower part of the glacier," Ed recalled, "was all hard, blue ice. I would chop a few steps with the ice-axe, rope up the clients and go on up farther. Sometimes we took the better ones a long way up to where there were ice towers, seracs and big crevasses and showed them the formations."

"It was slow work. The tourists could be a bit unsteady, so I had to cut big steps. Sometimes I'd cut as many as five hundred or more in a day. Once I spotted what looked like a stick coming out of the ice. I unroped, walked over, and found it was an ice-axe somebody had dropped into a crevasse. That's the way with glaciers; what doesn't come out the bottom comes out at the top. People who disappear into crevasses are found years later on the surface or at the glacier's tongue, perfectly pickled in ice like a frozen turkey. They look as fresh as the day they fell in, even if their relatives have gotten all wrinkled and grown white beards in the meantime."

"On one of my first trips to the glacier I had a couple of young people on their honeymoon. I climbed up with them, chopping steps for half an hour. They kept talking to me, but I didn't understand them because at that time all I knew was a few words of English like *yes* and *no*, and *bread* and *butter* — and of course, they didn't speak Swiss. I kept going higher into the ice-towers and seracs, and they kept pulling on the rope and stopping to ask: 'Guide, guide, is it safe to go there?' But I didn't understand so I answered, 'No, no, it's not safe — not safe,' and then kept going. 'Is it safe?' the lady asked again. 'No, no' I replied and went on."

"Finally, the young husband yelled and at the same time gave the rope a big tug. He looked real disturbed, and he pointed down with his hand. I figured something was wrong, something I didn't understand. So I took them down."

"When I got back to the hotel, I went to the head porter. He was from Leduc, near Edmonton, and had come to Glacier just for that summer. He was the only person who understood me a little and I told him what had happened. He pulled out a German-English dictionary and pointed out some words. Then I saw what I'd been saying was the opposite of what I meant. What I really meant was: 'It's very safe.' I had been all wrong with my first clients. I was so ashamed I never showed my face to those people again."

Ed spent the next two winters in Glacier where he shovelled snow, distributed mail and freight, helped in the kitchen, carried luggage for the rare off-season overnight guests and studied English under the wing of Mrs. Young. Sometimes he went climbing, but mostly he shovelled. In winter it snowed constantly at Glacier. By the time spring rolled around, Uncle Ed's transformation into a professional snow-plow was almost complete.

The trains came and the trains went, one a day from the East, one from the West, the only links with the outside. Sometimes, when there were many avalanches, the trains didn't come at all. On those occasions, Glacier House and its half dozen complement of part-time cooks, waiters, porters, janitors, scullery maids, bottle washers and, of course, the ubiquitous Mrs. Young and Ed with his snow-shovel, were completely cut off.

One day when there were no avalanches, Glacier House got a special guest. He was the Reverend James Chalmers Herdman, one of Canada's best climbers. He wanted to become Glacier's first winter alpinist. Uncle Ed eagerly dropped his shovel, picked up his ice-axe and led the intrepid visitor to the summit of nearby 8,091 foot Mount Abbot. Up near the top there was a cornice and Ed had to knock some of it off. Herdman thought Ed would fall. Fortunately, by this time, Ed had learned the right words to reassure Dr. Herdman in the spooky places. "I'm just making a safe route," Ed told Herdman, and the two then victoriously forged ahead to the top.

It was to be many years before winter mountaineering resumed at Glacier. What deterred Ed and other Swiss guides was the cold. Swiss winters, if snowy, were mild by comparison with those in Canada. This was especially true in the Rockies with their continental climate. In the Selkirks, it was a bit warmer because the prevailing winds from the Pacific reached them before becoming fully chilled. Yet even in the Selkirks, the winter was far more rigorous than it ever was in the Oberland.

Two winters and three summers far from his native soil wrought changes in Uncle Ed. He had served out his apprenticeship as a porter, had climbed scores of mountains, met hundreds of new people, learned English, unsuccessfully discharged his rifle a thousand times in the direction of goats and bears, and shovelled snow. When he first crossed the ocean, he had been a boy. He was to re-cross it as a man. In 1905, at the age of twenty-one, Uncle Ed sailed home. He was now ready to take the final guide exam.

Mountain guiding had become a regulated trade in Switzerland in 1856. After a long apprenticeship, any person wishing to obtain a certificate allowing him to work as a guide had to pass a stiff examination. The tests were administered under rules drawn up jointly by the government and the Swiss Alpine Club. Before you could take them, you first had to undergo medical evaluations and demonstrate that you were a person of good character who had never run afoul of the law.

The tests themselves were rigorous — and are even more so today. First came a week before a committee which questioned every aspect of your knowledge and qualifications, including First Aid. You were then turned over to a group of experienced senior guides, many of whom had served as instructors, who tested you out in the mountains for another week. Applicants had to demonstrate their proficiency as leaders everywhere, on rock, snow, ice, glaciers, in good weather and foul. They had to prove they could handle incompetents safely and keep them from trouble in emergency conditions. They had to pull people out of crevasses and haul them up steep cliffs like sacks of potatoes. Not only were they judged on their skills, but also on the basis of their patience, their courtesy, and their resourcefulness. A single mistake resulted in a warning, a repetition gave you bad marks, and one mistake too many meant failure.

Some people passed on the first try, others never made it at all. Uncle Ed had no trouble. He was granted his certificate, awarded his badge and handed his Fuhrerbuch.

The Fuhrerbuch is a guide's personal record; a list of his climbs with testimonials, favorable or unfavorable, by his successive clients. It can therefore serve as a reference source which people can consult in order to judge their prospective guide's reputation. A favorable Fuhrerbuch is as important for a certified guide as are laudatory references and good resumes for a successful business executive. And so, with Fuhrerbuch in hand and guide's badge pinned to his shirt, Uncle Ed returned to Canada in the early summer of 1906.

In London at the CPR offices on King William Street, right near the Bank of England, it was the old circus all over again with the nailed boots, quaint costumes, ropes, ice-axes and other esoteric material. Many of the same journalists and photographers were there to ask the same old questions. And the ship to Montreal was still jammed with the same stream of ragged immigrants, albeit with new faces. Nor had anything changed with the long train ride to the Rockies — the only thing missing this time was the wild Indian on his horse; he had ridden into the sunset.

There wasn't much climbing that year nor in the immediate ones following. Despite this, Ed began to collect a number of interesting clients, some notoriously well known.

"In 1906" he recalled, "there was this Mr. Hearst who owned all the newspapers in California. He came with a whole collection of pretty office girls who were always smiling and laughing. I liked Mr. Hearst — he was a good-time fellow. He had lots of money; he gave us big tips in $5 gold coins, which he said his father had mined. Naturally, with all that money we made a big fuss over him."

"Mr. Hearst wanted to camp up in the Asulkan Valley, where it was so beautiful. We had pony boys and horses to carry the tents and food up the trail. They wanted me along to take them on the ice. We led the horses to a campsite on the wooded moraine just below the last timber. I spotted a bear on the way up the valley and showed it to the girls."

"Time passed. We pitched camp and had dinner. Before we ate, Mr. Hearst walked around and gave each person a paper napkin and a small bottle of ketchup. Then he told us we couldn't drink the wine the hotel had packed. He thought there was something wicked about drinking wine and other spirits. I didn't mind too much because Mr. Hearst tipped in gold, but the pony boys were upset."

"For a while we sat around the fire and sang songs. It clouded over and looked like a big storm. Then night came. Everybody started for bed, first the girls, then Mr. Hearst. But I stayed up a while by the fire smoking my pipe and trying to figure how far up I dared take everyone on the ice the next day. Pretty soon Mr. Hearst came running back and said: 'Ed?' 'Yes, Mr. Hearst, what's wrong?' 'I'll tell you. The girls are scared. They're in the tent, and they're scared of that bear they saw; they think the bear will come around. Would you mind sleeping with the girls, Ed?' I didn't wait for more: 'With great pleasure, Mr. Hearst. . . . In the mountains, to sleep with girls! That doesn't happen often to us guides.' So I crawled in and snuggled with the girls. Just what went on in the tent I won't say, but outside the clouds had gone away and it was a nice, peaceful night — and, of course, there were no bears — just me."

"Next day we all went up the glacier some distance. That part is gone now — all melted away — nothing but rocks and alder. The glacier in those days was much more beautiful."

Hearst returned several times to the mountains, always surrounded with a harem of pretty girls. He stayed at Lake Louise and, to the girls' delight, climbed with the handsome Rudolph Aemmer. He also went out with the somewhat less handsome Christian Haesler.

Uncle Ed had his fill on the snow-plow brigade those two earlier winters, so he left his snow shovel with the somewhat discomfited Mrs. Young, although his brother, Ernest, soon followed his example at Glacier. For the next several years Ed spent the winter months in Switzerland where there was a bit less snow and a lot warmer weather. In effect, he now became a transatlantic commuter. Before the new arrangement was over, he would cross the Atlantic fifteen times.

In Switzerland instead of shoveling snow, Uncle Ed took up skating. He had always been a good skater: he could dance on ice and do all the figures. His father had been in charge of a skating rink in Interlaken, not far from his home, and young Ed had built a number of rinks himself. One day he saw an ad for an English-speaking skating instructor in Adelboden, not far from where he lived. Thanks largely to his new language skills, Ed got the job. He kept it for three seasons.

At noon on sunny days in Adelboden the pavilion and restaurant next to the rink opened and an orchestra would start playing for the skaters. People rested outside at tables, the real men drank their wine, beer, or Scotch, the sissies drank coffee, and everyone ate lunch. The music played, Ed danced around and taught his pupils how to waltz on ice. Ed had had an excellent dancing teacher and with her help, he transposed what he learned in the ballroom to the skating rink.

One day, the second winter in Adelboden, a huge bear of a man came up to Ed and said to him in English: "Didn't I see you last summer in the Canadian Rockies?" At first, Ed could not remember. He thought for a moment, then replied: "You may have. I was there." The man went on insistently: "You climbed with me." Then it all came back. Ed had been the fellow's guide on Mount Niblock. His name was Joseph Wood, Jr., and he had come to Switzerland for the Christmas holidays. Wood's words helped Ed make the most important decision of his life. Now, he had a name and reputation in Canada and therefore the roots of a career in that far-off land.

Snow, cold and lingering traces of homesickness were not the principal reason why Uncle Ed so often crossed the stormy Atlantic. It was, rather, that wonderful dancing teacher who was equally graceful in the ballroom and on the skating rink. Uncle Ed had fallen in love.

Her name was Martha Heimann, and her father was the Notary in Grindelwald. The Heimanns were Uncle Ed's distant neighbors when he was young. Martha was a clean girl with rosy cheeks and a very sensitive nature. She had spent a year learning to sew from the Vogel family who lived in a house beneath a cliff across the street from Ed's. On Sundays Martha often climbed to the top of the cliff and sat in the sun reading a book. Ed would watch her there from a distance. In time, he met her, chatted and took her dancing and, less frequently, out on short boat rides. After he went to Canada in 1903, Ed saw her only after his return and then only in winters, but their relationship kept growing warmer.

They were married in 1909 at a time when Ed was still commuting back and forth between continents. He had yet to make up his mind where he would settle permanently. But despite the unavoidable separations of the early years, Martha remained steadfast, like a good daughter of the Oberland. Their union lasted sixty-five years until she died at the age of 91 in 1974.

As Thomas Wolfe wrote, there comes a time in every man's life when you can't go home again. That time had now come for Ed. In the spring of 1912, accompanied by Martha and their baby daughter, Gertie, he left Switzerland and sailed to Canada, never to return.

CAJ XVI-195, Glacier House
CAJ XVII-43, Glacier House

CHAPTER
V

HOME IN THE RANGE

"Where is the true man's fatherland?
Is it where he by chance is born?
Doth not the yearning spirit scorn
In such scant waters to be spawned?
Oh, yes! His fatherland must be
As the blue heavens, wide and free."
James Russell Lowell, "The Fatherland"

The words of Joseph Woods in Adelboden were not the only, nor the most important, reason why Uncle Ed decided to move permanently to Canada. For one thing, he disliked the lengthy summer separations from his growing family. For another, the Canadian Pacific wanted year-round guides — and it was holding out a carrot.

The job of importing seasonal guides to British Columbia had always been time-consuming and expensive. Each man's round trip required tickets on European trains, free transAtlantic boat journeys, and similar rail transport almost across the American continent. It seemed much more sensible to give the guides a home near Western Canada's mountains and let fare-paying immigrants use the shipping space otherwise occupied by the Swiss. Besides, the novelty of the annual Trafalgar Square and Montreal publicity circuses had lost its original vigor. News reporters, now jaded and dwindling in numbers, were no longer inquisitive. The photographers sometimes didn't even bother to show up. On top of everything, some of the guides, notably Ed's father, were threatening never to go back to Canada at all.

The ideal site, obviously, was Golden. It was, to be sure, a tiny, isolated, backwash frontier village with a sawmill, where the trains stopped mainly to unload heavy machinery or take on logs and lumber. It could use the tourist attraction of resident Swiss guides. Besides, it was located in the pleasant Columbia Valley a couple of hours ride from Lake Louise and the Rockies on the east and

Golden in 1911. The railroad bridge connected the Columbia River Lumber Company with the CPR. Howard Palmer photo — Archives of the American Alpine Club (AAC).

Edelweiss Village at Golden, as seen from the railroad. Archives of the Canadian Rockies.

from Glacier and the Selkirks on the west. There must be a way, so thought the management, to persuade the guides to settle in the vicinity of Golden and at the same time preserve, if possible on a permanent basis, the publicity value of the Trafalgar Square fanfaronade.

Thus it was that, in 1910, some unmemorable CPR official devised a scheme that was to have far-reaching consequences for the guides. He planned a home for them which would be a lasting and visible symbol of Swiss presence in Canada. It should be, the reasoning went, sufficiently distant from the nearest adjoining locality to prevent the guides from mingling too frequently with their fellow humans. This would maintain their 'Swissness' and insulate them from local complaints about the CPR, which were legion. Thus immunized, they could be expected eventually to become the Company's faithful retainers.

Two miles north of Golden, in full sight of the track, on the flanks of a gravelly, soil-poor hill, the company erected what its dignitaries imagined to be a typical Swiss settlement which they called Edelweiss Village. There were altogether six structures whose facades distantly reminded the observer of chalets. Each had its own flagpole where one could display the Swiss emblem with its white cross on a red background. Each had its carved, gingerbread fancy-work. Each had its cuckoo clock beside the door. About the only things missing were a local chocolate factory, some cheese, and a Swiss bank.

Over the years thereafter, the trains came and the trains went; and with every passage, this locality was pointed out, complete with a brief pitch on the virtues and safety of climbing with the company's genuine Swiss guides. Unfortunately, the guides were not too happy, and gradually deserted the premises for more practical quarters elsewhere.

In those years the railroad was not the only access to Golden, though for most practical travellers, it seemed a monopoly. From the early 1880s there had been, however, a number of colorful riverboats. Some were skippered by pilots who later went on to the Yukon and other northern rivers; all were very shallow draft and ramshackle affairs. But they did navigate the upper Columbia, from Golden all the way to the lakes. *Dutchess, Nowitka, Klahowya, Pert, Marion, Kyak* and others carried freight and passengers through the twisted meanders of the swampy river. They did this well and at a profit, with the skippers often taking the winter months, when the river was low and frozen over, for extended visits to the major fleshpots of the continent. But all that ended in 1914 when the Kootenay Central branch of the CPR was opened parallel to the river. Had it not been for frequent station stops or to avoid hitting cattle, the trains could have covered in an hour the distance that took the stern-wheelers two days. From that date, the railroad, which was almost synonymous with the government, controlled all the lines

Arrival in Golden, July 1912.
Elise Feuz, Walter Feuz, Ernest Feuz, Rosa Häesler, Chris Häesler Jr., Clara
Aemmer, Rudolph Aemmer, Joanna Heimann. E. Feuz Jr., photograph.

of communication and transportation in the Columbia Valley.

It was early summer of 1912, when Uncle Ed's wife, Martha, just arrived from the Oberland, first saw the houses where the CPR expected her to spend the rest of her days. On sight of them, she turned to her husband and exclaimed; "Edward, I think I am going to faint. They look like monkey cages." Martha burst into tears. She was right; aside from attractive fronts and their grand view to the west, the chalets were little better than stables. They were cold and drafty in winter; hot and dry in the summer, and there were no nearby amenities so essential for growing families. Over the years, these improvements were made, but not nearly soon enough to retain the impatient Ed.

While the younger Swiss grudgingly allowed themselves to be paraded, they were certainly not the railroad's trained seals. They were not about to sacrifice their privacy and dignity. The guides pondered, as they puffed on their ever-present pipes, whether the CPR might be trying to pull them around on an economic chain the way they pulled some of their clumsier clients on a rope.

The mind of a Swiss mountaineer often registers certain forms of input slowly, but this is due more often to pensiveness rather than density. Slowly, therefore, Ed and his associates concluded that the time would come when the guides would have to fight for what they considered to be their rights, their pride and their independence, that most notable of Swiss characteristics. The war might be long and mostly invisible, but thanks to Ed's caution and restraint, it never got beyond the smouldering point. In the end the guides prevailed so graciously that their victory even pleased their formidable opponent.

Until 1911 Ed's father, as senior and original guide, had handled all the organizational and paper work of his colleagues in the annual migration to Canada. When he decided that year not to return to the New World, he turned those chores over to his eldest son, and from then on Uncle Ed did the staff work. He arranged for transport, travelling expenses and hotel accomodations. He paid the bills and kept the books. He haggled and bargained with the CPR. It was for him an entirely new business, but he grew into it comfortably, and by so doing he became spokesman for all the guides.

The first problem was to get away from those fake chalets which some of the locals had begun to call the 'Golden Ghetto'. The records don't show it, but on this issue Martha must have been impressive. "You see", Ed reminisced, "the Company owned about two hundred acres around the village. They wanted to make a real Swiss settlement there; which, I suppose, people could visit by paying the railroad an admission fee — something like a prototype Disneyland." [Ed never used the word 'prototype' because he didn't know it, instead he used a more colorful adjective; he didn't really know much about Disneyland, either, but he knew what it stood for] "It might have been a good idea", he conceded, grudgingly. "But whoever's brainstorm it was didn't think very hard. Everything about it was wrong — even the land. They offered us ten-acre plots because they wanted us to be farmers. But we weren't farmers, and even if we knew how to farm, we didn't want to. We were certified guides. For years we'd worked and sweated and froze, and carried huge loads, got rained and snowed on, and almost killed just to earn those certificates. We weren't about to change; not for the CPR, and not for anyone else, either. We were Swiss; we were born free; we were guides and we were going to stay that way. Nobody was going to tell us how to lead our lives."

"You know", Ed was heating up, now, "they even had the nerve to ask me to go home and bring over a few dozen fellow Swiss to take the extra farms on the bottom land, most of which was swamp; and live up on the hillside in that fake Swiss zoo. All publicity; and not a thought for how we felt. It just couldn't work."

"Also times were bad," Ed went on. "But there was worse. We already had as many farmers as Golden could support, and they raised the finest stuff you ever saw; potatoes, corn, peas, beans, even tomatoes. Trouble was; where to sell it? The nearest real city was Vancouver. That's four hundred miles west. In the other direction there was Calgary, but it was tiny, and it raised oceans of food, anyhow. Here in Golden, the only place you could sell produce was at the sawmill. Farmers? In Golden? They'd have enough to eat alright, but precious little of anything else. If the CPR thought I'd go home and beat the drum to bring my friends over here for that kind of life, they had a lot more thinking to do. Why, if I'd done that my neighbors would have dipped me in tar and run me out of town."

"And then those houses. They were no good, and they were in the wrong place. Not even a flat spot to walk around. We couldn't get to town except along the track. My daughter, Gertie, she tried to get to school in winter, and there was snow. She was walking on the track and the plow came along, pitched her up in the snow and almost buried her, just like an avalanche. She was lucky that the men on the plow saw her. They dug her out and took her home. One of them told Martha; 'please, lady, don't send your little girl to school in this weather'. But what could you do? They didn't close schools in Canada because of snow. And Gertie, she wasn't like me; she loved school."

"Yes, there was snow, even in Golden. That's another thing that got me. I was still shovelling the stuff, just like at Glacier. Only at least there wasn't quite so much of it."

After two years, Ed had had enough. He arranged to live in a house near the fairgrounds in town, and in the end, after more years, only Walter, the youngest, still lived in the Edelweiss Village

Golden was not much of an improvement. The only real connection with the outside world was the rail line. In winter, if there were avalanches in the Rockies or Selkirks, there could be no connection at all. Golden was unattractive as a tourist center, so nobody much stopped there. The few who did usually stayed in the barn of a hotel which the CPR had constructed. As in most other frontier towns there were few inhabitants an educated European would have called other than barbarian. The locals seemed to consist mostly of rough, tough, semi-educated, hard-drinking loggers and lumbermen of Scandinavian, Scots, or, rarely of French-Canadian origin, a few trappers, prospectors and rivermen, a couple of dozen railway employees, and at the big Columbia River Lumber Company mill, a collection of decidedly more civilized Chinese. These last, however, were carefully relegated by their Caucasian brethren to the bottom of the social totem pole.

It was, thought Martha, a far cry from Switzerland. And in midwinter Golden was a lot colder. There was no fancy skating rink where she could dance; just a rough surface over which the local people played a brutal game called hockey. About the only substitute for the drinking and dining pavilions with their refined tourists sipping Scotch whiskey and champagne, were several local saloons which served greasy potatoes, tough steak, raw liquor and sometimes passable ale — and where the customers engaged in fisticuffs and even bottle fights. In Interlaken and Adelboden, when the sun shone in winter, there had been those wonderful bands with their beautiful music. In Golden, it was far too frigid to sit out doors, some days, even when the sun was out; and the only tunes to be heard above the whistles of locomotives, were the roar of passing trains and the eternal whine of the sawmill.

It wasn't Interlaken at all, nor even the more primitive Gsteigwiler. For the first years Martha was wretchedly homesick. The children could take it because they'd never known anything else. So could Ed; and if he could, so would Martha. Homesick or not, she would stick it out.

From the dawn of economic history, employers and employees have had their differences. More compensation and better conditions are standard employee desires, while more output and lower cost are constant employer themes. Relations between the Swiss guides, with the peppery Uncle Ed at their head, and the Canadian Pacific, with its often distant, but somewhat paternalistic attitude, were to be no exception. Like most big corporations of that time and this, the CPR had many different spokesman, invariably hundreds of miles apart, some of whom were completely uninformed of the thinking and commitments made by others. Without any conscious decision-making, such organizations can appear to be intentionally deceptive.

Before moving to Canada, Ed, with his father's help, had hammered out a five-year contract, which guaranteed the guides yearround work with the company. But once the Swiss had moved into their village above the tracks, other CPR officials managed to overlook some of the fine print. There would still be jobs in summer, at $5 a day, which was considered a fortune in the era before Henry Ford created the $5 eight-hour shift; but the rest of the year? Well, the guides would be on their own. What could they do about this turn of events? They had no union, no friends, no money and no other Swiss.

Ed and his four compatriots had to do something. So they marched down to the big sawmill by the river, where a few good men were always in demand. "We took jobs" Ed related "alongside the Chinamen, piling slabs to keep steam up in the big boiler that ran the planers. Those Chinamen, of course they spoke no Swiss, and very little English, and we couldn't even understand that because they talked so funny. But we got along fine. They were all business, those Chinamen, even though nobody ever paid them what they were worth. We weren't paid enough, either, but at least it was a lot better than not working for the CPR."

"What we should have done was quit the guide business and stay at the mill. In time we'd have made good money. But then, as soon as spring rolled around and it looked like there'd be another summer in the mountains after all, then the CPR superintendent came in his special car from Vancouver, and said they'd be happy to have us come back as guides."

"Well, I began to think; maybe after all we had them by the short hairs, but instead of giving a good yank, like I should have, I said 'Yes', we'd go back. You know, when you have a trade you love, like mountain guiding, it's very hard to give it up, even if you can make a lot of money at something else.".

"My first mistake was to believe the CPR people when we moved to Canada. My second mistake was to think that they would now keep their word. But those bums didn't have any intention of holding to their promise, and next winter it was the same story all over again."

In fact, however, the CPR, not Ed, had made the mistake. The guides had been treated as ignorant peasants, with no resourcefulness, but resourcefulness under pressure, is the quintessential attribute of a guide. Ed now wrote a letter of grievance to the Swiss consul in Montreal. In it he explained how the CPR had dishonored an agreement with respectable Swiss citizens and was now cheating them out of their livelihoods.

Henri Martin was a native of one of those French-speaking cantons which Ed despised. But he was, nevertheless, first and foremost a Swiss patriot, and Swiss patriots, whatever their language, class or social differences, bank together. In those days Switzerland paid most of its consular representatives only token salaries. The consuls were usually selected from prominent Swiss businessmen already abroad. Not only did the post of consul enhance the incumbent's social and financial standing in the host community, but it also provided the Swiss government, and therefore its citizens abroad, with inexpensive services, some of which were very substantial. Accordingly, Martin, already a fixture in Montreal, knew the right people in the CPR, and how to get to them. No doubt he spoke softly, as is Swiss wont, but as is Swiss habit, he also got results. The guides had no further trouble with job security — ever. Nor did anyone ever again tamper with their privacy or independence.

Uncle Ed, like all good Oberlanders, especially guides, had finally found the CPR short hairs. He had pulled on them very much in the way he pulled on a climbing rope. If it ever became necessary, he knew just the place where he could arrange to pull again. From then on there was steady work. In winter, two guides were employed in Glacier, the others at Lake Louise, where in addition to other chores they also served as caretakers. Wives and children were based in Golden; so, of course, Uncle Ed grumbled about the two seasonal separations.

Things, in fact, were not as bad as Ed made them out to be, and as it turned out, he was, himself, responsible for some of the absences. If the CPR could double-cross on employment, it also had a paternalistic interest in trying to keep its employees' families together. That was the other side of the coin. The company created special jobs for guides' wives and children at the Tea House on the Plain of the Six Glaciers above Lake Louise so that in summer the guides stationed there would be close to their loved ones. And in the off months, when Ed acted as caretaker at the deserted Lake Louise property, he alternated between ten days on the job and ten days off. Ed reverted to his old habit of roaming the countryside in search of big game. He took out guided parties into the mountains to chase after elk, bear and moose. His clients had good aim because they invariably came back with antlers and grizzly hides. Uncle Ed, however, usually returned grumpy, and completely out of ammunition.

Summer work consisted of guiding, which is what the Swiss were all about. In winter the CPR piped the job whistle and therefore had the upper hand. When, at last, the guides were given winter work, the superintendent, with a big grin, handed Ed back his old snow shovel.

Sooner or later most people who start a family, guides included, become involved with real estate. First it's their home. Then, if they persevere and prosper, it can be something else. After his escape from the Swiss Village, Uncle Ed acquired property nearer town. So after a while did most of the other guides. The village was almost deserted of Swiss. While expecting the chalets to retain their symbolic value, the CPR decided to dispose of the property which now had little value except as a landmark. The company offered the place to Ed, but he'd have nothing to do with it, nor would most of the other guides. In the end, after some persuasion, Walter took

Tea House at Plain of Six Glaciers in early summer. Byron Harmon photograph, Archives of the Canadian Rockies.

it and lived out his years there. But if Ed had no interest in the Swiss village, Golden did prove to be the scene of one or two modestly successful ventures on his part into real property, and that property gave him and Martha a comfortable roof under which to live.

Farther afield pastures looked greener, and Ed was to have two big opportunities. The first never materialized because Ed felt uncomfortable about it. The second proved to be Ed's pride and joy. For almost three decades, into the 1920's, Glacier House had been the star diamond on the CPR's string of mountain hotels. It had glistened that long thanks largely to Mrs. Young. But as time passed, she began to dry up with age, just as Glacier's chief attraction, the Illecillewaet dried up beyond comfortable reach of the hotel. As a result of the far-reaching publicity effort that Ed had such disparaging words about, tourists now began to congregate in the Rockies at more modern places with more photogenic glaciers.

Mrs. Young retired in 1920. Thereafter things declined fast. The wooden hotel, now labeled a fire trap, had grown old and shabby; here and there the roof leaked and the sills under the dining room and other older parts slowly began to rot. For a few years more the CPR reluctantly heeded the wishes of a few old-time veterans and kept the place open, but in 1925 the hotel was closed. The CPR had younger and more attractive mistresses in the mountains; Yoho, Emerald Lake, Wapta, Lake O'Hara, and the two prizes, Lake Louise and Banff.

"You can have Glacier for a dollar" the Company told Uncle Ed.

"Take it," urged Walter.

Uncle Ed puffed on his pipe and thought. "What would I have done with it?" he told his friends in later years. "I was a guide, not a businessman. even with the other guides, we couldn't raise enough money to fix the place right. And if we had, how would we have gotten anybody to stay there? The only way into that place and out was on the railroad, and I knew damn well the CPR would tell everybody to go to their hotels in Banff and Lake Louise, and that there was nothing in Glacier except a musty old firetrap run by a bunch of peasants. Why, what with us mortgaged to our ears, they'd be pounding nails in our coffins. But that was where the real mountaineers wanted to be, and closing Glacier was the biggest mistake the CPR ever made."

So after a couple of years the CPR turned Glacier over to a Calgary wrecker who tore everything down and sold it off, lumber, nails, equipment, furniture, even the guides' shovels.

Hotels are not the most important kind of alpine lodging — and Uncle Ed knew it. He felt there was a vacuum in Canada's mountains because of the absence of high level accommodation for serious mountaineers. In Switzerland there had been those wonderful climbing huts in every stategic location where you could eat, rest, take shelter from storms and from which you could sally forth bright-eyed and bushy-tailed in the early mornings to have a leisurely day on the crests. In Canada there was nothing. If you wanted to climb something important like, say, Mount Temple, you had to get up at two in the morning and fight your way by dark through the bushes and boulders for several hours before you even began to climb. By the time you got on top — if you ever made it that far — your tongue was hanging out, your heart pounding and your legs were dead. You had no taste for the view, nor, for that matter, for the cheese, the salami, the smoked salmon and the bottles of wine the hotel had carefully packed for your pleasure. The only thing you thought about was how you were going to get home before dark. Something, Ed mused, must be done to make climbing, at least in part of the Rockies, more civilized.

The year was 1921 and Ed knew where to start. Back of Lake Louise were two big snow mountains over 11,000 feet. Everyone wanted to climb Victoria on the right and Lefroy on the left. They were separated by a col at 9,600 feet on the Continental Divide named Abbot Pass in honor of Phillip Abbot, the American from the Appalachian Mountain Club, who had stumbled over something while trying to climb Mount Lefroy and didn't have a guide. He fell off and was killed. Abbot had the unique distinction of being the first fatality in serious American mountaineering. It would not be long before he had plenty of company, completely, as Uncle Ed used to say somewhat approvingly, from among guideless climbers. If you could just get some cement up to the pass and a good stone mason and a few building materials, you could build yourself a hut which would make the place almost as civilized as Switzerland and of which people would be proud.

Ed and Rudolph Aemmer drew up plans. They showed them around here and there, mainly to the Natural Resources people, then to the CPR. There were no takers — it looked like too much work at too high risk for too little reason. "Forget it!" said the dignitaries.

Uncle Ed, like all good guides, never gave up anything easily. Besides, he had made an important friend, someone who could wangle concessions out of the CPR. This was an Englishman named Basil Gardom, and more importantly, he was a construction superintendent for the CPR in the mountain area. A great lover of adventure in the outdoors, an excellent organizer, a good agronomist, and a compassionate gentleman, he had gotten to know Ed and his fellow guides well when they worked as caretakers around Lake Louise during the winters. They had given him ski lessons. Ed showed Gardom the plans. Gardom was fascinated. "Let's do it," he urged. In no time he had mesmerized the reluctant CPR into granting approval.

Thus was built the Abbot Hut, to this day the highest permanent housing structure in Canada. Over the years it has sheltered

Out on the lower glacier the pack train moved easily. Abbot Pass is two thousand feet higher. W. Feuz photograph.

Ernest on the roof of Abbot Pass Hut, checking things for the summer season of 1926. W. Feuz photograph.

A cache, secure from most avalanches, was the end of the line for horses.
W. Feuz photograph.

thousands of weary climbers of differing generations. It stands today as Uncle Ed's most useful and lasting monument in the New World.

It was a job to build. From Lake Louise the only route to the pass, 4,500 feet higher, was up the glacier and into a narrow defile to the really steep part. This defile was overhung on the Mount Victoria side by ice-cliffs which collapsed at unpredictable moments covering everything below with big blocks of ice and other debris. Once above it you were safe, but it was still steep.

Ed headed operations. He hired a cool, sensible wrangler to lead lightly laden horses through the crevasses. One crevasse, the highest, was too wide for the horses and, unfortunately, completely spanned the slope. Ed built a strong ladder so he and the other guides could carry the loads over that obstacle. Above, the stuff was loaded on a sled which was then hauled up to the pass by a winch. Things that didn't fit the sled were backpacked up by the guides — in time about two tons.

If it had been a job to build, it was also quite a hut. Ed recalled: "On the outside it was all stone masonry, lined with three ply on the inside. The cabin had a big room for the kitchen and dining, a gentleman's dormitory, an attic with lots of mattresses. There was even a sleeping room for ladies." Ed winked, then resumed: "That was Martha's idea. She didn't want us repeating what I'd done with Mr. Hearst's girls.

"In the early days we had a big wood cookstove, which meant wood had to be hauled up on our backs. And somebody even put in a pump organ so you could have music, just like on the Adelboden skating rink."

The official inauguration took place in the spring of 1923. It was a gala affair. Twenty Applachian Mountain Club members, led by Boston Brahmin Dean Peabody, Jr., travelled all the way from Massachusetts to witness the event and pay tribute to their dead fellow-member for whom the structure was named. Uncle Ed and the four other Swiss guides led the way up through the dangerous places. Previously skeptical railroad officials tagged along behind.

At Abbot Hut Uncle Ed finally managed to say a few words between cups of hot grog: "Down in the valley, a house, a big house is just a big house. But up here, in the ice and snow, with all those beautiful peaks everywhere, this simple hut is home."

Ed climbed to Abbot Pass scores of times during his long career. Because he loved the mountains, he always enjoyed these outings. Most were so routine he never remembered them well. And he never managed to fall into a crevasse, at least not in this neighborhood. But there was one ascent that was to be memorable.

In order to maintain the hut's fuel supply, it was necessary to make frequent porter trips to Abbot Pass. Each person who brought up a suitable load of wood got paid $.50, which in those days was real money. The costs were recovered by charging tourists an extra $.50 apiece for each night's cooking fuel while in residence.

"One day," Ed recalled, "over in the kitchen at Lake Louise, when there wasn't much work to do, some of the boys had been given the day off. There were four of them, three Swiss including the pastry chef, Ernest Boker, and one French fellow. They'd never been up in these mountains and wanted to see the Abbot Hut. We guides were going up with loads of wood, and they asked if they could come along. I said: "Sure; we'll be glad to have you, and you can carry some wood and maybe even make a little money.""

"We started out from the Tea House, above Lake Louise, where my wife worked. We left at about 5:00 in the morning, each of us with a load of wood on his back. The path is right up the glacier and goes through a very narrow slot, maybe a quarter of a mile wide, between the two mountains, Lefroy and Victoria. There's a lot of ice, big chunks like a house, that tumble off the mountains, mainly Victoria. When they came down, they often fell right across the gorge. We called this place the Death Trap because it was so dangerous. We usually went through it as fast as we could. Also we always spread out so if some people got hit or buried there'd be survivors to help or dig them out. It was a spooky place, even for us guides. But we had to go through there to reach the pass. There was no other way."

They moved up the glacier in two parties, about three hundred yards apart. Ed led the first group, with Ernest Boker and the French boy, and Chris Haesler had charge of the second. At seven o'clock they were working their way through the crevasses along the bottom of the Death Trap. The loads were heavy so the men climbed slowly. The air was clear and all was still.

CRACK! It sounded like a bolt of lightning out of nowhere. Then from the Victoria side came a boom like thunder, a boom that reverberated across the canyon walls and grew louder until it was deafening. Ed hardly needed to glance upwards at the huge white cloud that rocketed towards him. At once the party broke and ran downhill seeking any ephemeral shelter on the edge of the gorge. But the plume of white death moved faster. One instant Ed was still in the clear, the next the hurricane winds of the avalanche picked him up and tossed him among the great, foamy waves of tumbling snow and ice. For a second he was on top, trying to dig in with his ice-axe. The next he went under. As he did so, he thrust up one arm. Everything came to rest and there was silence.

"I couldn't even move a finger," Ed recalled. "All that snow and stuff froze solid the second it stopped, solid as a rock. There was just a little pocket of air in front of my face so I could breathe, but the air wouldn't last long. Pretty soon I'd be dead."

"Then all at once I heard a scratching. A moment later my head was clear and I could see the sky. As I looked up, there was that

Avalanche pouring off Mt. Victoria in Death Trap. W. Feuz photograph.

French boy. He had seen my fingers sticking out of the snow where I had thrown up my arm. He looked pretty scared and he was crying. But he kept digging, digging with no gloves on, to get me out. His hands were so cold he screamed with pain; and still he kept at it. It was very difficult for him because I'd hurt my leg and it was twisted into the snow, and that snow was all frozen hard, the way it gets after an avalanche."

Back on the surface Ed looked around. Packs, ice-axes, all gear had been torn away and had vanished into crevasses. And there was no sign of the pastry chef!

Frantically, Ed and the French boy, still crying from the pain in his hands, searched among the great ice chunks of the avalanche. A half hour had now passed since the accident, and Ed was about to give up hope. Suddenly between two blocks of ice, Ed spotted Boker's hat. It was still on the pastry chef's head. The chef lay immobilized, just under the surface, with hands folded over his chest. To Ed's immense relief, he was still breathing. But he was temporarily blind.

The other party was equally battered. Chris Haesler had been thrown into the cliff by the force of the avalanche. One boy was bleeding badly where he'd been hit in the head by falling ice, and had also suffered a rupture. And Ed had sprained an ankle and could barely walk. But Saint Bernard, patron of guides, had protected them; everyone was still alive. Ed and Chris had yet to lose a client or companion.

They gathered a little strength. Then the two parties limped slowly back to the Tea House. Martha and Ed's daughters were there to meet them. Martha had heard the deadly roar a couple of hours earlier and had watched the white cloud descend. She knew Ed was up there somewhere, under it. But all she had done at the time was to turn to her daughters and say, stoically: "That must have hit your Dad. That's bad.". . .and then she had simply gone back to her business; a true daughter of the Oberland.

Soldiers and mountaineers rarely boast of their narrow escapes, but unlike soldiers, mountaineers often talk about them, mostly among themselves. They're not trying to evoke memories, however. Rather, they are in search of exchanges of information to discover ways to prevent a recurrence. In later years Uncle Ed often talked to others about his experience in that great avalanche.

"In my life I went up there hundreds of times, both before and after," Ed recalled. "I went up because it was my job and because there was no other way. Also maybe because I loved to climb. I was even there when I was eighty-five years old. But you always took a chance. You never knew when it might happen again. Ice avalanches are unpredictable. It's not a question of the time of day, nor of the heat or the cold. And don't imagine just because one avalanche has cleared a lot of stuff that there won't be another one on its heels. Maybe there won't, but maybe there will. It's a matter of pressure from the ice above, and nobody knows what those pressures are doing. So when the ice is ready to go, it goes; at dawn, at dusk, at noon, at midnight, or any time in between."

"We guides were either very good or very lucky — maybe both. From 1899 to 1949, when I retired, there wasn't a single serious accident to one of our guided parties. Sure, we had a few bruises here and there, and people got hit from time to time by pieces of that loose rock that make the Canadian Rockies famous. And, of course, there were narrow escapes. But never anything serious, like somebody getting killed."

"Nowadays most people don't use guides — and there's lots of accidents. In my time there was hardly ever an accident, and then only to guideless parties. I'm not against guideless climbing. I pretty much started that way myself, even if my father helped. But it means taking more chances, no matter how good you are."

"Even in my time there were a lot of young fellows who loved the mountains, but they just didn't have money for a guide. After 1921 our rate was $7 for a single day, and that was a lot for a poor boy in those times. So we'd give these fellows all the good information and advice we could, show them pictures, and then hope for the best. Mainly we tried to teach them to look out for traps, because the easiest way up a mountain can also be the most dangerous. We just didn't want anyone to get into trouble. And most of all we didn't want to have to go out on rescue missions or looking for dead bodies."

It was out of real concern for the safety of others that Ed until his dying day kept repeating to visiting mountaineers the details of the close call he had had that morning in 1924 on his way to Abbot Pass. Thanks to Ed's repeated accounts climbers like Norman Brewster and Ken Jones, who were neighbors and friends of the Feuz family knew the story almost by heart, and although they took more chances than Ed, they were always aware of his words of advice and acted accordingly. "Whether paid or not," Ed would say, "it is a guide's duty to instruct strangers." Some years later, Brewster put it differently, "Ed was a good teacher, a born teacher, perhaps; and he was also consistently gracious with young people who showed any interest in the mountains."

Beaver — Summer 1979, Edelweiss Village

CHAPTER
VI

WHO WERE THOSE GUIDES, ANYWAY?

"Beyond the East the Sunrise, beyond the West the Sea,
And East and West the wanderlust that will not let me be.
It works in me like madness, dear, to bid me say goodbye!
For the seas call, and the stars call, and oh, the call of the sky!

I know not where the white road runs, nor what the blue hills are,
But man can have the sun for friend, and for his guide a star;
And there's no end to voyaging when once the voice is heard,
For the river calls, and the road calls, and oh, the call of a bird!

Yonder the long horizon lies, and there by night and day
The old ships draw to home again, the young ships sail away:
And come I may, but go I must, and if men ask you why,
You may put the blame on the stars and the sun
and the white road and the sky".
　　　　Gerald Gould, 1885-1916 — *Wanderlust*

　　Statistics, a wise man once said, are the poison of a dull mind.
But if some consider them a road to perdition, they are for others
the highway to Nirvana. Whatever the case, you can use them to
prove just about anything you want. Uncle Ed used to wave around
a whole catalog of figures about the guides.
　　Depending on how you count, there are more than one thousand
mountains within what can be called the Canadian Pacific's "zone
of influence." About four hundred of these were first ascended by
parties led by European — mostly Swiss — guides in the period
beginning when Peter Sarbach came to Canada as the first professional alpinist, until Uncle Ed closed his Fuhrerbuch in 1949. At
that later time several hundred peaks still remained unclimbed.
Thus of all the mountains first ascended before 1950 close to 80%
were scaled by guided parties.
　　These climbs were made by no more than twenty-seven

predominantly Swiss guides of whom most came over from Europe for a few seasons only and of which just six, one an Austrian, settled permanently in Canada while still serving their vocation. Most of the time these guides were engaged in routine bread-and-butter repeat performances on peaks like Temple, Victoria and Lefroy in the Rockies and Sir Donald, Tupper and Uto in the Selkirks. This kept them so busy that only thirteen guides are known to have each made more than ten first ascents.

First ascent clients weren't numerous either. Less than 300 people, guides included, were responsible for all the first ascents in Canada prior to 1950. These people came principally from the United States, Britain, Canada and Switzerland, countries which in those days had a combined population in excess of 150 million. That works out to one exploratory mountaineer for every 500,000 people. The true alpinist of those days was a rare bird!

Of course it was Uncle Ed who made the largest number of first ascents, with over one hundred by the time he retired. His nearest competitors made only 62. Ed Feuz, Jr. made 25% of all the first ascents achieved by his predecessors and contemporaries combined. For sheer numbers, no one else came near.

Not all Ed's ascents were difficult. By modern standards most would be rated easy. But some, like South Twin and Sir Sandford were dangerously isolated. Every peak had at least one critical spot. On a few, like Amery, Ed's party got caught in very bad weather. On most, such as Quadra, there was hard work and the ever-looming shadow of responsibility.

Ed's fifteen distant rivals, in order, were as follows: Conrad Kain (Austrian) with 62 first ascents; then Christian Kaufmann with 45; Ed's brother, Ernest, 40; Rudolph Aemmer with 33; Christian Haesler, Jr., 23; Ed's brother, Walter, 23; Peter Kaufmann, a guide who came over briefly in the 1930s, 19; Ed's father, Edward Feuz, Sr., 17; Christian Haesler, Sr., 14; Joseph Pollinger 14; Hans Kaufmann 13; Gottfried Feuz, 11; Christian Klucker, 10; and Christian Bohren, 10.

The early guides got the cream, unless, like Robson and Sir Sandford, that cream was unknown or out of reach. Later arrivals, like Ed, had to scrounge around or venture afield.

The six men who stayed permanently in Canada had the advantage of year-round physical presence in their climbing arena while transient guides did not. But almost every guide who came over from Europe before World War II had a least the opportunity to make one first ascent.

Who were these guides, anyway?

With respect to the early ones, all that is left is the written record. But for the five Swiss guides employed by the CPR, there exists living testimony of some who knew them well. Oliver Eaton (Tony) Cromwell and his wife, the former Georgia Engelhard were quick to say:

"They weren't great guides in the sense that they climbed all over the world and got involved with the most famous alpinists. But they were ideal for what they did. They were much different from the usual European guides and displayed greatness in attempting countless new routes. They were excellent at finding their way around the mountains when there were no trails, maps, guidebooks or anyone who had been there before."

"Technically, they were never the equals of Armand Charlet, Gino Solda, Matthias Rebitsch or Raymond Lambert. They didn't have to be — but they did need to be strong and enormously resourceful, because on our climbs you could never 'go down to the village' for help; there were no villages around."

The twenty-seven European guides who brought professional mountaineering to Canada can be divided into two groups: the pioneers, who commuted; and the settlers who stepped into their predecessors' boots and stayed there until after World War II. Uncle Ed knew them all, some better than others. He was never bashful, either, to express his opinion — and Ed could be devastatingly opinionated. There were no namby-pamby niceties when he reached into the closet and pulled out the bones.

All early guides were employed seasonally. They came in late spring, spent the summer, and returned to Europe when activities ended with autumn. Some, like Peter Sarbach, visited Canada only once. Others, like Edward Feuz, Sr., kept returning year after year well into the twentieth century.

Uncle Ed could say this about the early guides. "Those fellows, like my father, had one real advantage. They belonged to a generation when people could still make first ascents in the Alps. They knew how to guide up a mountain that hadn't been climbed whether it was in Switzerland, Africa, South America or Asia. Those like me came later. We had learned to follow in others' tracks, but when it was a matter of going where nobody had been, we had to learn for ourselves. It is easy to repeat what others have done, but to do something *new*, well, that's a job, even if the next fellow calls it a piece of cake."

"I knew most of those early guides, and my father told me more. They lived pretty sober lives and they were tough — some of them didn't die until they were nearly 100. I met the oldest ones because they were still alive when I was learning the trade. Of course, I preferred the ones from the Oberland — except for the Kaufmann brothers, that is. I'm kind of clannish, you know; I was brought up that way and it sort of stuck to my ribs."

The prototype Swiss guide in Canada was Peter Sarbach, whom Professor Harold Bailey Dixon and Norman Collie hired for the 1897 season in the Rockies. Born in St. Niklaus just below Zermatt in the Valais in 1844, he was old enough twenty years later to have participated with Whymper in that greatest of mountaineering dramas that unfolded in 1864 on the Matterhorn. When he reached Canada he was 53, but like many older guides, still strong and vigorous.

He made the first ascents of Victoria and four peaks, including Lefroy where he avenged the death a year earlier of his old client, Philip Stanley Abbot. Thereafter Sarbach returned to Saint Niklaus where he died in 1930 aged 86.

Abbot's accident and Sarbach's subsequent success served to persuade the CPR that in the interest of its budding tourist trade, it had a need for professional mountaineers. A year later, through the Cook Travel services in Interlaken, railway officials got in touch with the Oberland guide Edward Feuz, Sr., Uncle Ed's father. With him and his old climbing buddy, Christian Haesler, Sr., they worked out an arrangement. The contract marked the start of continuous summer Swiss guide service, first at Glacier House, then at Lake Louise and Field.

In the early days, guides came and went, and eventually vanished. Even the older Ed Feuz, after crossing the Atlantic some twenty-six times, got tired of family separations, interminable train rides and chronic sea-sickness. After 1911, he stayed home until his death in 1944 at 85. Chris Haesler, Sr. had already gone back the previous year; but in 1918, following his wife's death, he returned to live in Golden with his son, Christian, Jr.

Edward Whymper appeared in 1901 with his own platoon of four Swiss guides for his first big season in the Rockies, all under contract with the ubiquitous CPR. It is possible the large number of guides reflected a subconscious recognition on Whymper's part that he had reached a sufficiently advanced age and saturated state of inebriation that he might well have to be carried up the mountains.

Whymper was a hard taskmaster and his bouts with the bottle didn't help. Of the four guides, only one ever served him again or, for that matter, returned to Canada. Besides, each guide had special reasons of his own for not returning. Joseph Pollinger had left valuable, high-paying clients in Europe, among them, at one time or another, Alfred Mummery, Leopold Amery, J. Norman Collie and even Henry L. Stimson. Moreover, he had sensitive culinary tastes which required the best of French and Italian gastronomy and which could never be satisfied by the New World's barbarian fare. Christian Klucker needed a forum at least as challenging as the high Alps in which to practice his special technical skills; and he indicated in his autobiography that this forum was not easily found around Glacier or Lake Louise, and certainly not at Banff. Joseph Bossonay, the only Frenchman in Whymper's act, had six lonely children in Chamonix.

There was a high desertion rate among Whymper's retinue, so each year he visited Canada, he had to beat the drum for new recruits. One of these was Heinrich Burgener, a son of the famous guide, Alexander Burgener. Like most of the others, Burgener stayed only one season during which he made four first ascents.

Other guides also made their appearances, either in the service of private clients or as employees of the CPR. Christian Bohren, of the older generation, worked in Canada only a few years in the course of which he had the distinction, with the elder Haesler, of making the first ascent and traverse of Assiniboine. The powerful Karl Schluneggar of Wengen spent a few seasons in Glacier, while the gentle, diminutive, meticulous Friedrich Michel was so home-sick he had to be sent back before his first season was over. Jacob Mueller, a veteran of the Caucasus and sometime guide for explorer-mountaineer E. W. D. Holway, was at Lake Louise just two summers before returning for good to his native Lauterbrunnen. Moritz Inderbinen, of Zermatt, much travelled and well-versed in English, served Norman Collie and Mumm, among others, in 1909 and 1913 and returned for one more stay in 1920. Finally, there was the jingoist Christian Jorimann of Tamins in Graubunden who worked intermittently as a guide from 1903 through 1913 for the CPR and who after 1914, to much local consternation, appeared as a fanatical backer of Teutonic imperialism — a sentiment he would have done better to suppress in this time and place. Somehow he weathered the resulting tempest, changed professions and, after proper apologies, was allowed to settle in Vancouver.

In those years there was also Ed's cousin, Gottfried Feuz, an excel-lent guide and frequently one of Ed's companions, notably on the

Jacob Muller *Peter Kaufmann* *Christian Kaufmann.*
Peter Schlunegger *Hans Kaufmann* *Edward Feuz*

E. Broman photo from Cafe Oberland in Wengen.

first ascent of Mount Tupper in the Selkirks. Though he and his wife were very happy when stationed at Glacier, the prospect of life in the Edelweiss Village at Golden was not to their liking, so after 1911, they went back for good to the Oberland.

Two guides merit special mention in part because of noteworthy achievement, in part because Uncle Ed was never to forget them until his dying day. They were brothers, members of a renowned Oberland guiding family, and their father had briefly visited Canada. They were Christian and Hans Kaufmann.

For two seasons, no doubt a record, the Kaufmanns had somehow managed to tolerate employment under Edward Whymper. When, however, their eccentric boss departed in 1903, they were left at loose ends. Edward Feuz, Sr., impressed with their record, as well as their English-speaking abilities, persuaded the C.P.R. to hire them.

The elder brother, Christian, was the more experienced. Probably his best-known client was Winston Churchill, who was yet to earn his laurels in other capacities, but whom he helped guide up the Wetterhorn in 1894. In 1899 he had accompanied the great Dr. Tom Longstaff for six enthusiastic weeks and somehow reluctantly stuck with Whymper in Canada in 1901 and again in 1903. The younger brother, Hans, climbed in Canada with Collie, Stutfield, Wooley and Weed, whom he considered "perfect gentlemen", when compared with Whymper. In addition to their command of English, both guides were tall and handsome. They were ideal for Canada and seemed ideal for the CPR.

If in later years you wanted to stir up a grandiose electrical storm, it was merely necessary to mention either of the Kaufmann's names in Uncle Ed's presence. He would inhale deeply on his pipe, puff out a cloud of blue smoke in which you could almost see the lightning flash, and then he would thunder: "They played a dirty trick on my good friend Professor Fay." Whereupon the wicked details would rain down on his listeners.

"Professor Fay," Ed prefaced, "was my friend, and he was famous. He started the Appalachian Mountain Club in Boston and later he was president of the American Alpine Club. He was a great advertisement for the Canadian Pacific because he brought out all the rich and famous American people to climb at Glacier and Lake Louise. He was a lot more valuable to the railroad and to us than a dozen of those press agents who interviewed us in Trafalgar Square and Montreal every year."

"Back of Moraine Lake there's a valley surrounded by ten peaks. The Geographic Board had just named the first peak Mount Fay in the professor's honor. It was unclimbed."

"Naturally, Professor Fay wanted to be the first to climb it. He hired Hans Kaufmann to take him up. But just then an English lady, Gertrude Benham, a very strong climber who had been all over the Oberland, sneaked up to Christian and asked him to get her up

Professor Fay at Glacier with the guides Peter Schlunegger on his left and Christian Häesler on his right. James Outram photo — AAC Archives.

there ahead of Fay."

"Christian knew the country. He'd been there with an American named Allen, who had made a map, and climbed several of the peaks. Those he hadn't climbed, Mount Fay included, he'd seen from Deltaform across the way, and he knew exactly how to find the easiest way up. Both brothers thought it would be a great joke to fool old man Fay."

"The two parties started out at the same time by different routes. Christian went the easy way with Miss Benham and romped up the mountain. Hans took the old professor up Consolation Valley where everything goes straight up. The two of them puttered around and couldn't get anywhere. So when they finally gave up and went back to Louise they found the others had made an ascent but weren't talking much."

"It was some while before Professor Fay found out what the Kaufmann brothers had been up to. When he did, he went straight to the big boss of the CPR: 'Either they go,' he stormed, 'or I won't come back.' 'Don't worry,' replied Mr. Van Horne, 'we'll take care of those bums.' They wrote my father a letter from Montreal: 'NO MORE KAUFMANNS' it said. That was the end of them — and good riddance."

Quadra Mountain and Consolation Lake, northeast wall of Mount Fay on the right. Byron Harmon photograph — Archives of the Canadian Rockies.

Over the years Fay's friendship with Uncle Ed kept growing stronger. On his last visit to Canada in 1930, now 84, Fay asked Ed, who happened to be with his brother Walter and Dr. Hickson, to accompany him ten miles up Prospector's Valley to examine the new Alpine Club hut named in Fay's honor. There the four spent the night and the next morning Ed and Fay parted forever. Six months later, the old professor was gone but not Ed's memories. Wrongs done to an Oberlander's friend are never forgotten.

Three quarters of a century after the Mount Fay episode, in 1980, there was an international convocation of guides in Banff held under the auspices of the Association of Canadian Mountain Guides. Some of the European participants journeyed over to Golden to meet the lengendary Edward Feuz, now 95. Politely they introduced Ed to the leader of the Swiss delegation who was described as "proprietor of a large Grindelwald hotel and the scion of a distinguished family of Oberland guides, Herr Christian Kaufmann." Ed looked at him, took a deep puff on his pipe, drew himself up to his full stature of five feet one inch, then exploded: "Dein Vater war ein Drecksackel!"

Mostly the guides came and went like clouds around the peaks. But there were six who planted their feet in Canada and stayed. All but one were Oberlanders.

Rudolph Aemmer (1883-1973) was Uncle Ed's closest friend since childhood, the only one somehow unrelated to the others. Rudolph's escapades with Ed went back to the Aarmuehle school where they had teased their hated teacher and tossed spitballs at her when she wasn't looking.

In later days Rudolph became an apprentice carver in ivory. He soon learned from Ed, however, that there were more exciting things to do in the mountains than to sit around all day with a knife in your hand. He became a member of the Swiss Alpine Club, earned a guide's license in 1907 and two years later joined Ed in Canada. It was a happy-go-lucky time for both. When not busy with clients, the two went climbing together for the fun of it — and, of course, ran risks they never would have dared when working with clients. When pressed, Uncle Ed might sometimes admit there were even a couple of minor accidents, even a broken leg or two.

Rudolph was by far the handsomest guide in Golden. One might almost have called him picturesque. He looked precisely the way a guide should. An inveterate pipe smoker, like Ed, he had friendly brown eyes, plump rosy cheeks and sported a magnificent black handlebar mustache. The gold band in his earlobe, with his dark and becoming tan, made him appear dashing and gypsylike. All this, along with his slow and deliberate manner used to provoke Ed into explosions of Swiss-German impatience. So handsome was he that in 1928 he almost became an overnight movie star. United Artists selected him as a double for John Barrymore in the filming near Lake Louise of segments of *Eternal Love*. Ed, however, always

Rudolph Aemmer acting as John Barrymore's double in the movie "Eternal Love", filmed on Victoria Glacier, Lake Louise, 1928. Archives of the Canadian Rockies.

Camilla Horn (leading lady in "Eternal Love" filmed at Lake Louise, 1928). Archives of the Canadian Rockies.

suspected the choice was made thanks to a cabalistic conspiracy among members of the Masonic Order to which Rudolph belonged. Whatever the case, women worshipped Rudolph just as they worshipped Barrymore — and Rudolph more than gladly reciprocated. Domestic jealousy never presented a problem for him — long after his marriage you always found him surrounded by pretty girls.

Women could, however, get impatient with him. He was slow, careful, meticulous — like all artists who carve. One morning, on the Illecillewaet Glacier he had gone out on a excursion with a group of ladies. As happens to every guide from time to time, Rudolph, in the lead, suddenly fell half-way into a hidden crevasse. His pipe dropped from between his teeth and vanished into the black abyss. At once Rudolph cancelled the excursion. For the rest of the day, the ladies had to sit disconsolately in the snow while Rudolph popped in and out of the crevasse in search of his missing property. Needless to say, the pipe was never found.

There was a very deep streak of gallantry in Rudolph. On July 16, 1921 Dr. Winthrop Ellsworth Stone, aged 59, President of Purdue University and elder brother of Harlan Fiske Stone who was to become Chief Justice of the United States, had set out with his wife, Margaret, to make the first ascent of Mount Eon in the Assiniboine area. Stone reached the summit alone having left Margaret on a

Ernest and Rudolph at one of the ACC Camps in the 1930's. Nick Morant photograph.

ledge about a hundred feet from the top. On his way back to her, he fell and was killed. The accident left the less experienced Mrs. Stone stranded alone at over 10,500 feet. It was two days before the Stones were reported missing. A massive search was launched, including packers, wardens, fellow climbers — and Rudolph. For a week operations continued without results. At last, on the ninth day after the accident, when hope was almost lost, Rudolph spotted Mrs. Stone alive just under the summit. She had stayed there without shelter or sustenance. Aided by Bill Peyto, Rudolph hurried up to her and with gentle hands, the two men brought her to safety.

Rudolph and four others received funds and a special citation from the American Alpine Club. Rudolph accepted his reward philosophically, as do most good professionals. "Real guides," he said, "cannot be heroes. When somebody gets into trouble in the mountains, we go after him, take the necessary risks, and bring him down. Nothing else counts." In 1950, fourteen years after the loss of both his children, Rudolph retired and returned to Switzerland. He was the only Golden Swiss guide to leave Canada. He never saw his old friend Ed again, for he died in Europe at 90 in 1973 without once returning to the land of his fame. Rudolph and his wife's remains were, however, brought back to Golden where they lie beside the bodies of their two sons.

Christian Haesler, Jr. (1889-1940) was a lover of nature and wildlife. He was the only son of Christian Haesler who had come over with the elder Feuz in 1899. He got his guide's license in 1911, but since he had neither a steady job nor a girl friend, Uncle Ed found him both. He introduced Chris to his first cousin, Rosa Margarita, and as soon as the two were engaged, found Chris a job as a guide with the CPR. Hardly had the fiances stepped off the train in Golden in the summer of 1912, when they were married.

Their life in Canada would be tragic. In 1924, Chris' father, who had returned to live with his son in Canada following his wife's death, committed suicide after a domestic quarrel. Thereafter, little by little, the entire family succumbed. The younger son, William Albert, perished in an explosion when he was experimenting with dynamite. The elder son, Christian Walter, who served in the Air Force in World War Two, died prematurely of a heart attack during the 1950s. There were no other children. Rosa became hopelessly insane, had to be confined, and soon died. Finally came the cruelest blow of all, the savage grizzly attack in the Yoho in the autum of 1939. Chris barely managed to make two or three more climbs the following summer, blessedly including the first ascent of a peak in the Rockies that now bears his given name. Three months later he, too, was dead.

Though a fine and widely admired guide, there was less drama in the life of Ed's younger brother, Ernest Feuz (1889-1960). In 1909, he arrived in Glacier with his guide's license and remained there under Mrs. Young's accommodating tutelage to "learn the

Guides Christian Häesler Jr., Ernest Feuz and Walter Feuz at ACC Camp. Byron Harmon photograph, Archives of the Canadian Rockies.

Walter in dapper pose at Lake Louise. Ken Jones photograph.

language". In 1912 he married Elise Schmidt, also an Oberlander, who gave him two sons and a daughter. The family stayed thirty years in the Swiss Village of Edelweiss which Uncle Ed so despised.

Men excel in different things. Many clients considered Ed the more capable guide, but there were exceptions, such as the outstanding German-American climber, Fritz Wiessner, who favored Ernest. Ed, however, was more audacious and inquisitive. Ernest, however, was the better woodsman and certainly the better hunter (which was not difficult). But he lacked Ed's easy ways of making friends and telling funny stories laced with a few well-timed exaggerations. He also had the handicap of living all his life in the shadow of his elder brother, who never let anyone forget who was senior.

"You know," Ed recalled, "Ernest once came to me with a problem. He had a lady client — a real, first class alpinist. Trouble with her was she never got tired and she climbed much too fast. She was always so close behind Ernest she kept butting into his rucksack — and that's irritating. I told him that if he were like the Kaufmann brothers, or his client were someone like Whymper, then the night before a climb he ought to eat a big bowl of baked beans and raw onions. But I said, 'You can't do a thing like that to a nice lady.' 'But how can I handle the problem?' said Ernest. That was where Ernest didn't have the best touch, no sense of public relations."

The youngest of the Feuz brothers settling Canada was Walter (1894-1985). He was ten years Ed's junior and arrived without employment in 1912, aged 18. Ed found him a job as bellboy at Glacier House under the ever helpful Mrs. Young. There he kept company with Joanna Heimann, Ed's sister-in-law, a bright lass who worked as a storekeeper. The two married and in time had nine children.

In his first years in Canada Walter became an excellent alpinist. He never obtained a Swiss guide's license, but Ed, Ernest and the others vouched for him with the CPR after 1920 when guide services were suddenly in great demand with the onrush of post World War I tourists and Ed found himself desperately short of help. Walter lived up to his brothers' standards, although his activities as a guide were somewhat sporadic. Like many persons raised in land lacking iodine, he develped thyroid trouble, and although eventually cured, he was frequently incapacitated. Walter had one additional handicap in his profession; no fuhrerbuch. His livelihood was the result of his two brothers' goodwill; not an always secure position.

Those few women climbers who considered Rudolph a bit too swashbuckling for their tastes often turned to Walter. One of these was Kate Gardiner, a seasoned English climber who was single and who, in addition, had plenty of time and money. In 1928 she went with Walter into the Southern Rockies. She returned in 1929 and

1930 and each time the two again headed into the rugged but dryer country south of Banff and Lake Louise. It was in those two years and in Kate Gardiner's company that Walter made 15 of the 23 first ascents ascribed to him.

There lived, however, another man who was neither Swiss nor Oberlander, yet for whom, despite his native prejudices and provincial preferences, Uncle Ed developed a profound respect and admiration. In temperament this man was totally different from the Swiss guides. To the extent they were cautious, so was he intrepid; to the extent they clung to tradition, so he sought innovation; to the extent they bowed to convention, so he constructed his own road and marched boldly along it. Such a man was Conrad Kain (1883-1934).

Kain was a born traveller, something of a professional hobo, bitten with eternal wanderlust. He had come to Canada in 1909 as a guide from Nasswald, an impoverished hamlet in the Austrian Tyrol. Over the years he held a variety of ill-paid, short-lived jobs, sometimes in mines or quarries, running a trap line, and, most frequently, with the Alpine Club of Canada. He was, however, too proudly independent, too great a lover of mountains, too much the gentle, philosophical anarchist to get himself chained to any formal institution. He guided, took what came his way — occasionally poached — and stayed poor.

Bound to no one, Kain travelled the map. Unlike the CPR's Swiss guides, he could work anywhere and with anyone he pleased, in Canada or abroad. In 1912, after a botanical trip to Russia, he visited New Zealand where he made several first ascents and where he was repeatedly to return. Equally skilled on rock and ice, his technical ability would have been a match for many of today's best professionals. Only Uncle Ed, whose career spanned many more years, guided a greater number of first ascents in Canada than did Kain.

Two of Kain's climbs were exceptional. One was Bugaboo Spire in the Purcells where the key move, even if no longer highly rated, still requires great mental fortitude. That first time, in 1916, when no one had been there before, and with, once launched, no chance to turn back, Kain must have felt excruciatingly exposed as he wormed his way upwards into he knew not where.

Kain's other great first ascent was Mount Robson. Mount Robson is not just the highest peak in the Canadian Rockies; it is one of the truly great mountains of the world. Kain had seen it close up in 1911 when on a surveying trip with Arthur Wheeler. He wanted to climb it. He was in New Zealand when Wheeler informed him the 1913 Alpine Club of Canada camp would be held at the foot of still unclimbed Mount Robson. Kain boarded the next steamer for Canada.

With two clients, William Foster, a CPR engineer, and Albert MacCarthy, a former United States Navy Captain, both excellent

Conrad Kain — his official guide photograph, 1910. Archives of the Canadian Rockies.

climbers, Kain attacked Robson by its North East face. The route had already twice defeated earlier parties. The key section consisted of an extremely steep, avalanche-prone snow slope. Kain started his party from its bivouac long before sun-up at an hour when conditions would be at their best. The route proved to be even more dangerous than he had expected. Even at that early time of day things were tumbling off. Kain went as fast as caution permitted. Finally he emerged, out of danger, on the still strenuous East Ridge which took the three men to the summit.

It was now late afternoon and the shadows were lengthening. To return by the avalanche slope was out of the question. What to do?

"Fear not and follow me!" Kain exclaimed. "I shall find a way." At this the three descended with the setting sun into the unknown darkness that rose up to them from Kinney Lake almost ten thousand feet below, on the other side of the mountain.

Not only had they made the first ascent of the highest and most formidable mountain in the Canadian Rockies, they had traversed it!

Robson was not scaled again for eleven years, by another, far safer route — and once more, the guide was Conrad Kain. But it would be long after World War II before the first ascent route was repeated. Even now some of the world's best climbers turn back on it — and a few have almost been killed.

By any route Robson is hard. Some years it cannot be climbed at all. It is probable that fewer people have to this day stood on the summit of Mount Robson than have reached the top of Mount Everest.

Uncle Ed in time would climb Robson. In 1939 he escaped from his normal turf to visit the north country. It was not a first ascent, but what was interesting about it was that he served as guide for one of the few women to get to Mount Robson's summit before World War II.

"I've saved Walter Schauffelberger (1881-1915) for last," said Uncle Ed, "because he tried to climb Mount Robson the same season Conrad got up, and because he was an excellent guide. He was from Zurich, a place where they have almost as many bums as in Geneva, but Schauffelberger was no bum. He gave up a prosperous tea business to go climbing full time. He tried to take his clients up Robson's Wishbone Arête, you know, the one everybody tried to climb and never did until 1955 — terribly difficult and dangerous near the top. They got caught in a storm and were lucky to get down alive after a horrible overnight bivouac. He still hadn't had enough: he tried Robson again from the south, but again the weather wasn't good. After that he returned to Switzerland where he disappeared one winter in an avalanche in the Bernina country."

"Schauffelberger was the only European guide out of almost

thirty who came to Canada and got killed in a strictly mountaineering accident — and that was in Switzerland. All the others, except Chris Haesler, who was really killed by that bear, died in bed."

"All of which," Ed moralized, "proves that guides are safe climbers and that if you want to live a long life, you should take up guiding, or, at least, good mountain climbing. That's the sure way to stay fit."

Then he winked: "There are those people who don't like us who complain we live forever."

It had been a long interview: Uncle Ed had refilled his pipe five times and we had each consumed three cups of tea. As we parted, Ed took from his table a handful of papers.

"I don't guarantee its absolute accuracy," he said, "because I am 95 years old and have more to remember than my brain can hold. But I think this list is complete and correct."

Ed thereupon handed us the document which is reproduced as Appendix "F" of this book.

AJ XVIII-96, Mountaineering in the Canadian Rockies
AAJ I-373, Charles Ernest Fay
CAJ XXVIII-189, Swiss Guides in Canada
CAJ XXIX-49, Swiss Guides in Canada

CHAPTER
VII

MOST WERE GENTLEMEN...

"The man Flammonde, from God knows where,
With firm address and foreign air,
With news of nations in his talk
And something royal in his walk,
With glint of iron in his eyes,
But never doubt nor yet surprise,
Appeared, and stayed, and held his head
As one by kings accredited."

Edwin Arlington Robinson, *Flammonde* from
The Man Against the Sky, 1916

The unique feature of Canadian mountaineering through the first half of this century, the one which most set it apart from simple Alpine excursions, was a colorful and noble institution known as the packtrain. It also provided, principally for people of at least moderate affluence, adequate leisure and a proclivity for adventure, the only practical and, if not luxurious, at least assured means to reach the flanks of any of the multitude of high and, more often than not, unclimbed summits situated far from that thin ribbon of steel, the CPR.

The packtrain belonged to an era when climbers and, indeed, all people, moved far less hurriedly than today. Aircraft, helicopters and ugly asphalt highways had yet to make an appearance in the mountains. When they did, the packtrain as an institution was doomed. Today it has been almost wholly displaced by the roar of engines, the beat of rotors, and the pervading stench of gasoline.

So long as you sojourned within sight of the railroad, it was more or less possible to conduct excursions in the fashion practiced in the Alps, albeit with somewhat fewer comforts. If, however, you wanted to go into the unknown and seek excitement, as Uncle Ed always preferred, you had to hire a pack train.

Packtrains were by no means a Canadian monopoly. They can still be found even today in such disparate places as Peru and Siberia. What was special in Canada was that in addition to servicing prospectors, hunters, surveyors and others, they represented the principal means for the transportation of climbing parties in the Rockies and Purcells. Without them there would have been few first ascents. The real work of the long approach marches, some of which covered a hundred miles, was done not by people but by domestic animals. Members of an expedition therefore carried no loads and could ride through the valleys in splendor.

There was often a choice of mounts: donkeys, mules or horses. The donkey, though docile, required far too much coaxing to be considered practical. However, persuasion sometimes could be achieved in the early hours with a light birch rod. But in the afternoon, when the creature tended to become overly obstinate, it was usually necessary to resort to an ice-axe — and sometimes even then without satisfactory results. Mules had both a bad reputation and a testy disposition. Besides, as one wrangler put it, "When Ed Feuz is along, one mule is enough". The suitable compromise, therefore, was the somewhat less sure-footed but always reliable horse.

The size of the train varied depending on the length of the journey, the number in the party, and the whims and ambitions of the participants. If, for instance, you wanted to bring your folding iron bed, your guitar and your portable toilet, you might have to rent an extra horse or two. On the other hand, persons of Spartan inclinations might dispense with all but the most essential pack animals. Thus the system had a great deal of flexibility. It was great. The horses carried the loads and the people. Nobody had to walk.

The days went by leisurely. At dawn, while the cook fried bacon and eggs, warmed up the previous night's bannock and boiled tea, the wrangler wandered off in search of whatever horses had managed (despite their hobbles) to stray out of sight. By nine, breakfast was eaten, food packed, tents and sleeping bags loaded and the indispensable rifle slung across the wrangler's saddle. Once more the expedition got under way. In the next hours the party crossed meadows, skirted open forests, sloshed through swampland, traversed sandbars and forded rivers. Mostly it forded rivers. Sometimes the riders even got wet.

By early afternoon — and certainly never late in the day — the chief packer, having scouted ahead, would return to the main party and announce the proximity of a good campground — whose precise location, however, he had in fact often known about for years. Once arrived there, the animals were unloaded and hobbled, tents were pitched, fire built, food prepared and whiskey uncorked. By dark everyone had a full belly and enough liquor to guarantee a good night's sleep. Such was the manner in which most climbers travelled in the good old days.

Uncle Ed rather enjoyed these outings. But there was one he preferred to recall over all others. This preference resulted strictly from the wise and gentle personality of his remarkable client, Leopold Charles Morris Stennet Amery. By birth, Amery belonged to a respected English family. By occupation, he was a statesman; by avocation, a mountaineer.

Amery had started out as a journalist for *The Times* for whom he wrote a seven volume history of the Boer War. Later, in 1911, he became a Conservative member of Parliament where he was to serve altogether thirty-four consecutive years. He took time out in World War I to fight with distinction in Flanders and elsewhere. In 1922 he was promoted to Winston Churchill's old post as Chief Lord of the Admiralty under the government of Prime Minister Bonar Law, a job he held until 1924; and, many years later, in 1940, he was to become Secretary of State for India. He travelled widely, wrote brilliantly, mostly on government and politics, and, like many other educated fellow-Britons, held strong and independent views which he never failed to express pungently in his numerous books and speeches.

The Amerys knew everybody worth knowing. In politics it was people like Churchill and the young Harold MacMillan, who were allies, and others like Lloyd George and Ramsey MacDonald, who were always friendly even if antagonists. There were scientists, like the Haldanes, men of letters like Sir Harold Nicholson, H. G. Wells and Rebecca West, educators (he was President of the Classical Association) and, of course, noted jurists like Sir Travers Humphreys, later Lord Chief Justice, whom the Amerys considered a friend, and a host of others.

As a sportsman, Amery climbed all over the world, though chiefly in the Alps. He was twice President of the Ski Club of Great Britain and in 1943, was to be elected President of the Alpine Club to which he had then belonged for forty-four years.

It can properly be said, to paraphrase Shakespeare's Malvolio, that he was almost born great, that he achieved greatness and that he had greatness thrust upon him. Yet unlike Malvolio, he never succumbed to the entrapping temptations of good lineage, ample wealth and high position. He was a quiet, modest man, rather small in stature, who talked little and observed much. Invariably, he was courteous and kind not only towards his peers, but to all who came near him. Thus it was that Uncle Ed came to consider him more as a friend than as an employer. Indeed, from the outset he addressed Amery not in any formal manner, but by his military rank of Colonel.

Mountains are rarely named after living persons. Amery was so much loved and highly respected that the Canadian Geographic Board decided in 1927 to disregard accepted tradition and christen in his honor a prominent, unclimbed 10,940 foot peak at the junction of the Alexandra and Saskatchewan Rivers half way up the wilderness of peaks, glaciers and forests that stretched over 150 miles from Lake Louise to Jasper.

Amery, though well beyond his middle fifties, was a vigorous and seasoned mountaineer. He had known Western Canada as a relatively young man, his first trip having been in the company of another distinguished British alpinist, Arnold Louis Mumm, and his favorite guide, Moritz Inderbinen, who had an English wife. Amery had also stayed at the original, tiny Lake Louise Chalet, twice remodeled precursor of today's grand Chateau. There Miss Annie Mollison, the manager had entertained the guests with her singing of old Scottish airs. It was, therefore, natural for Amery to regard the Geographic board's action more as a challenge than an honor: the mountain had been given his name, so, obviously, he must be the first to climb it. In the summer of 1929, he embarked for Canada with the intention of mingling a bit of business in Edmonton and elsewhere with a month's pleasure in the high and lesser-known Canadian Rockies.

Amery arrived in Lake Louise accompanied by Brian Meredith, a part-time Canadian Pacific publicity man and an ardent skier. Also in the party, fortunately, however, on a part-time basis, was Arthur O. Wheeler, the crusty former president of the Alpine Club of Canada, renowned as the mountain country's surveyor and cartographer. Like Amery, Wheeler knew everybody worth knowing, but unlike Amery, he was neither of comparable lineage nor of noble temperament. Rather, like many self-made men who suffer from incurable insecurity, Wheeler could not grow gracefully into positions of distinction and advancement. He was widely felt to pull rank at the slightest provocation.

The superintendent of the CPR mountain hotels, a Mr. Chester, had long since been appraised of Amery's plans and wishes. He had accordingly hired the best available pack outfit from the famed Brewster Company and had retained Ed Feuz to serve as the group's mountain guide in the high places.

The climbing party consisted of Amery and Meredith as clients with Ed Feuz as guide. In addition, there was Wheeler, with Ray Lagace, chief packer, Morgan Appleby, horse wrangler, Percy Bennett, cook, and a long string of pack horses and riding ponies. On the sunny morning of July 15th the cavalcade departed northwards into the great empty country above Lake Louise.

At the usual, leisurely packtrain pace, the party advanced the first day to Bow Pass, the second down the Mistaya. So far all had gone well. It was only towards the end of the third and last day's approach march that trouble occurred.

"We had just come to the place called 'the graveyard' " Uncle Ed recalled. "That's sort of a gravel desert opposite where you zig-zag up to Sunset Pass. Wheeler was always anxious to boss everybody. He dismounted, turned to me, and said: 'There, Ed, is your mountain.' 'Camp' he commanded, 'is here.' Well, the mountain was still awfully far away, it was only early afternoon, and there was a big river with high water from the melting snow which we still had to cross. I'd been here earlier with Dr. Hickson, and I knew that an hour's ride away on the far side there was a fine campsite with good water and feed grass and plenty of firewood. Here it was all rocks, sand and silty water. I said so to Mr. Wheeler."

"Wheeler, of course, knew better because he was both the Son of God and the Surveyor General, or something like that. When I contradicted him, he turned red and grew angry, and, of course, more insistent. Finally, I got angry, too. I went up to him in front of everybody and said to him: 'Mr. Wheeler, I'm the person who's going to climb that mountain with these two gentlemen, not you. I'm the one with the responsibility, and I'm the one who's going to be blamed if anything goes wrong. I happen to know the right campsite and that's where we're going.' The head packer, Percy Bennett, who was famous as a horseman and skier, turned to me: 'I guess that means we go on.' I replied: 'Sure. I know the place. I've been there before. Mr. Wheeler hasn't. My job is to take the Colonel up the mountain, and that's where we'll start.' "

"Wheeler's red face turned deep purple, just like a peacock. He backed off like he'd been hit with a club. For once in his life he'd learned he wasn't boss. Percy mounted his horse and crossed the river. Everybody else followed, Wheeler angrily tagging along last, of course. An hour later, I said: 'Percy, we'll stop right here. There's lots of feed and good water.' We were in a lovely spot, a real little paradise, a few miles up the Alexandra River. Besides, it had turned kind of cloudy and the weather didn't look too good."

"The Colonel, Meredith and I started from camp a little after three the next morning. We moved up through the trees in the dark. I knew there'd be a storm because clouds were low and the air felt heavy, damp and warm. I kept going because I figured as long as we were in timber we could return easily if things got bad. But they sure didn't improve as we climbed higher. Just above timberline I stepped to one side and looked up at the mountain. 'Colonel,' I said, 'it doesn't look like a very nice day. I think we should turn around. We really need a nice day to do a first ascent. You won't be able to see anything or have any fun.' "

"The Colonel sniffed around a bit. Then he turned to me and said in his gentle English way: 'Edward, we don't turn around in Switzerland, do we, when we climb mountains?' "

" 'True,' I replied, 'we don't turn around. But over there you know the route by heart and the way is usually marked. Nobody has ever climbed this mountain, and I've got to find a way — and I can't find one if I can't see through the clouds and mist. It's all very difficult here, Colonel. But if you really want to go up, just say 'yes', because I'm ready, and I'm not about to overrule you, not yet anyway.' "

"Amery thought a minute. Then he said: 'Let's go!' "

"So on we went. And the weather, of course, got worse."

"Finally, we came to the last cliff band, maybe three hundred feet below the top. It was snowing hard by now, and blowing even harder. Clouds were everywhere and I could hardly see anything. I tried climbing to the right. No luck. I tried another side and found a gully full of snow-ice. I cut steps as far as I could and brought up the Colonel and Mr. Meredith. I did that again, twice more until we came out of the gully. Here the ground was almost level, but we had another problem. Because the snow and wind were so bad, we had to crawl to the summit. The snow stuck to our caps and faces, and we couldn't see more than ten or fifteen feet."

"When I got to what I thought was the very top, I stopped and made the other two take shelter behind some rocks and try to keep warm. Then I built a big stoneman as a sign we'd been there. I told the Colonel this was the summit, but he wasn't too sure."

"Things were bad as we started down. Between the clouds we could see the valley. It was all black down there. Slowly, very slowly, we descended. You have to be terribly careful in a storm, everything is slippery and you have to watch every step, and still move as fast as you can. Nobody is ever a real mountaineer until he's gotten caught in a tight spot in bad weather and gotten himself and the people with him safely out of it. That's the real test for climbers and also for guides; the rest is all window-dressing."

"The Colonel was wonderful. He really proved that day he was a true mountaineer. After that, I would have gone anywhere with him. He never once complained, never even raised his voice or got excited. It was hard to believe in a few more years he'd be sixty. But by the time we reached the first timber he was so tired he could hardly lift his feet."

"It was late now and still the storm went on. I took out the little folding lantern I always carried and tied it on my back so the Colonel could see where to walk in the woods. For another hour we went down through the trees until I turned and said: 'Colonel, I think we should stop for the night, make a fire and go home in the morning. You are tired, it is slow in this rain, we'll never get to camp this evening, and we'll end up walking all night. Out here in Canada, Colonel, when things get like this, we usually stop. I've spent nights up high in lots of worse places. Here we can build a fire and be comfortable.' "

"But he turned to me again and said in his quiet, gentle way: 'No, no Edward. We don't do that in Switzerland, do we? We go right on down to the hotel.' I replied: 'Yes, but there you have trails, and at the end of the trail, there's a hotel, just like home, maybe better. Here you have nothing. I can't see where I'm going, and you're too tired.' "

Edward Feuz and Col. L.S. Amery on Mt. Amery, 1928. Photo by B. Meridith, Archives of the Canadian Rockies.

" 'Oh, let's go on, Edward,' he said. 'Alright,' I agreed, 'we'll go on.' "

And so they did, all three of them. But about half an hour later the Colonel's stubborn streak of grit and pride finally melted into modest common sense. He turned to his guide, and, once more in his quiet, gentle way, said; "Edward, I think you were right. To stop is a splendid idea."

They went over to where there was a little stream and dry wood. Ed built a big fire, brewed tea and doled out a nice cup to each of his weary clients. In five minutes Amery was fast asleep. Ed woke him once more to eat, then again he fell asleep, this time with a big smile on his peaceful face. Ed stoked the fire all night to keep everyone warm and to dry their clothes. At daybreak he woke his clients. "Colonel, a cup of tea? We can start for camp now."

All the way through the woods Amery smiled. He was still smiling, silently, when Wheeler walked up to greet them as they came into camp. He continued to smile and say nothing while the great surveyor berated guides in general and Uncle Ed in particular for not planning things better and keeping clients out all night.

"We climbed the mountain and we're back safely," Uncle Ed observed. "What's the fuss all about?" A few rays of sunshine and a hearty breakfast restored cheerfulness. Amery was so happy he set aside both that and the following day as a time of rest.

Next morning, to general surprise, there was another party camped at the far end of the meadow. It was Jim Simpson, already a legend of the Rockies, who was there with a group returning down the Alexandra from a trip to the Icefields.

Amery remembered Jim well from a visit years before to his camp at Bow Lake. Jim had moved to Canada from Stamford in Lincolnshire in 1896 when he was nineteen and had by now become the dean of explorers, trappers and packers in the Rockies. If you let him get started, he could talk incessantly. But his stories were so fascinating and numerous that none of his listeners ever reported a moment of boredom, a single interruption or the slightest redundancy.

Hearing of Amery's presence, Simpson wandered over from his camp. To Wheeler's discomfiture, he immediately cornered the conversation. Amery, who never said much anyway, unless it was important, listened spellbound. Simpson had a field day. So did Amery.

The party split the morning of July 21. Wheeler and Meredith, short on time, joined Jim Simpson as far as Bow Lake and then continued south to Lake Louise. Amery, Feuz and the bulk of the packtrain headed for more adventures at Castleguard Meadows. Having tested his client's reliance, Ed had by now projected the climb of a new route up the south ridge of Mount Bryce. This spectacular mountain, at the edge of the vast Columbia Icefield on North America's hydrographic apex, bore the name of another British statesman and mountaineer who, unlike Amery, had never had a chance to ascend the peak named after him, but who, like Amery, was at one time President of the Alpine Club. Bryce earned immortality in the footsteps of his French predecessor, Alexandre de Tocqueville by writing a famous, friendly and insightful treatise on the United States government entitled *The American Commonwealth*.

Unfortunately the approach march across the head of the Bush River proved lengthy, the terrain was unfamiliar, and the weather very spotty. When, late in the day, they reached a point only a few hundred feet below the summit but still a long distance away, Ed turned to Amery:

"We've given it a good, sporting try, Colonel, and if you insist we'll go on. But we'll risk going through the same thing we had the other day. I think we've had enough and should go home."

"This time, Edward, I won't argue with you," Amery's voice was as gentle and firm as ever. "We've done the really hard part, so I think we can call it a day."

For the next couple of days the weather was atrocious. When Ed finally stepped out of his tent there was a foot of snow all around. Climbing was out of the question.

Amery came up to Ed: "We can do nothing today," he said. "But you know, it's been weeks since I washed and I do really fear I'm beginning to smell. Is there any way I could take a bath?"

Always resourceful, Ed replied: "At your orders, Colonel!"

While the cook heated up buckets of water, Ed dug a hole outdoors in full sight of the snow, lined it with a rubber tarpaulin, mixed in both hot and cold water until it reached a pleasant temperature, and just as the sun came out, called to Amery, addressing him for the first and only time by a different title:

"Your *Lordship*, your bath is ready. There is even a brush and soap."

As Amery said, it was just like Switzerland, except that the Canadian bathroom had a more grandiose backdrop.

But something seemed to bother Amery. He had with him a picture of his wife which was always there and which he kept right beside his cot. Finally Ed inquired, "Anything wrong, Colonel?" Again Amery spoke quietly:

"Well, you know, Edward, when we got up on my mountain, that bad weather we had — it did bother me a little." Then, with a slight gleam in his eye: "Do you think we were *really* on top?"

"We can settle that easily," Ed replied. "Tomorrow looks like a beautiful day. We can climb Mount Saskatchewan, which is easy, and from the top we'll be able to see your mountain, right across the valley. I'll show you the stoneman I built, and you can judge for yourself."

The next morning was glorious, with warm sun, crystal air and not a cloud to be seen. In due course the two men sat together on the summit of Saskatchewan at almost 11,000 feet. Ed handed Amery his field glasses. "Look across the valley, Colonel, over there. What do you see?" Amery looked through the glass, then put it down. Then, without the slightest trace of emotion: "Yes, you're right, Edward, your cairn is on the very top. It looks well against the sky."

Amery wanted to visit Maligne Lake in Jasper before ending his holiday. Jasper was technically in Canadian National territory where CPR guides were not welcome. Uncle Ed had misgivings, but Amery refused to be concerned.

The trip took a few days, first over Jonas Pass, down Poligne Creek and beyond the height of Maligne Pass. By now they had solid good weather, the kind every experienced mountaineer comes to know he can count on for many days.

"It's a shame to stay in the valley in this kind of weather," Ed observed. "I said to the Colonel: 'Let's have another climb tomorrow. Let's climb that peak just north of the pass that stands straight in the air. Nobody's ever been up it and it doesn't even have a name. From there we'll see Maligne Lake. Surely you have enough time left, Colonel?' 'Oh yes,' he replied, 'several days.' "

"So we went up, and it was another beautiful day. There was still a lot of fresh snow from that storm a few days earlier which made for hard work, but near the top it was bare because everything went straight up. When I got over the hard part I brought up the Colonel and said: 'Now you go first.' 'But Edward,' he protested, 'you're the guide!' 'Never mind, you be guide for a change. I want you to be the first to step on the summit of this mountain.' He smiled and went ahead, never saying anything. And he was so happy."

"The view that day was great. We could see most of the mountains in the Northern Rockies. There was Forbes and Bryce, the great peaks around the Icefields, Mt. Fryatt and the Ramparts, and the great big one, Mount Robson. The Colonel told me how he'd tried to climb Robson in 1909 with Hastings, Mumm and their guide Inderbinnen."

"We named the mountain after his 10 year old son, Julian. But later the Geographic Board got a few things mixed up. They're a good outfit, but sometimes people back in Ottawa get confused, and it isn't always all their fault. Anyway, the name got changed to Llysyfran, and another peak, a little bit higher, is called Julian."

The men descended to Maligne Lake where they hired a boat to ferry them around. Unfortunately, the boat developed engine trouble, so instead of climbing Mount Sampson as planned, they went up a smaller, closer summit, Mt. Leah. But throughout Colonel Amery could see the mountain he had named after his son, and he was supremely happy.

Ed and Amery parted company at the pony house below Medicine Lake. There was a car waiting. Amery left by motor to rejoin the world of politics and statescraft. Ed, for his part, headed south through his beloved mountains with the packtrain. It had been an eventful month. He had made three first ascents and almost a fourth, he had refreshed his memories of many favorite old haunts, and he had even trespassed into new ones.

As Uncle Ed rode down the trail behind the pack horses, he reflected at the good fortune that had given him many splendid companions. They were all so beautifully educated, so wise in the ways of the world, so independent of spirit, so gracious and so unassuming. There were people like Dr. Herdman and Professor Fay, Howard Palmer, Edward Holway and Roy Thorington, each with his own, special, different background, yet all of them interesting, courteous and kind. Real gentlemen! But somehow, in later years, Colonel Amery seemed to stand just a little above the rest. Maybe it was his firm, quiet way. Maybe it had something to do with the distinction also achieved by his son, Julian.

Uncle Ed had felt uneasy that a big mountain should be named in honor of a mere child. You never know what the young fellow might do that could disgrace the gesture. But Colonel Amery's faith in Julian proved amply justified by events.

At the age of nineteen, Julian was already a war correspondent in Spain. At twenty, he carried out special missions for the British in the Balkans, joined the Royal Air Force as a sergeant, transferred to the army, saw service in Egypt, Palestine, the Adriatic, then in China where he was an aide to General Carton de Wiart, and, after the war, married Harold MacMillan's daughter and followed his father into politics. Like his father, he has had a distinguished career in Parliament and at various times in the British Cabinet, being at one time or another Minister of Aviation, Minister of Public Works and Minister of Housing and Construction; like his father, he has written extensively; and above all, he has carried on the family interest in skiing, mountaineering and other outdoor sports. As these words are written, he is still serving as a Member of Parliament.

When, after World War II, Leopold Amery was offered a place in the peerage, he turned it down for the sake of his son's career. In those days all titles of nobility were hereditary, and acceptance would have jeopardized Julian's status in the House of Commons. Such a gesture is not properly appreciated in republican countries like Canada and the United States, but in Britain a chance to join the peerage is rare, and to turn it down represents real sacrifice.

So much for happy endings. All families have their tragedies, and the day would come when Leopold Amery's would have far more of its share than it deserved. In later years Uncle Ed would sometimes mumble darkly about them, but he was never specific. [NOTE — E-4]

AJ XLII-32, A Month in the Canadian Rockies
CAJ XVIII-1, A Month Between Lake Louise and Jasper

CHAPTER
VIII

"...AND A FEW WERE NOT"

Arthur Wheeler blew his Feuz
When Whymper guzzled all that booze.
So Uncle Edward took up his axe
And gave old Whymper forty whacks;
And when he saw what he had done
He gave Art Wheeler forty-one.
Tarara-boom-de-ay...etc."
          (From an old Golden, B.C. folksong, author unknown)

As members of the human condition mountaineers have always been something of an aberration. They are not your average man-in-the-street. Their personalities are unique and often egocentric. If they perform loyally in small teams with intense self-discipline, through their veins runs a strain of anarchism defiant of most convention. They are the intellectual heirs of the rough, proud alpine peasants of Uri, Schwytz, Unterwald, and Bern — Uncle Ed's lineal ancestors — who between the 13th and 15th centuries cast off the Hapsburg yoke and established the freedom of what became the Swiss Confederation.

A touch of anarchy can be good. It spurs defiance of tyranny, hones novel ideas, promotes self-reliance. Its defect is to fan suspicion for all desirable institutions, to deter mass cooperation and to reject help in times of real need. In its most pernicious form, the frustrated anarchist reverts to despotism when his associates refuse him the things he believes to be his own.

Most individualists, including climbers, manage to achieve a healthy balance whereby they retain freedom yet conform to the needs of a rational social order. Leopold Amery represented close to the ideal; and most of us surely aspire to stand in his steps. A few people, however great their merits, can never quite do so, yielding all too often to chaos or tyranny.

There was a man, a real man, born on the Old Sod in Kilkenny,

Ireland. Though of some social status, like most of his compatriots, he began with little in a land where people had been known to starve. He emigrated to Canada, worked night and day, often under atrociously primitive conditions. He defied convention, ever seeking better innovations that might help man's progress. In time he became a highly respected and well informed cartographer of his adopted country. Whatever he started he finished with the attention of a perfectionist. He had Irish emotions, Irish sensitivity, Irish grace and, more frequently than some would like, an Irish temper. With his peers he was courteous, refined, captivatingly entertaining. Above all, he could sparkle with the charm characteristic of his tribe. In short, he knew how to behave like a real gentleman.

He had, however, another side. Towards his subordinates, indeed towards anyone he considered an inferior — and this included Uncle Ed — he could be savage. Having risen from humble beginnings, he seemed to despise those of comparable origin who failed to match him. He had a brilliant, impatient mind which tolerated no delay. Those in his employ or at his orders often found him abusive, arrogant, conceited and autocratic. In short, when not on good behavior, he epitomized the anarchist turned tyrant. His name was Arthur Oliver Wheeler.

From the start Wheeler had planted his feet firmly on the road to greatness and distinction. With Edouard Gaston Deville, who hired him, he turned the new process of photo-topography into a widely accepted science. He mapped the Canadian prairie, then the foothills, finally the intricate main ranges. A superbly illustrated book was merely one of the by-products that issued from his surveys of the Selkirk mountains. His crowning achievement, a task that occupied decades, was the mapping of the Alberta-British Columbia watershed, in the course of which he delineated over 600 miles of the master range of the Rocky Mountains. It was, for Wheeler, a labor of love, and it served to transform him into a seasoned, if always somewhat eccentric mountaineer.

There were other accomplishments which, in fact, he preferred. In 1906 he founded the Alpine Club of Canada, over which he presided for many years. He created its journal, supervised the construction of its huts, and directed its annual camps. He obtained its recognition as an affiliate of the prestigious English Alpine Club and he won it international status at the 1907 Allied Congress of Alpinism in Monaco where the Prince awarded him the Cross of the Order of Saint Charles. Not bad considering his impoverished Irish background, and a lot better, so he believed to his dying day, than the guiding achievements of an Oberland peasant.

By Ed's account, Wheeler caused the guides much grievance. There was, for instance, the Alpine Club camps, a perennial affair which Wheeler started in 1906 and over which he presided even when, as frequently occurred, he was physically absent.

Camp scene at the first Alpine Club of Canada summer gathering; Yoho Valley, 1906. V. Fynn photograph, Archives of the AAC.

The camps proved to be one of Wheeler's most successful innovations. No national club anywhere had ever organized an annual camp for its members and the public — especially in the wilderness. Wheeler's idea was to provide a base in an outdoor setting where persons of relatively modest means could spend an inexpensive fortnight's vacation in the clean air of a beautiful mountain setting, and where they could reach big summits in the safety of appropriate supervision. It was, in short, the average person's form of mountaineering.

Until Wheeler came along mountaineering in Canada was almost exclusively a rich man's monopoly. There were no facilities for the masses, people with dirty fingernails and faces who toiled on farms and in factories. Either you were Mr. or Mrs. Moneybags and paid for a luxury suite at Glacier, Lake Louise or Field, handed out tips to Uncle Ed and his associates and on occasion rented an expensive pack-train from Brewster or Jim Simpson to venture into real wilderness, or you were out of it. Most people were out of it.

When the ACC instituted its summer camps, things began to change. The CPR, ever seeking commercial opportunities, quickly smiled on Wheeler's creation because it noted that, rather than competing with their hotel business, the camps enhanced passenger traffic by attracting a previously untapped class of customers. It also served as yet another advertising gimmick. In time, the camps drew from all kinds of people, including even Mr. Moneybags who, after a fortnight's whooping it up at Lake Louise, sometimes liked to rough it. By and large the ACC camps, as Wheeler intended, catered to the middle and lower-middle class.

The camps proved popular and became an annual tradition. They lasted two weeks, usually bracketing the last days of July and the first of August — a period which Wheeler, after long experience, judged the most propitious part of summer. Over the years they were held in various convenient and scenic spots never far removed from the railway, but always in alpine surroundings. The CPR was the area of preference, but occasionally there were outings in the Grand Trunk's (later Canadian National) north country.

Canada in Wheeler's day was deeply conservative. Not surprisingly, the ACC camps reflected this tendency. True, faces changed from year to year, although some became permanent fixtures and slowly fossilized. But operations of the camp always remained much the same. A fixed formula, perfected in early days, governed all activity until long after Wheeler's death. Any visitor who attended the camp in 1956 and even thereafter, was at once projected back in time and could observe how things had been done half a century earlier when Wheeler had begun the concept.

By all accounts these things were done remarkably well, even if anachronistically. Camp was invariably pitched in a large alpine meadow. In the center stood a canvas shelter of captive-balloon proportions. Inside were tables, chairs, a massive bulletin board and a big bell to summon the multitude. The structure served both as refectory and meeting place. Beside it was a well-worn cook tent, usually a bit charred. On a few occasions, when the cook had sneaked a nip too many and people weren't watching, it had been known to burn down altogether, this despite the frantic efforts of the working staff. It was, in fact, the only tent that ever needed replacement. Nearby were a couple of supply and equipment tents. One of them held first-aid equipment and could be converted if necessary into a dressing station.

On either side and well separated by the administrative center were two clusters of sleeping tents whose number varied in accordance with the quantity of people in attendance. Each housed five or six persons. The larger cluster, always on the true right, or starboard side, was reserved for men. The smaller cluster, at first never more than one or two tents, was set apart exclusively for ladies. Behind each cluster, but well out of sight so as to conform with accepted standards of propriety and decency, were the latrines. These were always well stocked with toilet paper, lime, and, for the ladies, other necessities. Men and women were thus properly separated. Under no circumstances was any mingling of the sexes permitted during sleeping hours.

Far off and all alone, well back of everything, was situated a special tent for the packers and the guides who attended at Wheeler's behest and at CPR instructions.

In the evenings, after the day's climbing was over, everybody, guides included, assembled around a big bonfire and sang songs or listened to President Wheeler or other dignitaries recite their old adventures in the distant wilderness. Uncle Ed, however, considered many of these stories fabrications. He also grumbled that the camps lacked the spirit of real pack-trips because at the ACC camps liquor was a scare commodity. When Ed wanted a drink, he usually had to snitch one from the cook, who always took the precaution of bringing his own supply.

There was a sense of tradition and, above all, solidity about the camps. The leak-proof tents were solid. The tables and chairs and, most especially, the bulletin board, were solid. The climbing gear was solid, the food solid, the camp managers and the Club members and their guests solid. On cold days even the drinking water was occasionally solid, and in the limestone country of these mountains, it was always hard. The guides were especially solid. It was a solid institution. Above all, reigning supreme, both in fact while he lived and in spirit after he died, was the camp's goateed patriarch, Arthur O. Wheeler.

One of Uncle Ed's jobs, at least in the early years, was to serve as guide at these camps, this under orders from the CPR. Invariably the task interrupted his lucrative seasons at Glacier or Lake Louise where he had leisurely clients, some of several years' acquaintance, who were, in addition, always interesting and a few of whom even had the power to move the world. In the big hotels, after a single day's excursion, people like Mr. Hearst tipped with $5 gold pieces; here, Ed was lucky even in a fortnight, to collect thirty pieces of silver, and usually in $.25 denominations — if he was tipped at all. Uncle Ed didn't really like the ACC camps. "I felt as poor as Jesus Christ," he lamented.

Fifty years later, he was still growling. "Those people at the camps were the cheapest skinflints I ever had. They took all my time when I could have been with rich Americans and Englishmen who were regular clients and knew me well. Those tips at the camps were nothing — maybe $10 for two weeks."

"I had to work night and day, and again listen to a damned bell, the way I did when I was fifteen years old. Most of the people didn't know a thing about climbing. I had to teach them how to walk on snow and in places where there were no trails. They were from Calgary and Winnipeg and didn't even know how to use their feet."

"In 1906, the first year, I had to drag a lot of idiots to the top of Mount Whyte (now Vice-President) in the Yoho just so they could qualify for Club membership. And those women wanted to climb in skirts that touched the ground. Naturally, the dresses caught on rocks and got torn and the women tripped and sprained their ankles. And then I got blamed! For two days, Gottfried, my cousin, who was there with me, and I argued with the managers to stop that nonsense and make everybody wear knickers. That's the only time Wheeler agreed with me. But of course when the fuss started, he wasn't even there. He'd gone up north on some kind of survey when he should have been at the camp doing his job as president of the ACC."

"Some of the other guides at the camp, they came and went. But those first years Wheeler made me come every summer. I finally beefed to the CPR. 'Let's change this thing around' I said. 'I'll go one year, then Rudolph, then Ernest and finally Chris, and then we start over again.' So things were done that way and it was fairer."

"But even when I wasn't supposed to be at those camps, they sometimes managed to rope me in. In 1910 I was engaged as guide for Dr. Hickson, and Gottfried and Conrad Kain were doing the ACC's dirty work. Hickson heard that Tom Longstaff, the famous English climber who knew all about Everest, was at the camp near Moraine Lake and wanted to meet him, so I had to go. Besides, Hickson wanted to climb Mount Quadra because it hadn't been done before."

"First thing I knew, Hickson told Wheeler his plans, and Wheeler said right off we must take Dr. Bell and Mr. Gordon with us; so it meant two guides instead of one, and a big, clumsy party of five instead of two."

"Quadra has four tops. We had to climb three to get to the highest. That took a long time, what with five people and several rock cliffs to climb up and down. So it was very late afternoon when we came down to the glacier."

"I decided we'd be safer to descend the Fay Glacier to Moraine Lake and around the Tower of Babel to camp. But it was very steep, pure ice, and we had to chop steps for over two hours. It was dark when we reached the rocks below Mount Babel and the going was difficult. I told them, 'I'm not going farther in the dark. I can't see the best way and I don't know where to step. We'll just sit here on a ledge until it gets light. It'll be uncomfortable, but it won't kill us.' "

"It was cold up there and we shivered for three hours. Down below we could see the Alpine Club Camp where they had a huge fire burning and everybody was warm. So when the moon came up and we could see a little, I got everyone started and we reached camp before breakfast."

"As soon as we got in Wheeler collared Gottfried and me and read us the riot act. 'What kind of guiding is this when you keep people out all night?' he stormed. I said: 'Mr. Wheeler, you can talk like that to Gottfried, even if it's unfair, but not to me because I'm working for Dr. Hickson, not you. You're the one who slowed us down by making us take more people. Besides, you don't know what things were like up there, and when I'm on a climb as guide, I'm the boss, not you.' " That shut Wheeler up — enough anyhow so he didn't speak to me again that day.

"Wheeler wanted to boss everything. Whenever things went wrong, he blamed us guides. Back in 1901 when he worked for Wheeler doing a survey, my father fell into a crevasse. Then after he'd scrambled out, he said guides often had that kind of trouble in Switzerland. I did the same thing some years later. That was Wheeler's excuse for saying we guides didn't know our business."

"If anybody was reckless, it was Wheeler. I once took some people from the London Alpine Club — people who'd climbed in India and all over — up to a mountain. Wheeler came along. When things got difficult, everybody roped up except Wheeler. He refused. I said to him: 'Mr. Wheeler, you should rope up. It's a lot safer.' 'That's a lot of . . . . . . nonsense' Wheeler retorted, 'and you know it.' I didn't argue. But on the way down, when I was in front chopping steps in a steep place, I suddenly heard something behind me. It was Mr. Wheeler. He'd slipped and was sailing down the slope. There was a thousand foot cliff about fifty feet lower down. For a second I wondered if it wouldn't be a good riddance to let him go all the way. I guess my instincts as a guide got the better of me. I jumped right on top of him and he stopped. 'Now will you get on the rope?' I asked. But all he did was curse. He never went on a rope."

"When it came to mountains, he couldn't tell a hard one from an easy one. Back in 1906 at that first Alpine Club Camp where the women were always tripping over their skirts, Wheeler and I got to talking about Mount Tupper, that beautiful sharp spire that rises out of Rogers Pass in the Selkirks. It had never been climbed and I wanted to try it."

" 'Don't you do it,' said Wheeler, 'I know everything about those mountains. I've seen your Mount Tupper from all sides, even measured it. It's just one wall on top of another, pure quartzite. There's no man this side of Hell will ever climb it.' "

"That gave me ideas. There was a German fellow named Koehler I'd climbed with in the Yoho, a good, strong member of the Deutscher Alpenverein. He came to Glacier, where I was stationed. I said to him: 'See that mountain over there? It's never been climbed and there's a nice place just below it where we can spend the night. Want to try it?' 'Ja Wohl!' said Koehler and we were on our way."

"We had a bit of a fuss about boots because he'd already shipped off all his gear but we finally found a pair that fitted. I took my cousin Gottfried along to be on the safe side. But even that wasn't necessary. Wheeler just didn't know what he was talking about. It was an easy climb and a lovely one. Good rock, good holds, good weather — and fun. I'll never forget it."

"The only way to deal with Wheeler was to stand up and almost pull that silly goatee of his, and most people didn't have the guts. One who did was Fred Stephens. I really admired that guy: he was great. He was one of the best packers around, he really cared for his horses. Wheeler once hired him to carry his survey gear up the

Mt. Tupper across the Rogers Glacier, 1910. H. Palmer photo — AAC Archives.

Miette and on down the Snaring River. Wheeler decided they should camp at Centre Pass. That's about as desolate a spot as there is in the Rockies, just wind and rocks and no animal feed — sort of like the 'Graveyard' where we'd have stopped with Colonel Amery if it hadn't been for me. Wheeler and the rest of the party with the fast saddle horses charged up the pass. Stephens, following behind, came to a lovely meadow with good feed for his horses, so he camped there."

"Wheeler and the others had kind of a cold night of it at the pass with no tents, no food and no sleeping bags. At dawn, Wheeler wanted to find out what was wrong and rode back down the trail. He found Stephens just packing up and he said: 'Mr. Stephens, I always heard you were a good man, but you're not.' 'Mr. Wheeler,' Stephens replied, 'I always heard you were a son-of-a-bitch, and you are.' With that Fred unloaded all his animals and led them back to town. So there was Wheeler and one or two others, all alone with a ton of junk and no horses to carry it. Served him right!"

We prodded Ed further:

"And what more can you tell us about the old gentleman?" we inquired.

There was a pause, a puff of blue smoke from the pipe. Finally:

"Wheeler was never a gentleman."

Another long pause, another puff of smoke, and then a change of subject.

"There was also Edward Whymper. He's the guy that got Wheeler into the English Alpine Club. I didn't know him well, but he was no gentleman either."

If not the best alpinist of his time, Edward Whymper was certainly the most renowned. The son of a famous artist-engraver, he became a first-scale engraver in his own right. At twenty, in 1860, he was commissioned to make drawings of the Alps for the second edition of *Peaks, Passes and Glaciers* and it was then that he developed his first love of mountaineering. Not well remembered by the public are some of those first ascents: the Pointe des Ecrins in the French Dauphine, the Aiguille Verte, the highest summit entirely in France, and surely his most daring climb, and countless others. For him this was a time of boundless energy and great expectations.

Then came the Matterhorn, for years his fixation and at the youthful age of twenty-four, the climax of his climbing career. In time it would also lead to his moral and physical destruction. It's a well told story. On the descent four members of his seven man team fell from near the summit. The rope broke, the fall could not be arrested. Whymper, the leader, was one of three survivors. Many people blamed him for the tragedy, unfairly, as is the public wont. The memory of that terrible, dramatic event tormented his sensitive artist's nature for the rest of his life. From then on he rarely laughed again.

Edward Whymper at Field, B.C., 1901. CPR Archives.

If notoriety accompanied the Matterhorn tragedy, so did fame. As an engraver, author, lecturer, self-made scientist and celebrity — indeed, a man of many accomplishments — Whymper now embarked on a lonely career that took him all over the world. He was the first man to climb on four continents and the first serious climber to visit the Arctic. But these journeys gave him no joy and more and more he turned inwardly. Always in the dark of his mind were the shadows of Croz, Hadow, Hudson and Douglas, their arms spread, sliding towards the abyss with no one to stop them.

Whymper took to the bottle. First one drink, then another, then a pint, a fifth and, finally, over a quart a day. He had, fortunately, an iron constitution; and his mind, when sober, remained sharp and clear. But as time passed and as happens all too often with victims of alcohol, he became increasingly morose, suspicious, misanthropic.

He employed guides on all his journeys but seldom treated them well — hardly did he recognize them as human beings. Since the Matterhorn disaster he had lost faith in humankind, and in guides most of all. For him they were a lazy, greedy, scheming tribe of brigands who merited treatment as drudges.

Guides continued to climb with Whymper because of the prestige associated with his name and because it gave them a chance to travel with decent pay thrown in. But in time, Whymper's reputation in the guiding profession, in Europe and elsewhere, reached a very low level.

In 1901 Whymper came to Canada on a publicity assignment for the CPR. He arrived complete with four of those brigand-guides as he called them. They were Christian Klucker of Sils Maria in the Swiss Engadine, Joseph Pollinger of St. Niklaus, near Zermatt, Christian Kaufmann of Grindelwald in the Oberland, and Joseph Bossoney of Chamonix, France.

The party camped in a variety of places: Vermilion Pass, Yoho, Ice River Valley and a few other spots. Wherever they went, horses bore the equipment, the food and the bottles. Mostly the horses carried bottles. The guides did as Whymper told them, and grumbled. But they scouted around, climbed various mountains and did a variety of onerous chores not in their contract. Finally, on September 8th they mutinied and Whymper sent them home.

Whymper for his part either slept and had bad dreams about the Matterhorn or spent his time in camp slowly draining his precious bottles. Years after his journey, one could always identify a Whymper campsite by the large number of discarded liquor containers that littered the area. There were so many, it was said, that, had their contents not been consumed, you could have collected enough to open a prosperous liquor store in the Lake Louise-Vermilion-Yoho-Ice River quadrangle. In short, the guides got their peaks, Whymper his booze, and the CPR very little.

As he grew older and increasingly introverted and as his attachment to John Barleycorn intensified, Whymper developed peculiar habits which sometimes discomposed those who happened to be in his vicinity. During his first sojourn at Field in 1903, Uncle Ed had the unusual privilege of witnessing one of Whymper's entertaining capers.

Ed had just arrived from Switzerland, spoke only a few words of English, was completely unfamiliar with Canadian mores and was, moreover, an impressionable and rather conservative lad of nineteen. In later years he recalled the incident well. Whymper was staying at Field as a guest of the CPR on another of his contract tours. The railroad was to receive from Whymper more than it expected.

Early one evening the hotel guests, in requisite attire, had gathered as was customary in the lounge next to the lobby to enjoy pre-dinner libations. Uncle Ed was on the premises attending to minor chores. All at once polite conversation was interrupted by a piercing female scream of terror from the corridors above:

"RAPE!"

A split second later a dishevelled middle-aged Victorian lady streaked past the assembled guests and ran breathless to the reception desk; "Help! There's a MAN! He chased me down the hall. He was STARK NAKED!"

The manageress, one of the Mollison sisters, smiled, unperturbed. "Oh, madam, not to worry" she said. "That must have been our good friend, Sir Edward Whymper. He's not so young as he used to be and he has his little eccentricities, you know."

On September 10, 1911 Whymper arrived in Chamonix. He held a press conference. "I am seventy-two years old and I am finished. Every night, do you understand, I see my comrades of the Matterhorn slipping on their backs, their arms outstretched, one after other, in perfect order at equal distances — Croz, the guide, first, then Hadow, then Hudson, and lastly Douglas. Yes, I shall always see them . . ."

Three days later he withdrew sullenly to his hotel room and locked himself in with a couple of cases of brandy. On September 16 what was left of him was carried out feet first. His remains were laid to rest in the local cemetery alongside those of countless lesser mountaineers, most of whom had been killed on the peaks, and a large number of guides, including even a few whom, in his last, anguished and unthinking years, he had treated so shabbily.

AJ XXIV-490, A Week in the Selkirks with the Alpine Club of Canada
CAJ I-169, Alpine Club of Canada Camp
CAJ II-31, Ascent of Mount Tupper
CAJ III-52, Ascent of Mount Quadra

CHAPTER IX

LADY MOUNTAINEERS WERE ALWAYS LADIES

". . .The reason firm, the temperate will,
Endurance, foresight, strength and skill,
A perfect woman, nobly planned,
To warn, to comfort and command. . ."
William Wordsworth, "Perfect Woman"

Uncle Ed often had mixed feelings about the pedigrees of some of his male clients and those of more than one fellow guide. But in his youth as we have seen, he had once spent a night in the Selkirk's Asulkan Valley in a tent with several of William Randolph Hearst's young ladies. The experience had been so pleasant that ever after he never doubted anything about the women with whom he climbed. 'The ladies," he insisted, "were always ladies." He loved them for it.

"We had a lot of women climbers in my time," Ed said. "They were a delight for all us guides. When the client was a lady on those dull excursions like Lefroy and Temple, which we'd been up thirty times, everything would begin to sparkle and look new again. But the greatest joy of all was the women we had on first ascents because they were so much more eager than men."

"A lot of people nowadays believe that in my time there were no women climbers, or at least very few. A few years ago a fellow named Chris Jones wrote a book called "Climbing in North America". Even if it only mentions my father's name and mine once, it's the best thing of its kind. I recommend it. But it's biased, because he writes about four hundred men, one dog and only eight women alpinists. I don't know much about those men and the dog, but he's wrong when he says there were only a handful of women mountaineers."

"When I saw what Jones wrote, I checked my records. In my time almost a quarter of what you call 'exploratory mountaineers' were women. If you count all the first ascents in the CPR's area of the Rockies and Selkirks, you'll find there was at least one woman on about a quarter of all first ascent parties, including the hardest climbs. Two of those women each made more first ascents than any but five professional guides, and only three male amateurs did better. That may not be good enough for modern women, but it sure is a lot better than Jones made it seem."

"The women climbed as well as the men — except, of course, for those ladies with the long skirts who kept tripping over their clothes and spraining ankles at the first Alpine Club of Canada camp — and they changed into something more practical in a hurry. Most ladies were not quite so strong, pound for pound, especially in the arms and shoulders; and most could not handle heavy loads. I've seen men carry packs equal to their weight all day without grumbling, but put a forty pound load on the average hundred pound girl and she's likely to lag behind. But women have better balance than men and, on delicate rock, better ability with their fingers."

"The real strength of women climbers is in their morale. Men can panic when things go wrong, but women rarely do. I think they have greater survivability. I know they have greater enthusiasm."

"Of course, too much enthusiasm gets you into trouble. There was a famous French diplomat, Prince Talleyrand, I think it was, who told his agents; 'Above all, no excess of zeal.' Well he could have said it to most women climbers — and quite a few men. The women can be too anxious to get what they're after. When I was a small boy, the older guides talked about a famous case in the Italian Alps, when an English woman, Alice Rosa Barker, died. The weather was bad, it was cold, she didn't have the right clothes, her guide wanted to turn back, but she insisted on going to the top. On the way down she collapsed and died in her guide's arms. And her niece, who had stayed down at the hotel, she died, too, when they told her about Miss Barker. Just a couple of years ago, there was that American girl, Nanda Devi Unsoeld, the daughter of a famous mountaineer, who just had to climb the mountain she was named for, India's highest peak. She was on a big expedition and had excellent companions. But she'd been sick for a month and was told to stay in base camp. She refused, and her father wouldn't stop her. So, she went up with him until she was exhausted. She had real guts, but should have known better and been a bit more patient. Instead she died."

"On the plus side, women's morale can help a lot. In a mixed party they're the ones who keep the men's spirits up. Men get discouraged and give up a lot sooner than women. If it hadn't been for that French girl, Denise Badier, I don't think Lito Tejada-Flores and his party would have gotten down those overhangs in that big summer storm on the Petites Jorasses near Chamonix in 1965. The Genevese guide, Raymond Lambert, and Marcel Galley would surely have never made it that winter week in 1938 after they traversed the Aiguilles du Diable on Mont Blanc if it hadn't been for the courage of Erica Stagni. Women can be real heroines in places where men turn tail and run."

"All I can say is that men are in some ways stronger and women in others. I think it all balances out. But some women are just plain strong, like Annie Bergenham, who lived right here in Golden, and used to go out in the bush with her woodsman husband, Pete. She could carry as big a load as he did and just as far and fast."

"One thing is sure; none of us guides ever had a woman client who behaved like Edward Whymper, or that map-maker, Arthur Wheeler, whom I never liked. They didn't try to boss everything, they didn't lose their tempers, as Wheeler did, and they didn't get drunk they way Whymper did. All our women were real ladies. So if we had a grumpy man on the rope one day and a smiling lady the next, it all balanced out for us."

Ed overlooked a few things. In his time, most people who wanted to make first ascents, hired guides because it gave them a better chance for success. Besides, there's a kind of magic when people of opposite sexes get together to share an adventure, especially one that involves an element of danger. For some reason, both men and women in a mixed group perform better than when accompanied only by their own gender. And when the wind howls and the spindrift seeps into your underwear, and you're out in the middle of nowhere on a ridge or a big icefield and can't see ten feet away, and you find a hole out of the storm, it's a lot easier to snuggle up with someone of the other sex than just to sit around and swap jokes.

"We guided hundreds of women up peaks like Lefroy, President and Sir Donald," Ed continued, "and it was always a pleasure. Rudolph Aemmer got the bigger numbers because he was so handsome the ladies thought he was John Barrymore. I had other thoughts about that, of course. But Ernest and Walter and I, we three brothers and our friend Chris Haesler, well, at least we got the cream, the best lady climbers, the ones who were after first ascents and who could also be very generous with their pocketbooks. So again, among us guides, it all balanced out, too."

"Back in the old days, mostly before my time, the great women climbers in Canada were people like Henrietta Tuzo, who gave up climbing when she married, and Gertrude Benham, an English lady. I guess, though, that Miss Benham was less a lady than the ones we guided because she helped the Kaufmann brothers to pull a dirty trick on my friend, Professor Fay."

"Miss Tuzo's real claim to fame is that she was Canadian-born, perhaps the first real Canadian woman climber; and she came at a time when there were a lot of first ascents to be made. In 1906, she made the first ascent of Mount Tuzo, 10,658 feet high near the Valley of the Ten Peaks, which they named after her. She also made the second ascent of Mount Collie, 10,325 feet the same year. Her father was a doctor in Victoria, but she was educated in England, was married there, and then moved back to Canada with her husband. After that she stayed interested in parks and nature but didn't

John Barrymore (left) and Rudolph Aemmer during filming of "Eternal Love" at
Lake Louise, 1928. Archives of the Canadian Rockies.

do any more climbing. I guess she figured that marriage and mountaineering don't mix; but that's not so. She climbed with those
Kaufmann brothers, too, and I never got more than a glimpse of her."

"Sometimes Rudolph would go off with a dozen women and
show them how to chop steps, or climb in and out of crevasses,
like the time he dropped his pipe and spent the rest of the day looking for it while everyone else stood around waiting. But he took
a few on first ascents — for instance the Crosby sisters on Princess
Mary and Smuts and Haiduk and Prince Albert. There was also a
Miss Pillsbury, who was a flour girl, I'm told; and the Hendrie sisters
and Miss Wilcox on Mount Maude, and also Mrs Eddy and Mrs
Fynn. But mostly, his were day clients who only did the standard
things."

"Three women mountaineers of my time were way above the rest.
One was an American, another an English lady, and the third, by
far the best, was a native Canadian."

"The American was Georgia Engelhard. She was tough and wiry
and climbed so fast she often had us guides puffing to keep up.
In her youth she made a lot of first ascents, mostly with Ernest in
the Selkirks. She's still alive, over in Switzerland, married to the
Philadelphia climber, Tony Cromwell."

"Miss Engelhard had a lot of talents besides climbing. She was born in New York in 1906 and at the age of nineteen was Phi Beta Kappa at Vassar. She spent most of her life as an artist, first a painter, then a photographer, with time out to become a professional horse trainer, and, of course, to climb mountains."

"Miss Engelhard was interested in exploration, and in those days, the early thirties, there was lots left to explore, much of it not even on the map. My brother, Walter, once took her up the Spillimacheen River to find the Bobbie Burns granite mountains, back of the Bugaboos. Nobody had climbed them. All the old mining trails were gone so they spent a week fighting the bush, the swamps and the slide alder. They ran out of time and food before they got more than a look at the mountains."

"Like a lot of women, Miss Engelhard never gave up. In 1939, my other brother, Ernest, the one she had already run ragged in the Selkirks, heard a knock on the door. There was Miss Engelhard, and puffing up the hill a hundred yards behind her, was her friend, Dr North. 'You're taking us up Bugaboo Creek, Ernest,' she announced, 'and this time we'll get Bobbie Burns and twist his tail.' So, off they went, charged through the bush to timberline, and across all the glaciers to climb the best peaks. Then they came tearing back across the glaciers and out again, first Miss Engelhard, always fresh as

"Ernest Feuz, the Swiss guide whom I have climbed with for eleven seasons, and myself on porch of guide's house, Lake Louise." G. Englehard.

a daisy, then Ernest, still game, but anxious for his days off, and finally, much later, Dr North, with his tongue hanging out."

"I climbed with Miss Engelhard," Ed said, "once in 1938 and again in 1941 when we made first ascents. Each time we went up by a huge mountain with lots of towers, all separate peaks — Murchison, it's called. Ernest warned me before we left; 'You've got a fine lady, but watch out. When she starts uphill, she goes like a rocket. What she needs is a mountain goat, not a guide.' Luckily for me she had her regular boyfriend along, Tony Cromwell, who knew her well and felt the same way I did about running uphill. He and I talked the situation over. 'Maybe we could get some hobbles from the packer,' he suggested 'or we could sneak a few rocks into her pack'. But that was just talk, even if we could have put the rocks in very easily."

There was an English woman Ed wanted to climb with, a lady whose whole life was more dedicated to the mountains than that of any man. She was Katherine Maude Gardiner. Her father, Frederick, had been one of the most notable alpinists of his day. He had been the first to climb Mount Elbruz in the Caucasus. No summer passed without a visit to the Alps where he climbed with guides of the famous Almer family. Many times his daughter had gone with him. Though she learned mountaineering and loved the outdoors, she could not always join him. Her mother was an invalid and Katie felt duty bound to attend her, until she died in 1926. By this time Katie was of such an age that the only life left for her was in the mountains.

Frederick Gardiner had also been a smart investor. Among other things he owned stock in the Canadian Pacific Railroad. When he died in 1919, he left a substantial fortune. Katie was well off and free to do her thing.

Miss Gardiner, travelling, as expected, on the CPR, arrived for her first Canadian climbing season in 1929. She was entirely alone. She hired Walter Feuz and a couple of packers and spent a fortnight examining the rugged country south from Banff towards the Crowsnest. She also made a few ascents in the Purcells. What she observed of her companions she liked, and what she saw of the country she enjoyed.

For two more seasons, with Walter as guide, she ventured south into unknown country, making altogether fourteen first ascents, ten of them over ten thousand feet — a quarter of the summits of that altitude between Banff and the United States border. If she were to return again there'd be precious little left for others. So later, in 1935, she went into the lovely Bugaboo granite country west of the Columbia with Bill Harrison, Walter, and Ken Jones, the latter Canada's first native-born mountain guide and one of the best skiers of his time.

By now Katie had become one of the most formidable alpinists to visit Canada. There was, therefore, no way she could escape coming to Uncle Ed's attention. He'd heard nothing but good about her, but never had a chance to cross her path. "Then, one day I came over Abbot Pass from O'Hara," he related, "and had gone down to the Tea House where my wife worked and where she'd seen that big avalanche off Mount Victoria which nearly killed me. Along the trail I saw some fresh tracks with Swiss edge-nail marks. So I asked Martha; 'who's got Swiss edge-nails around here?' 'Oh,' she replied, 'It's that English lady, Miss Gardiner; she's staying at the Chateau. She just left here.' I jumped up and ran down the trail. We talked for hours as we walked back along the lake."

"After 1936, Katie was all mine. We had a tremendous time in the mountains. Miss Gardiner liked to go places where nobody'd been, especially those that reminded her of New Zealand, a country she loved. But much of the back country, like the Selkirks around Arrow Lakes or most of the Monashees, just doesn't have worthwhile climbing, at least after all the bush you have to fight and the mosquitos. Where there were good peaks, like in the Battle Range or the Sir Sandford country, there were no trails for horses, and even if you cut one, the animals were likely to trip on alder roots and break a leg and have to be shot. So you'd have to put everything on your back, which is always too much, spend the nights swatting mosquitos, stumble over logs, tear your hands on Devil's Club and cut your way through the slide alder for days on end. By the time you reached timberline your food was almost gone and you were almost dead. All this to climb one or maybe two good mountains. It wasn't worth it."

"Things changed with the Depression. The unemployed fixed over the old Government Trail into a road around the Big Bend and this made it easier to get near a lot of country most people couldn't reach before. If you had enough courage, gasoline and a tough car and didn't mind clouds of dust, you could drive a couple of hundred miles in eight or ten hours and go from Golden around to Revelstoke. If you were smart, or had a pass like me, you stuck with the train. That trip took half the time and you rode in comfort — even play cards and have a snack."

"1937 rolled around" Ed continued, "and so did Miss Gardiner, this time all the way from New Zealand. She had an American friend from Philadelphia, Lillian Gest, who had a car at Lake Louise and was an important member of the American Alpine Club. They asked me to take them up Mount Bryce. I said it was still a bit early in the season, we all needed to get in condition, so why not go into a place which would remind Miss Gardiner of what she called the 'Southern Alps', the mountains of New Zealand?"

" 'You want to see some real bush?' I asked. 'Well just come along with me, and I'll show you some beautiful mountains nobody's ever been near.' I brought along another guide, Chris Haesler, and we all climbed into Miss Gest's car and bumped along for hours over the gravel road to Sid Webber's little fishing lodge on Kinbaskit Lake in the Big Bend country. We shook the dust off and then Pete Bergenham rowed us across the lake and left us on the far side with mosquitos and no-see-ums in the wildest forest you ever saw. We sweated two days to reach timberline. But up there it was a real paradise with lovely alpine meadows and the usual little lakes and a few trees, but still too many bugs. We left them behind, though, when we got up onto Mount Trident. Then a day or so later, a bit cut up and scratching our bites, we were back at the car; everyone was very happy."

"You could now cut a couple of days off the old packtrain trip to the Icefield country and Mount Bryce because the Jasper Highway had been pushed as far as Bow Lake. There we met Jimmy Simpson, who was as ready as ever with stories of the Canadian wilderness. Back in 1929, he'd had fun with Colonel Amery around these mountains, and now he put on an even better show for a couple of ladies. He had a top-notch packtrain to take us to Thompson Pass. We camped just about where I'd stayed with Amery eight years earlier. The old bathtub I'd built for the Colonel was still there. I wanted to suggest the girls might like to use it; but then I thought I'd better not. They might think Chris and I had been on the trail too long."

"The weather hadn't changed much since Amery's day — it was awful. Miss Gardiner had climbed all her life in every sort of weather — she'd even spent a week in a crevasse on the Fox Glacier near Mount Tasman in New Zealand trying to keep safe from a terrible storm, singing songs and cheering up her three companions. So, like all old-timers in the mountains, she had become a fair-weather alpinist. Not that she didn't know what to do if caught in a storm, she just preferred to avoid it. She had learned the greatest virtue of all mountaineers, patience."

"The weather got slowly better, so we did a few climbs like Mount Alexandra. But the clouds were so thick on top we almost lost sight of each other on the rope; if it had not been for the cairn we would never have known we were on the summit."

"Bad weather gave us time to move our camp high onto the south side of Mount Bryce, much closer than the last time when I was there with Colonel Amery and we didn't quite make it. So, when it finally cleared, we left at two o'clock in the morning, Miss Gardiner on my rope, Miss Gest with Chris. The snow was excellent; we reached the top in no time and were back in camp after less than twelve hours. Those two girls were strong; both knew how to move right along, but luckily for Chris and me, not as fast as that Georgia Engelhard."

"It was twenty-five years since Sir James Outram and his guide, one of those Kaufmann brothers I didn't like, had been there on the first ascent. Ours was the second, but we'd taken a much harder and more beautiful route — and we were a lot older than they had been. Three of us, including Miss Gardiner, were 49 or over; which proves that in mountain climbing you'd better never underestimate the power of either women or older people."

"After Bryce we made more first ascents on our way back to Louise. Then Miss Gest had to go home; but Miss Gardiner never had enough; she kept me on way into September climbing old and new routes up in the Pipestone country. She was very generous, but later I thought that maybe she had a reason."

" 'Ed' she said, the day she was leaving, 'I want you to take me up Mount Robson. It's time an English woman climbed it.' "

"Oh, Miss Gardiner, I'd sure like to, but I work for the CPR and we're not allowed to do anything north of the Columbia Icefield. That's government territory and they have their own guides, the Fuhrer boys. You'll have to hire one of them." [Note — E-5]

In the next year, Kate Gardiner tried Robson twice with the Fuhrers, and twice they had to give up. Early in 1939 she wrote Ed in desperation: "Those fellows in Jasper just can't get through the icefalls. I've got to have you. You handle the CPR from your end, and I'll handle it from mine."

Ed was tempted. It could cost him his job, yet by any route Robson was a big prize, and an even bigger one if a CPR guide were to take a lady client where CNR guides had been unable to climb. Ed went to the hotel superintendent, Mr Chester, who was staying at Lake Louise. At first Ed was blunt, matter-of-fact — Miss Gardiner wanted him, and he wanted to accommodate her. Chester balked, but Ed kept at it, day after day. His sly, Oberland mind began to conspire. The CNR might not like it, but the publicity, if any, could help the CPR, instead. Chester's attitude wavered from hostile to skeptical.

"You know," Ed finally volunteered, "Miss Gardiner always uses CPR facilities when she travels." Then casually, he pulled out his trump card; "She's also a big stockholder." He got up as if to leave. Chester grabbed him by the lapel. "Not so fast, Ed. What was that last item? Sit down." He walked to the cupboard and pulled out a bottle of whiskey. "Ed, have a drink," he said. Then he added; "You better take Chris Haesler with you — and above all, no near misses and no advance publicity. But if you get to the top, we're all going to have some fun."

"It was early August" Ed resumed "when Chris, Miss Gardiner and I stepped off the train at Robson Station. The other two went ahead to hire horses at Hargreave's ranch for the trip up to Kinney Lake. The ranch was a beautiful place where they raised foxes. I stayed behind and looked through my field glasses at the great mountain rising ten thousand feet up from where I sat. I looked all over for a couple of hours, until I figured a way through the crevasses. Then I went down and joined the others at the ranch."

"Mr Hargreave was a big, tall man who could sort of overawe little fellows like me. First thing he asked was to let his son come along. I refused. It was a dangerous, difficult mountain, I told him, and never having been up it I didn't know what to expect, so I didn't want inexperienced climbers along. Hargreave understood. Instead he lent us his daughter to make camp for us at Kinney lake and look after the horses while we were up on the mountain."

"It took a long time to go from Kinney Lake to our high bivouac — on the south side of Robson. We had a lot of food and equipment — Miss Gardiner called it 'swag' — and it was a long way up, maybe 6000 feet."

"We stopped on a rib right next to the first problem, a big gully which reminded me of the Death Trap on the way to Abbot Pass. There were chunks of ice and stuff coming down from the seracs above. We spent a miserable night, even though it was clear. A cold wind blew on one side, and on the lee the packrats kept us awake trying to get at our food. One even ran over Chris' face. So we were up early, which was part of the plan, anyway."

"I must have figured the route pretty well from down on the railroad track. We had no trouble at all, just a walk in the snow and a lot of step cutting on the final ridge. At the top I turned around and held out my hand to Miss Gardiner; 'Welcome,' I said, 'to the first British lady up the highest peak in the Canadian Rockies.' She smiled; then she reached into her pack and pulled out a bottle of wine she'd hidden from us. 'And here's to us old-timers,' she beamed. 'We old folk can beat the young ones any day!' I hadn't thought of that. All three of us had been around for half a century already. I'll bet no party on Robson before or since can match that record."

"It must have been a tough climb," said Chester, when Ed got back to Lake Louise. "Hard?" Ed exclaimed, "why with Katie Gardiner along, it was a piece of cake."

If Uncle Ed had a warm place in his heart for women mountaineers, they in turn had similar feelings about their guide. A couple of months after that trip, in Warrington, near Liverpool, where the bombs were now beginning to fall, the soon-to-be President of the Ladies Alpine Club cited the words she had written in Ed's fuhrerbuch on August 28, 1939: "I have been fortunate to spend part of another summer climbing in the Rockies with Edward Feuz as my guide. On a packtrain trip we made the ascents of Mount Freshfield, Prior Peak, Mount Pilkington in the Freshfield Group, climbed Howse Peak and made the first ascent of White Pyramid. From O'Hara we climbed Hungabee. From Bow Lake, Mount Olive, St. Nicholas, an unnamed peak; on the way over the glacier from there to Twin Falls making the ascent of Mount Collie. We also made an expedition up north to climb Mount Robson and I cannot speak too highly of Edward's great kindness and care of me, nor of his patience under bad weather conditions and his wonderful mountaineering. I feel it has been a great privilege to climb with such a famous guide and such a skilled mountaineer and shall always look back with much pleasure on the various expeditions we have made together."

Kate Gardiner could not fight on the front lines with her countrymen in World War II; even if she had been a man she would have been judged too old — Robson or no Robson. Instead she quietly joined the Red Cross and reassumed the task of boosting men's morale, a job she had taken up years earlier in the big crevasse at the foot of Mount Tasman. In time she would return to New Zealand where on January 24, 1974, aged 87, at her home in Hastings, she would die peacefully in her sleep.

"I've had the good fortune to climb with the best American and British women mountaineers who came to Canada," Ed resumed. "But my one great disappointment is that I never made any ascents with a Canadian lady who outpaced all the others, native and foreign alike. Her contribution was as much to exploration as to mountaineering, and in the first half of this century that was what Canadian climbing was really all about."

"Still," Ed continued, "I heard a lot about her, as you have, too. I'm talking about Phyl Munday, and it's important to tell her story, but you better look into that yourselves, because she was never one of my clients."

We hadn't thought of Phyllis Munday because our minds were too much focussed on Uncle Ed's territory in the Southern Rockies and Selkirks where Phyl rarely climbed. But Ed was right. Far more than Georgia Engelhard or Katie Gardiner, it was Phyl Munday who truly understood the Canadian wilderness for she came to live in it, to respect it and to love it. Phyl was from Vancouver and soon after she started climbing met and married Don Munday, another outdoors oriented person of that city.

Husband and wife both loved all aspects of nature from nearby seas to equally nearby mountains of the Coast Range, but the hills had priority. Only a minor adjustment was needed to perfect what soon became Canada's greatest married climbing team.

The era was still one where the man of the house was invariably considered the senior partner, but in the case of the Mundays this relationship ended at the doorstep; anywhere beyond it they were on equal footing. Few occasions ever arose during their many adventures when Phyl failed to take the lead as required. A woman of extraordinary curiosity, Phyl also had great courage and physical strength. If a forty pound load seemed the limit for a hundred pound woman in Uncle Ed's estimation, he would have been astonished to watch Phyl Munday tramp, day after day, through tangled bush and treacherous icefields with a seventy pound load on her back — twice the legal limit for guides in the Oberland. And when the day was done she invariably helped pitch camp, build a fire and then prepare wholesome meals for her companions. Nor, years later, was Phyl capable of telling how many times she had travelled on dangerous peaks and glaciers, under blistering sun or in the gloom of storm or night, for twenty, thirty or even more hours, without sleep. Georgia Engelhard could climb fast, Kate Gardiner could persevere, but only Phyl Munday could endure.

It was no surprise that she should have been the first woman to climb Mount Robson, back in 1924 with Conrad Kain as guide.

The weather was perfect, the climb uneventful. Phyl on the first rope, followed in Conrad's steps. As he reached the summit he turned, and gallantly held out his hand to Phyl: "There lady," he exclaimed, "You are the first woman on top of Mount Robson!" Phyl's only words were; "Thank Heaven!" For her this was the culmination of a four year ambition.

In 1925, the year after Robson, Don and Phyl, now guideless, explored the Cariboos, sighted by them the previous season and where only two parties, one in 1916, the other in 1924, had ever visited. Aside from the big snowfields, large glaciers, several high peaks and, of course, the lure of the unknown, the area, from a mountaineering standpoint, was not especially challenging. Rather the trip served as a preparation for things to come, for on one notable climb, that of Mount Sir John Thompson, the pair ascended and then descended a total of 10,000 feet in an elapsed time of seventeen hours.

Rockies and Cariboos were one thing, but what really fascinated the Mundays were the Coastal Ranges which ran from their own back yard northwestward for almost five hundred miles. Even a quarter into the twentieth century people knew little about those mountains. The approaches were formidable, the weather atrocious, and, besides, not many were interested because the area was generally believed to have only a handful of peaks over ten thousand feet. Hitherto travellers and explorers had been content to sail the coastal waters because it was easy, or, far more rarely, to try to navigate the rivers, which was hard. Except for a limited area near Vancouver, nobody climbed high.

Shortly after the Cariboo trip, on a late afternoon, Don and Phyl and their companion, Tom Ingram, after a tiring climb high up Vancouver Island's Mount Arrowsmith, sat down for a late picnic lunch. As they looked north into the mists, the clouds briefly parted and there, maybe 150 miles away, but clearly visible, rose an enormous rock spire never before reported by cartographers or mountaineers. The vision lasted a mere instant, yet for Don and Phyl it marked the start of an adventure lasting for decades.

North of Vancouver the coast for a considerable distance runs westerly. It is punctured at intervals by long, narrow inlets, the Canadian counterparts of the Norwegian fiords. Flowing into these are mighty rivers whose waters have been swollen many fold by the drainage of the great mountains through which they have cut to reach the sea. Two of the most formidable, each running in a southerly direction, are, on the east, the Homathko which empties into Bute Inlet, and, about thirty miles farther west, the Klinaklini which flows into Knight Inlet. Based on all the Mundays' conjectures, the "Mystery Mountain" they had sighted and temporarily so named, together with any satellites, must lie in an unexplored quadrangle of about 700 square miles between those rivers and perhaps ten to thirty miles north of tide water.

Unknown as yet to Don and Phyl, they were about to discover the most savage mountain range in provincial Canada, and one of the world's most formidable. Here, shrouded by almost eternal mist, were great, as yet unknown, granite spires, the rivals of Chamonix' needles, which soared skyward above huge chaotic glaciers that dwarfed anything in the Rockies, the Interior Ranges or even the Alps. Their protection was guaranteed by the climate, the almost impenetrable surrounding forests and ferocious torrents.

By way of comparison: in the Canadian Rockies, with over 20,000 square miles of peaks, there are only four summits that exceed 12,000 feet, and three of these rise from a base of about 6,000-7,000 feet, while the fourth starts from at least 3,000. But in that secret area between the Homathko and the Klinaklini, barely 5% as large as the Rockies, Don and Phyl Munday were to find at least six, and perhaps as many as ten summits as high or higher, including the master of them all. Unlike the Rockies these peaks, rather than rising out of an elevated plateau, begin their journey skyward only twenty miles from the sea.

There would be many Munday expeditions and each, after more hardship than reward, would slowly help unravel what now became Canada's greatest geographical riddle. In that country almost everything was hostile: there were treacherous tides, deadly quicksands, dangerous torrents, tangled forests, crevassed glaciers, endless storms, long hours, always hunger, and sometimes even thirst. There were to be many encounters, some unpleasantly close, with ever-present grizzly bears. Phyl Munday, her pack at seventy pounds, played her role gallantly in everything. By all accounts she proved, over the years, to be the real heroine of the story.

Year after year Don and Phyl, with various companions, kept venturing deeper into the mystery country seeking to unlock its secrets. First by water, up the Homathko, then on repeated missions up the vast Franklin glacier, finally towards the end, by land from the east side of the range. Often almost alone, never without peril, the pair uncovered piece by piece new country and found new mountains, including their original, elusive quest, the great peak which they helped to name Mount Waddington. To many a geographer's surprise it turned out to be the highest summit in Provincial Canada. Even today it is considered, together with slightly lower Mount Robson, to be one of the two most formidable mountains in North America outside of Alaska and the Canadian sub-arctic. Don and Phyl, to their misfortune, never got to climb Mount Waddington, but over time they managed to make first ascents of many of its difficult neighbors. Their great reward, however, was the supreme satisfaction of discovering and exploring for the benefit of future mountaineers and geographers an alpine region which is matched only by a very few of the world's finest mountain areas.

With the Waddington area explored the Mundays turned elsewhere — though still in the mesmerizing Coast Range — to the Silverthrone area, the Homathko snowfield and many another spot. Don and Phyl were no great alpinists technically, but they knew their mountains as well as anyone, and loved the wilderness more than most of us.

Time passed. Don died in 1950. But for Phyl there was still a lot of living. In 1956, with Sir Edmund Hillary, the first man up Everest, she flew around her beloved Waddington region whose peaks so resembled, yet so outrivalled, Sir Edmund's New Zealand Alps that he almost expressed envy.

"You know," Ed Feuz told us as we terminated our collective recollections of the Mundays, "even with planes and helicopters not many people go into that Waddington country today. It's mighty isolated, the climbing is as hard and dangerous as anywhere in the world, the weather is atrocious, and you've got to have a real expedition and lots of time if you want to accomplish anything. But there's a hundred years' worth of new routes for people, like Phyl Munday, who have the guts to go there."

"She still lives in Vancouver; I suppose thinking a lot about the good old days in her favorite mountains, leaping crevasses and chasing away bears. Phyl is the only person, let alone woman, who is an honorary member of both the American Alpine Club and the Alpine Club of Canada, where she is the Honorary President. She's quite a lady."

AJ XLII-70, A Canadian Pack Train Trip
AAJ I-459, Some Climbs in the Selkirks
AAJ III-221, Mt Trident
LAJ 1936-23, A Fleeting Visit to the Rockies
LAJ 1939-20, Mt Bryce, Canada
LAJ 1940-5, Mt Robson and Other Climbs

Phyl Munday. Archives of the Canadian Rockies.

CHAPTER
X
FIELDS ON THE ICEFIELDS

Salut, glaciers sublimes, vous qui touchez aux cieux
Nous gravissons vos cimes avec un coeur joyeux.
La neige se colore, l'air est pur, l'air est frais,
Allons chercher l'aurore sur les plus hauts sommets...

Old Swiss Mountaineering Song

Oh, hail to noble glaciers that reach unto the skies,
We climb your lofty pinnacles with joyful hearts and eyes.
The snow is turning roseate, the air is pure and clear,
So let us seek the break of day on mountains far and near.

Rough Translation by A. J. Kauffman

They were young, they were strong, they were pleasantly rich. They came fresh from Harvard with noble ideals. But for the moment there was excitement, wonder, and discovery in everything they saw, in all that was brisk, new, and sparkled before their eyes.

They stepped off the train at Lake Louise, complete with a specially imported Zermatt guide on a warm early summer day in June, 1924 and immediately fell into Uncle Ed's welcoming arms.

"You must be Ed Feuz" said the first of the three. "My name is Bill Field (some people call me Oz), and this is my brother, Fred, and our friend Lem Harris. And over here is Joseph Biner. He's a Swiss guide, like you, and has climbed a lot in the old country with Lem and his father. Lem brought him along so you wouldn't have to do all the work."

Harris and the two Fields had booked a pack outfit from Max Brooks in Banff for a month's camping and climbing in the country north of Banff and with the big peaks of the Columbia Icefield as the principal objective. They had engaged Uncle Ed through the CPR. Biner, whose first experience with America had included a visit to the Coney Island rollercoaster, attended as a useful supernumerary whom the elder Harris supplied both as an extra element of security and as a courtesy to an old climbing companion. The trip, so Bill told Ed, would be the first expedition of the newly founded Harvard Mountaineering Club, still something of a dream in the thoughts of those few people in Cambridge, Massachusetts, who had an inclination for serious mountain climbing. So the expedition needed to be a good one.

Harris and the Fields differed totally from Ed's usual clients. Mostly they were either beginners who needed prompting and instruction; or they were graying, experienced alpinists who had begun to slow down. There was neither slowness nor awkwardness in the Harvard boys. All three were athletic, outdoor types, they already knew much about camping and horses, they'd had at least some mountaineering experience — even if not enough to satisfy Ed — and all three were bursting with enthusiasm. It was, thought Ed, like turning loose a pack of hunting dogs after they had been penned for weeks in their kennel.

In that far-away time it took several days for a pack train to travel from Lake Louise to the foot of the Icefields at Castleguard Meadows. The exact length of time depended greatly on the amount of new windfall, river channel changes, and most importantly, snow melt in the mountains. There was a march to the source of the Bow River, then down the Mistaya, across the North Saskatchewan and, finally, up the Alexandra. The trip involved no mountaineering and no bad bush, but a lot of swamp, and travellers had to know their horses and how to handle themselves and their mounts in swift, deep and icy rivers. There was a lot of water to deal with between Louise and the Icefields, especially in summer when the snow was melting above and the streams were in flood.

"Those boys were good riders — and how they could swim!" Ed related. "But Biner worried me. There's a world of difference between approach marches in the Alps and in the wilds of Canada. Over there you go on foot, there are good bridges over the torrents, and you're never far from help. Here, you have big rivers where you have to coax your horses, and they don't always coax. Sometimes, where the trail is washed out and where there are too many fallen logs you have to go right into the water."

"I knew Biner was a good Swiss guide, like us, and up on the glacier he could do anything, but he couldn't swim a stroke and all he knew of horses had been from feeding them in the stable, and he had no experience in camping. But he tried hard, and he always stayed with me near the back of the train helping the pony boys while Max scouted ahead with the Harvard fellows who were always trotting around and getting into every sort of mischief."

"Things went along better than I had expected until the fifth day when we were all going up the middle of the Alexandra River, where the water was so white it looked like a storm at sea. All of a sudden I spotted Max hurrying back to me: 'Hey, Edward, where's Joseph?' he asked. I turned around. No Joseph in sight. 'Why Max,' I said,

Packtrain fording the Saskatchewan River. W.O. Field photograph.

Joseph Biner and Ed at Castleguard Camp. W.O. Field photograph.

'he was right behind me not ten minutes ago.' 'You better go back and have a look. He might be in big trouble.' "

"I turned my horse downstream until I could look around the bend. There, in the middle of the current, with water up high around the horse's legs, was Joseph. He was sitting there alone on his beautiful big white pony, with one hand on the saddle horn and the other holding his mane, not knowing what to do. He looked just like a statue of Napoleon. Joseph and the horse were just standing there in the water. I said to him in Swiss 'What's the matter? Why aren't you coming along with the rest of us?' 'Oh,' said Biner, 'I saw all the water moving by and I thought I was going upstream.' 'Listen, Joseph, you're grounded and don't know it, but I'll fix that.' I went to the horse's rear and gave him a couple of whacks with my leather strap. Off they went back to the pack train."

"After that Biner always stayed right behind me. He was learning that when you climb in Canada the problems can be very different from the Alps. He needed to get back into his element, high on the peaks, not down in the torrent on a horse. The pony boys were laughing behind his back and calling him a real dude. But Biner soon got his wish."

"After seven days on the trail we camped in the Castleguard Meadows, just below the Icefields. The Harvard fellows had spent all afternoon chasing marmots and looking for goats, sheep and bear — mostly bear — only they never seemed to spot anything. They were disappointed. 'Ed,' Bill suggested, 'let's go up South Twin right away. That's what we've been after ever since Roy Thorington told us about it at the last AAC meeting in Boston. It hasn't been climbed, and it's 11,700 feet. But it's a long way over, I know, maybe fifteen miles on the ice.' 'Tell you what we'll do,' I replied. 'We'll leave this evening, go up Castleguard Ridge, get on the ice before midnight and just march across in the dark when everything's frozen solid.' "

"Those fellows — how strong they were! We hardly ever stopped. By daybreak we were in the crotch between the Twins. First we did South Twin, all snow but with a very narrow, steep ridge near the top which took two hours because a high wind came up and we had to dig in with our axes to keep from being blown off. It was good to have Biner along under conditions like this; he really knew his stuff. On top Fred and Lem planted the American flag. Then we all climbed down to the col between the Twins for lunch."

"It was still early. Bill Field, who learned a lot about glaciers and later ran the American Geographical Society in New York, turned to me: 'Can we go up North Twin, too?' 'Might as well do it,' I replied. 'We'll be late getting back anyway, and we'll never have a better chance.' " [Note E6]

"Fred rebelled; 'No, no, Ed, we're not going up there. We've had enough for one day.' But Bill and I won out. I just got going up the slope, pulling Fred behind me while Bill pushed. Harris was smarter about it; he just turned to Biner and said 'Joseph, we're not here for glory, if you want to turn back any time, it's alright by me'. So then they followed after. It turned out to be all very easy, even Fred was beaming when we reached the top."

"It was a long trip back. The snow was soft now and our faces were burned by the sun, the reflection off the snow and the terrific wind. By late afternoon the wind died down, but we were sinking in a foot at each step. It was after midnight when we came into camp. We had been on our feet almost twenty-four hours and had travelled roped together over thirty miles, most of it at more than 10,000 feet."

"We took a day off, then climbed Mount Castleguard, which is very easy. Too easy for Harris and the Fields. They were beginning to fidget around camp and were back chasing the gophers and marmots and looking for invisible grizzly bears. I said: 'Let's take the whole crew, packers too, and all go climb Mount Columbia. It's the highest thing in the Rockies next to Mount Robson. It'll be another long day, but mostly an easy walk. There'll be eight of us, with Max, Ernie Stenton and that old fellow, Soapy Smith."

"Well, it was a long day, all right, but it wasn't easy. Those pony boys felt about as comfortable on a mountain as Joseph Biner did on a horse. Mount Columbia is where Joseph got his revenge for the way they had called him a dumb dude, and every time the packers goofed, I would watch him laugh."

On the Columbia Icefield side of Mt. Castleguard, Ed Feuz Jr., Fred Field, Lemuel Harris, Joseph Biner. W.O. Field photograph.

140

"Even on the flat of the Icefield those packers felt unhappy. Pony boys know their business, but most of them just don't enjoy steep places. I guess Jim Simpson and Tom Wilson were about the only exceptions, and even they never climbed hard mountains — just a few snow bumps and easy walk-ups."

"Columbia had been climbed twice before, each time by the big snow face on the east side. But when we came near I saw conditions had changed: there was a huge crevasse that went completely across the mountain. So we took to the rock on the south ridge and made a new route."

"The rock was all rotten, steep too, and with eight people, three of them cursing and complaining all the time, mostly scared to death, and one guide snickering, it took us five hours, twice as long as it should have. We were gone for twenty-three hours, and had to use the lantern for quite a while. When we reached camp all three packers turned to me and said: 'Never again!' "

"The Harvard boys felt just the opposite, of course, It took only one day of rest after each of those twenty-four hour climbs — the longest I ever made — and they were ready to go again."

"We were all sunning ourselves at camp in late afternoon the day after our trip up Mount Columbia when Biner asked me if all the rock in Canada was as bad as on Mount Columbia. He had expected to find good stuff like they have around his home village of Zermatt and he wasn't too happy. I had to tell him that most of

Mt. Columbia. Photo by Glen Boles.

the Rockies was like this, but those mountains he saw off to the west, when we were up high, the big Selkirk peaks, they were made of real rock. Just then Harris spotted what looked like an army of pack horses coming up the valley from the south. It was Sir James Outram who had made so many first ascents, including Columbia, around the turn of the century. I had never met him before, but this was his last visit to the mountains he loved. Soon he would go home to Victoria and was dead within a year."

In the lead, was a tall, gangling man with long legs that almost scraped the ground. He seemed uncomfortable. Close behind rode an attractive young lady who handled her mount like a professional jockey. As the first rider approached, Ed recognized the square face, the deep-set brown eyes, the bushy brows.

"It's Henry Hall!" Ed cried. Then he turned to the Fields: "He's an old friend of mine, I've been trying to teach him how to climb for almost ten years, ever since his father told me to do it right."

"Edward," said Henry as he dismounted, "What a pleasant surprise. We're on our way up to the ACC camp at Mt Robson but Henry Schwab and I would like to take a trip up on the Icefield while the others look around the cave and enjoy the scenery here for a couple of days. I hope you're taking good care of those Field boys and young Harris I sent you from Harvard. They need a good, experienced man like you to show them around." Henry looked at the young lady:

"Edward, you've met my wife, Mrs. Hall. You and Walter took us up Mount Victoria together a couple of years ago." Then, addressing the others: "Bill, Lem, Fred, I believe you've already met Lydia?"

Henry babbled on so casually Uncle Ed barely paid attention. He overheard him saying: "They've had a bit of a fire at Lake Louise."

"Henry's OK, but sometimes he makes you think he's a bit of a windbag." Fred remarked when they were out of Henry Hall's hearing.

"Maybe that's true," I replied "but the fact is I've known him for years and he's a real man. But it takes some knowing to understand him. He's kind, and he's generous, he's concerned, and he's the best friend of mountaineering in North America, one of the best in the world. He may not be the greatest technical alpinist, and he may not climb as fast as you fellows, but he's strong, he's solid, and he's reliable — and he loves the mountains even more than you or I do. I'll bet he'll do more for mountain climbing than all the guides and climbers who've been out here in Canada put together."

Henry was more than a mountaineer. When he arrived at the Icefields in the summer of 1924 at the age of 29 he was already a seasoned professional trustee, a conservative caretaker of his own and other people's money. His was a prestigious, time-honored career he would pursue throughout life and in which he would practice those cautious financial policies that have made so many proper Bostonians rich, and those, like Henry, who were already rich, richer still.

Summit of Victoria, 1937. Edward Feuz, Edwin Muller, Henry Hall. Photo by G. Englehard.

Henry's love, however, was the mountains; and Ed's words proved prophetic. For the next half century Henry served as a Councilor, Director or Officer of the American Alpine Club and made it grow into an internationally honored mountaineering organization. Henry understood better than anyone of his time that exploratory and innovative alpinism was a young man's sport. He also knew that most young people, however talented, rarely have money. So wherever there were youthful climbers with ability, ambition and noble dreams, as in the Harvard Mountaineering Club, the Appalachian Mountain Club, the Sierra Club, and elsewhere; there, too, was Henry, aways quiet, always in the background, but always ready to help. Without Henry modern North American expedition mountaineering would never have grown to its present stature. Yet no one, perhaps not even Henry himself, will ever know precisely where he assisted and by how much. Minya Gonka? Nanda Devi? K-2 in 1938 and several times later? Mount Everest? The power which created the 10th Mountain Division that broke through the Appennines in 1945 and helped defeat Germany? Mount McKinley? Mount St. Elias? Hidden Peak? And how many others? The laurels went to the climbers. He always remained in the shadows. Only the poor and simple alpinists of this world, like Uncle Ed, have ever expressed their gratitude and appreciated the greatness of Henry's generous anonymity.

Henry's visit to the Icefields was partly a training exercise. He was getting ready for a big expedition the following year. It was to be Mount Logan, the highest unclimbed peak in North America, second only to Mount McKinley — and he needed practice. A few brisk outings on the Icefields might be good training. Mount Columbia — that would be a good start.

"We were up there yesterday," Ed volunteered.

That evening, alone with the Fields, Ed confided: "You know, Henry likes to sleep late. The snow will be getting soft when they reach it and they'll sink in to their knees. My bet is they'll never make it."

Ed was right, as he usually was in such matters. The Hall party never got started until sun-up. It therefore spent the daylight hours sloshing around where at night, two days earlier, Ed's party had raced across a brick-hard surface. Late in the day, scorched by the sun and with their boots soaking wet, Henry's party deferred the ascent of Columbia to another occasion.

"For the Harvard boys, however, North Twin, South Twin, Castleguard, and Columbia had been mere appetizers. In the next days they made first ascents of Mounts Outram, Epaulette and an unnamed peak near the twin Kaufmann Towers. The evening after this last climb they were camped near the Mistaya Lakes. Early the next day, just as everyone was thinking of what to do, Ed looked down the valley and spotted a big string of horses crossing the Saskatchewan River. 'Who's that?' Fred asked. Max Brooks, our packer, replied: 'That? I expect that'll be Caroline Hinman,' then he added casually: 'They call her Timberline Kate. She runs some kind of a school in New Jersey and every year she hires my partner, Jim Boyce, and goes off into the mountains with a bunch of students. She'll be coming along up with a whole battalion of girls.' "

At this there was a great cheer. "Girls!" those boys all cried. "Edward, we've changed our minds. We're not moving. Why, we haven't seen any girls for over three weeks!"

"Before they could reach us, the girls had to ford the Howse River. The water was high and everyone got soaked. So for the next day they wrapped their hair in towels and there were panties and bras and I don't know what else hanging up on lines all over camp. The Fields were delighted. They chased around the clotheslines and had a wonderful time. We staged a huge party. We put a big table in the tent, and Max and Jim baked an enormous bannock three feet long. It was just great; guides, pony boys, the Harvard fellows and those girls, all together. There must have been twenty, and not an ugly one in the lot, and precious few men, just the Fields, the packers and I. It was just like that night in Mr. Hearst's tent, all over again."

Everyone was photographed, even Biner, a devoted family man, who very much resisted the whole concept of posing with a bevy of young American lovelies for fear of the blackmail possibilities young Harris might extract from him back home.

After this pleasant interlude the party split; Harris and Biner had to return to New York to join some others for a late season trip in the Alps. The Fields, however, would continue climbing; their eager eyes now focussed on the still untrodden Mount Patterson. "The reason nobody'd climbed Patterson" Ed reminisced, "was that you couldn't get there. It was across the Mistaya Lakes which were too wide for the horses, and the approaches were all swamp. 'We need a boat, but we don't have one' I said."

" 'Never mind' Bill Field replied. 'We'll build a raft.' And off he and Freddie went along the shore looking for logs. We had no nails — besides, they'd have been unsuitable. So I took some of the lash rope from the pack train and a couple of long climbing ropes. 'That should do fine' I told them. The work took all day. They cut poles and made a paddle, and those boys even fashioned a sail out of a blanket. In the end they had not one raft, but two."

"That crossing was the high point of the climb — perhaps of the trip. We pushed and paddled and poled and trimmed sail, and the Fields hooted and hollered all the way. We climbed as high as we could that afternoon, made camp, and then went up to the summit easily the next morning. Up on this mountain, I looked over to the east, beyond Mount Murchison, and saw a bunch of big peaks that looked interesting. 'Where are those mountains?' I asked Bill, who had some kind of a map; 'I've never seen them before.' He took a lot of pictures and the very next year he and some other Harvard boys went in there to climb. Then my old friend, Howard Palmer,

Fred Field and Ed crossing Mistaya Lake. W.O. Field photograph.

Lake Louise Chalet, circa 1920. Byron Harmon, Archives of the Canadian Rockies.

went in there with my brother, Ernest, and got up a couple of big ones. They all went up the Pipestone River from Louise, not over the Bow Pass like we did. Not nearly as much snow in there, but the rock is better, Ernest told me. It was ten years later before I got to see some of that country myself, when I was up on the Murchison Towers with Henry Hall."

"Then we built a couple of cairns, so that one could be seen from each valley and then back across the lake on our logs that evening. It was real fun for those youngsters, but not for me, most of us Swiss don't really take to the water. The boys wanted to cross the Mistaya for still another climb for the third time on this trip, but I didn't trust those flimsy rafts and I was able to talk them out of it."

"What a wonderful trip. Those Field boys, you'd never have guessed they had money. They spent it, all right, but it never showed. I heard that later on the younger one, Fred, got into some strange causes, but I don't blame him. There are a lot of things wrong with the world, and when you try to straighten them out you sometimes make mistakes and take the wrong guides. He may have gotten a funny slant on life as a youngster; he told me his uncle gave him a solid gold razor on his seventh birthday. For me, what counted was their friendship. That trip with those fellows wasn't work at all for me. It was more like a real vacation. I hadn't done anything like it since Rudolph and I had sneaked off climbing together years before." [Note E 6]

But on the return journey Ed's thoughts were neither on the Fields, nor Harris and Biner, nor on the Icefields, nor Mount Columbia, nor Sir James Outram, nor even the girls. "I wonder," he reflected as they approached Lake Louise the afternoon of July 30, "I wonder just how bad a fire Henry Hall was talking about."

AAJ III-152, The Second Ascent of Mount Bryce
AAJ IV-87, The Murchisons Revisited
App XVI-144, Mountaineering on the Columbia Icefield
HM II-66, A Visit to the Clearwater Group, 1927

CHAPTER

XI

STEWARDS OF EMPIRE

"Notte e giorno faticar,
Per chi nulla sa gradir,
Piova e vento sopportar,
Mangiar mal e mal dormir,
Voglio far il gentiluomo
E non voglio piu servir.
O che caro galantuomo. . ."

> Lorenzo da Ponte:
> Laporello's Lament from Mozart's *Don Giovanni*
> Act I, Scene I.

Night and daytime do I slave
For a man who does not care.
Wind and rain I have to brave,
Sleep and food are always rare.
It's the peerage that's my dream,
Let me cease to be a slave,
Gallant men get all the cream. . ."

> Rough translation by A. J. Kauffman

"Henry, I smell smoke."

The snores stopped. There was movement under the blankets. Then a sleepy voice:

"Nothing to worry about. Must be the guides having a bonfire. Go back to sleep, Lydia." The snoring resumed.

"Henry!" This time she nudged him, "I SMELL SMOKE!"

"Why Lydia, I do believe you're right" Henry sat up in bed. "Let me take a look in the hall."

He opened the door.

"Hello! There's smoke all over! I believe the Chateau is on fire."

"Henry, what are you waiting for? Let's get out of here. We can rappel out the window on your climbing rope."

Fire at Lake Louise, 1924. W. Feuz photograph.

"Why Lydia, we can't do a thing like that. It would be undignified." Then he added: "We must pack up quickly and walk down the stairs the way we came in. Here, let me put away that nice photo we took of you on Mount Victoria two years ago."

Four or five minutes later Lydia and Henry, with their worldly goods in hand plus that of some friends who were off climbing, emerged on the hotel lawn, coughing a bit from the smoke as they walked. By now flames were rising out of the windows in the employees' quarters at the northeast corner of the rambling structure. Henry moved the baggage to a safe place on the far side of the newer concrete wing, then, since there seemed little anyone could do, he joined other hotel guests to watch the show.

About the time Lydia first noticed smoke there had been a commotion at the guide house. The hotel manager, Mr. Delahanty, had come running:

"Fire! Fire!" he screamed, "Hurry! Hurry! Man the pumps!"

Rudolph and Walter, the only guides in residence, jumped into their clothes and hooked up the big hose to the hydrants. Rudolph aimed the spout point-blank at the flames while Walter opened the valve. A great cataract of water streamed into the fire. The initial burst of pressure was so great it nearly sent Rudolph tumbling

Walter Feuz and Rudolph Aemmer. Even when putting out a fire, the guides kept their pipes — symbol of status? — in action. W. Feuz, photographer unknown.

backwards head-over-heels. But his struggle availed nothing. The wooden structure was bone dry and the fire was out of control. A whole brigade, let alone two volunteers, would have been helpless. There was nothing to do but watch, keep warm (which, under the circumstances, was not difficult) and cheer as everything except the fireproof concrete annex went up in smoke.

As the flames intensified, Henry quietly approached Delahanty: "I do hope you got out the hotel safe," he said, almost in a whisper. "I'm a professional trustee, you know, and I've had experience with those things. They just can't be built to withstand that kind of heat for very long." Then he added: "Too bad about the old hotel. I do hope you had it well insured."

"Don't worry, Mr. Hall. We took care of the safe. And as for the hotel, it's my bet the Company will start rebuilding in less than a month."

Just a few days later Uncle Ed would be standing near the same spot sadly and silently surveying the remains. The central part, the old annex, the north wing, they were gone, and all that remained were charred bits of wood and cinders. The whole ground was littered; the lawns and even the nearby forest. The only thing left standing was the big, fire-resistant concrete wing where Rudolph and Walter had concentrated their efforts when they saw it was all that could be saved and where Henry Hall had secreted his bags. All those many winters when Ed and his colleagues had tended the structure and shovelled snow with loving care now seemed wasted. Suddenly the CPR's prize mountain jewel was nothing but ashes.

The grounds were deserted. Even the undamaged concrete wing stood lonely and empty and silent as a wraith. A few guests had been moved to nearby Deer Lodge, the rest had gone to Banff or, like Henry Hall, had fled north into the bush. Would it ever be the same again?

Uncle Ed extinguished his pipe and wandered to the guide house to clean up from his trip to the Icefields. What, he wondered, could be happening to these great hotels which had served the Swiss guides so long and so well as the center of their careers and the source of their income?

Glacier — Field — Lake Louise. Glacier, if it did not in the meantime suffer the Chateau's fate, was to close within a year, Ed had been told. Field, too, was nothing but a firetrap. And Lake Louise, beautiful Lake Louise — would it ever be the same? All three spots had a special place in the guides' hearts.

Glacier always evoked the early days of Ed's apprenticeship, the endless winters in the snow-banks with pipe in mouth and shovel in hand, the fruitless hunting trips, the gripping loneliness that stuck in his throat and which he had slowly overcome, the conquest of a new language, and the kindness and compassion of Mrs. Young. And now Glacier House was to close and be torn down, and the grounds returned to the squirrels, the marmots and the occasional prowling bears.

Mount Stephen House in Field meant somewhat less, except that it had been the scene of his maiden look into the eccentricities of de luxe Canadian hotel-keeping. It was here that before his astounded eyes he had watched that greatest and most awesome of alpinists, Edward Whymper, streak naked through the corridors seemingly in pursuit of terrified Victorian matrons. It was also here that Ed had been initiated into the wonders of his favorite occupation next to mountaineering, British Columbian big game hunting.

His father's friend, the elder Haesler, had served as Ed's mentor. Chris wanted to capture a live mountain goat. His scheme had been to dress Ed up in a snow white costume, like the specter of Hallowe'en, complete with gloves. They tramped around for hours above timberline, one in his hunting clothes, the other in his awkward masquerade outfit, until they spotted a conveniently situated she-goat accompanied by offspring. Chris shot the elder goat. The kid fled. Chris then posted Ed under the dead animal with instructions to lie quiet, and withdrew. After about an hour the kid returned to feed on its mother's milk. Ed grabbed it by the leg and carted it victoriously over his shoulder back to Field.

There was a big fuss over the creature, and after the first moments of fear the goat began to enjoy the attention. The guides bathed her, soaped her, rinsed her, dried her, curled her hair and even put a red ribbon, complete with fancy bows, around her neck.

Bohren and Häesler with Ed's goat near Field, B.C., 1902. CPR Archives.

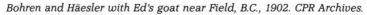

They then placed her on display near the train platform. She became very tame. Finally, one day, an old, sticky fellow with long hair and bewhiskered face approached Chris: "I'm a curator from the Philadelphia zoo," he announced, "and we have no mountain goats. I'll pay you $500 for yours." That was more money than most of the guides saw in six months, and reflected the rarity of this species. In no time the deal was sealed, goat and curator were headed east on the Montreal Express, and the guides divided the spoils and discussed what they intended to do with their windfall.

In the autumn of 1914, with the slack season rendered even slacker through the outbreak of war in Europe, the guides were called upon to help the work crew redo the kitchen and clean out a vermin-infested basement beneath it. Uncle Ed growled. It wasn't part of the contract. He could see little relationship between guiding appreciative and smiling tourists up beautiful high mountains and exterminating ugly and ungrateful cockroaches in a hotel cellar.

The job took months. Modern insecticides being unknown, it was necessary to lace the walls with arsenic and then seal all holes and crevices with plaster. The remedy proved little, if at all, effective, but at least it provided the illusion of security, and the authorities could always claim that measures had been taken. Rudolph, however, claimed that roaches ate plaster for breakfast (and sometimes cement for dinner) and that the whole thing was a waste of time. Ed concurred. Even if it involved animals, the task was not his idea of an autumn hunting expedition.

The roaches were everywhere, not in batallions, but in army groups. There were big ones, little ones, and medium ones, and even king-sized roaches and wee, wee, wee ones you could hardly see but which could scoot around even faster than the big fellows. They crawled all over, even on Uncle Ed's hands and face and into his underwear. Ed's old trick of sticking a spruce needle up a horse fly's rear didn't work with roaches, at least it never produced worthwhile results. All you could do was stamp — provided you moved fast — and Ed felt this was far too sudden a fate for such pests.

God only knew, thought Ed, why they settled at Mt. Stephen House. Canada's air was far too pure and the winter climate too cold to act as an attraction. How they had come was another story. Uncle Ed to his dying day insisted they had arrived at the turn of the century in Whymper's and the Kaufmann's baggage. "After all," he used to say "those three fellows were born half-roach."

There were, thought Ed as he mixed plaster and swatted insects, far too many odd things the CPR imposed on the guides which were no part of the contract. Shoveling snow, for instance. It was all right, of course, as long as you kept jokers out of it like Joe Danniken, a fellow-Swiss but no guide, who had charge of the boats at Lake Louise, and was full of Rube Goldberg ideas. One year in Glacier he lit on the novel thought of flushing the snow off the roof with the fire hose. The scheme worked perfectly. It had, however, one important flaw. The water from the saturated snow avalanches

Walter, Joe Danniken, Ed, Ernie Boker, Rudolph, Ernest and Chris at Lake Louise after Glacier was closed. Nick Morant photograph.

Snowfall was so heavy at Lake Louise that chunks had to be removed from the roof by sled. W. Feuz photograph.

Cutting the ice with "proper tools". W. Feuz photograph.

flooded the basement. Pails, buckets and small hand pumps then had to be rounded up and the job of bailing was three times as hard work as normal snow removal. Forever afterwards Joe was referred to as "that scheming bastard".

After Glacier House closed and a modern and glorified Chateau Lake Louise finally rose like the Phoenix on the ashes of the old, Uncle Ed and CPR dignitaries hammered out a new agreement. In return for various considerations, the guides would henceforth act as official off-season caretakers of the various CPR summer facilities such as Emerald Lake, Yoho, Storm Mountain and Twin Falls. They would, as needed, clear the roofs of snow, they would inspect the interiors, they would look after the furnishings. And because the Chateau had insufficient refrigerating equipment, they would also cut ice on the lake and pack it in sawdust in the Lake Louise icehouse so summer guests could chill their whiskey, their martinis, Canada Dry ginger ale or even branch water.

"That ice," said Ed, "was a terrible job. The hotel used 300-400 tons of the stuff each year — enough for a small avalanche off Mount Victoria. It was the labor of Hercules. We'd wait until the ice got thick enough, say three feet. Then we'd just about break our backs shoveling off an acre of snow from the lake surface — and God help us if it started snowing again! After that we'd bore a hole in the ice until we could see the fish. That was done so we could get saws in; and then we'd start sawing big blocks. We hired people who had horses to haul it — first the Brewsters, then a Ukrainian fellow named Slabodian, who had a strong constitution and a team of Percherons. The horses, unfortunately, were not house-broken. Whenever they had to move over the ice one of us had to follow close behind with a broom and dust pan to remove all traces of any accident."

"When we were in Lake Louise" Ed added with a malicious look in his eye, "we guides never put ice in our drinks. The American guests with their iced libations always wondered why, but we just said we preferred our Scotch and soda the way the English do."

Each block of ice weighed close to 700 pounds. Even with horses, it took a lot of jockeying and sliding around to get the slabs into the icehouse and pack them in sawdust so they would be well insulated. "It kept us in shape in the winter," Ed said, "but it was a lot more work than the CPR ever gave us credit for."

In the early days the hotels had been open year round with a full staff even in the slack months — a most uneconomical practice. The help was all Chinese, however, and, therefore, low cost; and the managers were all women — therefore, in those days, also low cost. There had been Miss Mollison at Louise who used to entertain guests by singing Scotch songs, another Miss Mollison at Field, and, of course, the unforgettable Mrs. Young at Glacier. With time things changed. The CPR decided to close its hotels in the off seasons. That's when the guides had really started in as caretakers.

156

Harry Slabodian and his team. W. Feuz photograph.

"We were watchmen" Ed explained, "and in our rounds we had to punch time clocks with keys wherever we went. The CPR wanted to keep tabs on us, I suppose. I don't know how many keys we had to carry, but we looked like those young fellows with pitons and chocks who climb big walls in the Yosemite. We'd never punched clocks in our lives before, we'd never had to. We came from a country where they *made* clocks. Besides, we were guides. Guides are people you trust, no matter what they're doing. Here they treated us as though we were loafing or had our fingers in the cookie jar."

"Besides, those clocks were hard to see in that big, dark, empty hotel. Most were hidden away in closets surrounded by dry wood-work, and because the electric current was cut off in winter, we had to go around with kerosene lanterns to find them. I wondered for a long time how we could put an end to this nonsense. Finally, the insurance man arrived and I had an idea. I took him on my rounds. I turned up the wick on my lantern so it almost smoked. At every clock, I put the lantern down close against the woodwork and maybe near some drapes, and then I'd have to spend a minute fumbling for the right key. At each stop, I'd tell the insurance man: 'It's a terribly dangerous job in here, more dangerous than guiding. We have to use these lanterns because there's no electricity; and we have to go up and down dark stairwells and into cubby holes to see if everything's O K. I'm only a watchman, of course, but I think it would be better and a lot safer just to close the place up tight in winter and let it go at that.' The insurance man said 'thank-you' and left. He never came back. But next year they locked the hotel

Ed displaying his ice skating skills at Lake Louise. W. Feuz photograph.

*Walter Feuz below ice cave on Victoria Glacier. Byron Harmon photograph —
Archives of the Canadian Rockies.*

in the fall and told us there'd be no need to go around and punch clocks anymore."

"But that led to the next problem. One spring the workmen who maintained the tram road between the station and the hotel came to start work and couldn't find their tools. They said we'd stolen them. Just why we'd want to steal a lot of picks and shovels, earth-moving equipment, I never knew. Other people said we stole linen from the hotel rooms, not that we had any use for that, either. So that summer when I saw the CPR hotel superintendent talking to Walter down by the boathouse, I wandered over and collared him, and we sat down for a bit of a talk. 'The trouble here,' I pointed out, 'is that there's no system. When the doors are locked for winter everything's left lying around. As my old friend Colonel Amery used to say, 'that's not the way we do it in Switzerland'. What you should do is have the help take an inventory of the linen before they leave, stow it all in one or two bedrooms, and lock the doors so nobody can get in, not even us guides. Same with the tools: have the carpenter build a box, put them in it, and seal it with a padlock. After that, we'll take care of things. The superintendent saw I was making sense. Beginning the next fall, that's how things were done. The system worked fine, and it still does, because that's how it's handled even today."

It wasn't, however, all work and no play in the off season. There was time for skating, and skiing, and many other activities. Figure skating had always been one of Uncle Ed's specialties. He had started years ago in Adelboden at the rink where there was that wonderful orchestra, and bright alpine sun, and you could sit out-side and sip whiskey and soda and be really civilized. He'd tried to keep it up in Golden, but the only rink was invariably swarming with wild screaming teenage savages who played a barbarian Canadian game called "hockey" — big sticks flying through the air, and cracked skulls, with skaters going every whichway.

One winter Ed learned there was to be an ice carnival in Banff — a welcome sign for Ed that western Canada was slowly gaining in refinement. He asked his old friend and boss, Basil Gardom, who had promoted the Abbot Pass Hut, if he might go. "You go right ahead," said Gardom, "and be sure to skate with my lady friend from Vancouver. She's a real champion — learned to skate in Switzerland." The two danced together over the ice and the judges awarded them a gold medal. Winter, Ed conceded, could have its rewards — even with the CPR.

The guides skied a lot, but in those days rarely served as profes-sional instructors. Walter was an excellent jumper and Ed could sometimes emulate him. Mostly, however, they practiced tech-niques they had learned years before from the English and the Norwegians in the Oberland: the stem turn and the graceful if archaic telemark. Sometimes, too, they would harness up horses and ride behind on skis in the now almost extinct sport of ski-joring.

And, more rarely, there were cross country excursions, the first of their kind in Western Canada, up to Mount Abbot or Asulkan Pass near Glacier.

Even on the job it was not all drudgery. Sometimes there were unexpected opportunities. Indeed, it was as a caretaker-watchman-on-duty that Uncle Ed achieved his crowning and perhaps only triumph as a nimrod.

The autumn had come and the brisk, cold air reminded Ed the moment had arrived to unlimber and oil his old hunting rifle and buy a few hundred extra rounds of ammunition so he could blast around in the general direction of assorted deer, elk, mountain goat and grizzly bear and maybe even "get lucky" for a change. But here he was, stuck with mundane chores in Lake Louise with Walter and Ken Jones. So he spent a lot of time grumbling.

One afternoon brother Walter happened to look out the window:

"Hey, Ed, come over here. There's a moose on the lawn."

Ed, with Ken close behind, sneaked up to the window and looked out. Sure enough, there, before their eyes, not fifty feet away, stood the largest bull moose any of them had ever seen. He seemed indifferent to the men and was quietly munching the vines on the walls of the Chateau.

"No need to chase him away" said Ken, "he's just eating the virginia creeper. It's all weeds and the CPR wants to get rid of it anyway."

"Virginia creeper, my hat!" Ed responded. "Those are hops. I was just about to collect them to make Martha and me a touch of home brew. We've got to get rid of that beast. I'll shoot it!"

Ken interrupted: "Ed, you can't do that. This is Park territory. The wardens will lock you up and throw the key away if they learn about it. Tell you what, I'll go out and scare it away."

Ken exited. A few moments later he reappeared on the lawn with a paddle from the boat house. Ed watched with a grin as Ken went to the animal's rear and whacked it over the rump. The moose's reaction, however, was somewhat different than expected. It wheeled around, lowered its antlers and headed for Ken, who forthwith vaulted like a nervous matador into the hotel's neutral territory.

For two days, though it seemed like weeks, the moose controlled the grounds while the besieged caretakers holed up in the Chateau. Day after day the "hop" supply dwindled. There were endless conferences, but no solutions. Finally Ed could stand it no longer.

"I don't care what you fellows say. I'm going to chase that thing out of here for good." From a dining room closet Ed pulled out a rusty, single-shot .22 caliber rifle and a few rounds of ammunition. "That ought to be enough to pepper him and get him away from my hops" thought Ed. So with Walter and Ken watching curiously, Ed pushed open a window, aimed his weapon point-blank at the moose and fired a single shot.

To Ed's astonishment and dismay, the moose collapsed on the snow-covered lawn.

"Get that thing out of here!" Ken screamed. "If anybody learns of this, it will be the end of my hunting guide license."

Ed put down the rifle. He and Walter headed for the moose, shouting, yelling and throwing snowballs as they came. Slowly and unsteadily the moose rose to its feet and wobbled a short distance towards the riverbank in the direction of the guide house.

"No! No! Not that way!" Walter screamed. "Over there, over there, into the woods!" At those words the moose fell again.

Ken Jones came up. The three made a further, supreme effort. The moose slowly stumbled a few steps past the guide house, reached the edge of the trees, and fell a third time. It never got up again.

"Get that carcass out of here," Walter shrieked. "The wardens could be here any minute."

"There's no way we can move it!" Ed answered. "That thing weighs a ton. We need Slabodian and his Percherons, and he isn't here."

Ken was more practical. "I'll handle it," he volunteered. He disappeared into the building and shortly came out with a couple of razor-sharp knives, a cabinet maker's saw and a large axe. 'one of you fellows go stand sentry on the carriage road, and I'll butcher it all up. Then we'll run the tough parts through the grinder and also make some hamburger. We can split it three ways and smuggle it home for our wives to cook."

By late afternoon Ken, covered with sweat and blood, had finished the grizzly job. All traces of the moose were gone. All but one, that is.

Whenever we talked with Ed in later years at his house, we always wondered about the big trophy over his fireplace, the one with the long nose and glass eyes that stared down at us and the huge antlers that stretched almost across the room. We had never dared to ask, but in our hearts, we now knew.

CHAPTER
XII
THE ENDLESS VALLEY

Voici le jour, la montagne s'argente,
Le glacier luit comme un vaste miroir,
Allons, allons, epouse diligente,
Ma carabine et mon vieux chapeau noir.
Prepare aussi mon petit sac de toile,
Mets-y du pain, c'est tous ce qu'il me faut.
Pourquoi pleurer? N'ai-je pas mon etoile?
Quelqu'un me gardera la-haut. . ."
Le Chasseur de Chamoix, old Valais mountain tune.

Aside from immediate next of kin, the two things dearest to the heart of most men, guides included, are their homes and their friends. Home in the broad sense is not limited to the place where you hang your hat. It encompasses the geographical area of your main activities and comes to include the district, the province and the land to which you belong — in modern terms, your "turf".

Home, to the peregrinating Swiss guides and in the narrow sense, was Golden, the sleepy way-station with its sawmill, half-way to nowhere along the CPR track. Home however, soon came to mean the almost endless Rocky Mountain Trench and its surrounding mountains. Despite its isolation, the district around Golden had unlimited potential.

Golden lies about mid-point in the broad valley formed by earth movements, which extends roughly in a north-south direction from beyond the Mount Robson country to the United States border, and which separates the Rockies from the Interior Ranges. The trench, as it is known geologically, acts as a conduit for four rivers that carry all the water flowing from the great moist mountain chains on either side. From south to north these rivers are the Kootenay, which flows south, the Columbia, which runs north about two hundred miles before abruptly heading in the opposite direction, and the Canoe which merges into the Columbia at its elbow. Farther on, the Fraser River occupies this trench for a similar distance. The Columbia is by far the most majestic and historic of them all.

The valley's climate is anything but uniform. North of Golden the country becomes increasingly pluviose and at the same time wilder even than the surrounding mountains. In Ed's day the dominant rain forest was almost impenetrable. In winter, snow and cold — cold that was often more intense than at higher altitudes — stopped all but the most intrepid trappers. In summer the mosquito population ruled supreme and deterred not only men, but also elk, moose and grizzly bears. A series of awesome rapids virtually blocked navigation. Loggers considered the timber overmature for commercial exploitation; and prospectors never discovered anything more valuable than fool's gold. The place was, obviously, worthless; therefore no one built any roads. Even today there are no significant permanent settlements from the vicinity of Golden north, until you reach the new Mica dam, well over a hundred miles distant on the far side of the Columbia's Big Bend.

South of Golden things were dramatically different. The valley slowly dried, the cedar, spruce, fir and hemlock gave way to lodgepole and jack-pine, which in turn eventually surrendered to grass and sage brush. Everywhere, however, the land was rich and there was always plenty of water for anyone with the need and incentive to build irrigation ditches. In the Rockies there were deep veins of coal, while along the Interior Ranges lay intriguing deposits of gold, silver and other metals. Outside Cranbrook, the Kimberley Mine was to become one of the world's great lead and zinc producers. In time it would be operated by Consolidated Mining and Smelting (COMINCO), in large part a fiefdom of the ubiquitous CPR.

For Golden the best was that the Columbia could be navigated south, almost to its source in this rich country. Beyond that, a little digging might even link it with the Kootenay and make river traffic possible all the way into Montana, Idaho, and perhaps even back into Canada, and at the same time open up a lot of rich agricultural bottom land. To be sure, these rivers meandered all over their valleys in unpredictable fashion, thus forcing boats to ignore the postulate that a straight line is the shortest distance between two points. There were also shoals which seemed to shift almost daily. These were not serious barriers. With the CPR's main line now cutting through the mountains east and west, it was profitable, long before Uncle Ed came to Canada, to operate a small fleet of sternwheelers between Golden and the big ranches and settlements in the south country — places with quaint English Lake Country names like Invermere, Athelmere and Windermere.

Even a budding tourist trade developed thanks to the natural beauty, the outdoor life, the warm summers, the clean air, the fishing in the streams and lakes, and the discovery of curative thermal springs at the foot of a narrow gorge in a place soon called Radium. So promising was the countryside that as far back as 1882

William A. Baillie-Grohman, a renowned big-game hunter of Austro-British parentage, finally took steps to connect the Columbia and Kootenay for navigation, and then drain the swamps for agriculture by building an interfluvial canal across the height of land that separated the two rivers. The CPR feared the increased flow of water northwards might flood its roadbed, even wash out bridges then under construction, and therefore took political steps to terminate the project before it became commercially successful.

Water travel is inexpensive — but slow. Ed's era had already succumbed to speed. In summer it took two days for the best and fastest of these vessels, the *Dutchess* and the *Pert* to cover the seventy miles from Golden to Windermere, with an overnight tie up at Spillimacheen, the half-way point. In winter, everything that didn't dry up was frozen solid and the paddle wheelers lay ice-bound and aground at their piers for months while Captains Armstrong, Taylor and the others, like traditional sailors lived the good life, carousing at local bars, singing ribald songs and pursuing available damsels. Thus the boats simply could not meet the demands for speed, nor could they provide reliable year-round transportation.

Still, the great valley represented the only practical north-south route between the 250-odd mountain miles that separated Calgary and Lethbridge in the east from Trail and Revelstoke in the west. The CPR also badly needed an escape route for any of its traffic that might get stranded in the Columbia valley by avalanches in the Rockies or Selkirks. The company accordingly decided to build a branch line, the Kootenay Central, to connect Golden with the CPR's southern east-west line at Cranbrook.

For years after it was completed in 1914 the line never carried heavy traffic, but what it transported was mostly high-quality priority freight and therefore profitable. Even at the outset the trains looked like vestiges of the earlier days of railroading. There were two services weekly in each direction with stops everywhere so that the Golden-Windermere journey still required seven hours — at the net speed of ten miles per hour. In addition to the coal-burning locomotive, a typical train consisted of sundry freight cars plus, just ahead of the inevitable red caboose, one or two antique wooden passenger cars in which illumination at night was provided by kerosene lamps. The rolling stock was always in good repair, but never represented the CPR's transcontinental quality, and passenger service was terminated around 1950. Those who rode the line, in effect travelled in the past. The whole thing was a sort of glorified Toonerville Trolley.

The train's arrival at the various way stations was invariably a gala event for local inhabitants. As the locomotive whistle announced the approach, men, women and children would flock to the station, more often than not in holiday garb, to watch the fun or to help load and unload, and often simply to cheer. As trains passed through the open rangeland cows would low, sheep would bleat, donkeys bray. All too often the service fell behind schedule when the track was blocked by cattle. In such cases it was necessary to grind to a halt and send trainmen ahead to chase away the offending trespassers.

Actual construction of the line was no great problem. Compared with Kicking Horse Canyon or Roger's Pass, the job was child's play. The chief concern was to prevent the track from meandering as extensively as the river, and to avoid major swamps. Twists and turns were inevitable, and the finished product bore at least a distant resemblance to a migrating python. The task was carried out under the supervision of one of the company's best location engineers, Alexander Addison McCoubrey.

McCoubrey was a lot more than an engineer. He became in time an avid mountain climber. He imparted his love of the sport on many a fellow Canadian, among them his second wife, Barbara, and his only son and namesake, Alec. Over the years he would gradually step into Arthur Wheeler's shoes as President of the Alpine Club of Canada and play an important role in the development of its huts.

In the process he and other members of his family got to know the Swiss guides well and Uncle Ed best of all. If nothing else, they shared a common employer in the CPR. But it was climbing that would unite them, and over the years, McCoubrey not only became one of Ed's clients but also one of his fast friends.

Often, as he surveyed the Kootenay Central roadbed, Alex's eyes would wander towards the high, unknown summits to the west, mysterious even if not far away. Thirty years earlier, loggers and prospectors had pushed trails into those hills and worked their flanks, but no one, aside from the Topographical Survey, had done any climbing. The Purcells, as these mountains were called, had more than 250 summits, of which more than sixty rose to above 10,000 feet and ten, it would in time be discovered, exceeded 11,000. The glaciers were more extensive than the Rockies at this latitude because of the damper climate, and the rock was much superior — in the Vowells, the Starbirds and especially the Bugaboos, climbers of future years would find granite faces almost as pure as the walls of Yosemite and as challenging as the spires of Chamonix.

Most engineers have inquisitive minds, and McCoubrey was no exception. In 1914, with his railroad job completed and a few days free time on his hands, he decided to make a quick trip into the Purcells. He needed a solid companion so he went to Uncle Ed.

Ed knew little about the region. Aside from rare glimpses from high points in the Rockies, it was all new to him. McCoubrey was the first man he'd met who really wanted to climb there. For Ed, there was another problem. Until the rail line was opened you had to travel up the valley by water. A series of stormy transAtlantic crossings had removed from Ed any desire for further navigation, be it by sea or by river. He basically distrusted boats of any size or shape. Ed claimed you never had any control over embarcations of any kind if something went wrong. In 1907 he'd nearly drowned when his canoe tipped over on the way back from Mount Begbie. Why take a chance with the *Dutchess* or its competitors? River steamers, he kept repeating to Alex, as he puffed on his pipe, were notorious for catching fire: what about the *Sultana*, the *Sea Bird* and the *General Slocum*. And sometimes they didn't even wait for fire to start; they just blew up, like the *Magnolia*. Besides, more people drowned in the upper Columbia in a single summer than got caught in accidents on the nearby mountains in a decade. Water, Ed always insisted, was not his favorite drink.

Completion of the Kootenay Central totally changed Ed's attitude towards the Purcells. He climbed eagerly aboard McCoubrey's train. The pair got a few horses, wandered up Horsethief Creek, then followed an attractive side stream and soon found themselves at timberline. Ed sniffed around; "Nice country," he said. "No bad bush like the Big Bend." Then he grinned; "and hardly any mosquitos." In the next couple of days he and McCoubrey made first ascents of Delphine, the range's fifth highest peak, and Mount Slade. After that time ran out for McCoubrey, so they had to return. But Ed was intrigued by this new area — he especially liked the good rock, quartzite, like Mount Sir Donald. Besides, there were signs the country might be a paradise for big game. Ed was to come back to climb in the Purcells four more times, and in addition, he and the other Swiss guides would carve out a special preserve where they took hunting parties in the proper legal season, and sometimes at other moments as well.

Ed was in the Purcells with McCoubrey twice more. In 1924, eight years after a brief and relatively unproductive venture into the Bugaboos with Dr. Hickson, he joined McCoubrey and his wife on a journey where they made the first ascents of Mounts Hamill and Lady Grey. They had two intriguing adventures, but not on the peaks. On one occasion Ed, leading through a thicket of slide alder with McCoubrey cursing behind, almost stepped on an unsuspecting grizzly bear. The animal stared briefly at the Swiss intruder, uncertain of what course to take. Apparently it disliked both the volume and tone of Ed's voice because after snorting loudly, it lumbered off and disappeared in the tangle.

The second adventure also concerned animals, this time a beast of burden. While crossing an old bridge over Toby Creek, then under repair, one of the horses broke through the rotting boards. The creature's body lay trapped at the bridge surface while its legs kicked helplessly between the planks and the torrent below. Ed and the pony boys pushed, pulled and yelled, but nothing happened.

AA. McCoubrey 1924.
Archives of the Canadian Rockies.

Summit of Peak #3, head of Hamill Glacier, first ascent. Edward Feuz, Jr. and
Mrs. B. McCoubrey, 1924. A.A. McCoubrey photograph, Archives of the
Canadian Rockies.

Bugaboo Group from the northwest. G. Englehard photograph.

Finally the unlucky beast was unloaded, harnessed to the other animals and again there was a mighty heave, this time with horsepower ahead, manpower behind, and Ed's voice lending encouragement to all. "One, two, three — GO!" The bridge shivered, boards creaked, timbers started, and behold, slowly the trapped animal regained the surface and wobbled onto its feet. "No problem," said Ed, "just minor bruises."

In 1928 the Alpine Club of Canada held its annual camp at the Lake of the Hanging Glaciers, in the very heart of the Purcells. It was Ed and Walter's turn to serve once more as the organization's reluctant guides. Fortunately for Ed, the McCoubreys were there, and he climbed with them as much as possible, even if he had to neglect a few of the other denizens in attendance. Together they made three first ascents, including a new route on Mount Farnham, the range's highest peak. Ed went back to the Purcells only once more, in 1941, again with an old climbing friend, Roy Thorington, who brought with him Tony Cromwell, who climbed often with Ed thereafter, mostly in the Rockies.

Ed enjoyed the Purcells; good rock, open forest, reasonable trails, pleasant campsites, but in fact his heart was elsewhere, chiefly in the Rockies. He also wanted to leave something for other less affluent guides than he, people like Conrad Kain. Conrad was a true friend even if not from the Oberland, and he was a fine climber and excellent guide. He had no steady income, often he nearly starved. Why compete with him?

The south country was tame, Ed reflected, not as tame as Switzerland, but still most pleasant. It was ideally suited for civilized people who liked a leisurely drink after a hard day's climb and sit around the campfire to debate the fine points of European alpinism or discuss intellectual problems such as the geological origin of Lake Athabaska or the possibility of corneal transplants. You didn't get rained on all the time, and while there were mosquitos, you could find ways to avoid them. It was perfect country for people like the McCoubreys, Dr. Stone, Tony Cromwell, Roy Thorington, even Conrad Kain — after all Conrad was an Austrian, and in that country even people from the poorest villages somehow get tinged with a few Hapsburg refinements.

There was also the big country north of Golden — a place to test your manhood, but not a neighborhood you wanted to stay in too long or frequent too often — Ed only went there three times. It was wild — as wild as anything can get. It was, in fact, too wild for most wild beasts, but it never got too wild for wild, wild men, the heirs of the French "voyageurs"; people, for instance, like Peter Bergenham.

"Bergenham," Ed would say, "that's a man you never forget." Most persons who knew and admired Pete could agree. They would often add, however, that Pete represented one of the few modern links between man and the lower animals. Ed, himself part cave-man, did not entirely agree. He admitted, however, that there existed in Pete something primitive of the kind he'd occasionally read about in novels by Edgar Rice Burroughs.

Whatever the case, Pete Bergenham was doubtless the greatest woodsman ever to roam the lengthy Rocky Mountain Trench. Some people considered him the most formidable forest man to inhabit Canada since the era of George Simpson's voyageurs. For decades Pete was the only person capable of dominating the mosquito, alder and devil's club country north of Golden to the bend of the Columbia — and if there is any area in Canada rougher than that one, there exist a few people who would like to know about it, among them the ghost of Pete Bergenham.

Pete, like guides and climbers, was by nature an anarchist. He could only work for himself, which meant that after he'd done a few odd packing, rafting, canoeing and logging jobs, he would vanish back to his trap line. To Pete's discomfiture, trapping regulations underwent important changes during his lifetime. When Pete started out, you trapped wherever you wished. There were no boundaries. That was just fine for Pete because he didn't believe anyone should ever be fenced in. In Pete's world trappers went out to catch as many animals as they could, and let God, or the Devil, whichever came first, take charge of replenishing the supply. The result was that fur-bearing animals became threatened with extinction.

When at last, the government took alarm, it decided to auction off specific districts which then became the exclusive trapping preserve of the leasors. They could operate as they pleased; kill off all the animals in a single season, or take out only as many pelts as would not damage the next year's supply. But, because they were now restricted to a specific area, most trappers quickly learned to "farm" their turf, that way, they could guarantee themselves an annual income.

Not so Pete Bergenham. At the outset, he would have nothing to do with the new system. When finally, events forced him to obtain a legal trapline, he found himself left with the dregs, a barren area where beaver were rare and marten rarer still. Somehow he had to make up the loss. Accordingly, he poached in the Parks — mainly Glacier Park. He was never caught.

Bob Mann was a life-long Park Warden, first at Stony Creek on the Beaver, then at Glacier, and finally, as Chief Warden of the Mount Revelstoke Park, and a long-standing acquaintance of Pete's. He reported that one winter Pete was busy poaching up the Beaver Valley, inside Park Boundaries, and while no one could prove anything, everybody knew it. Bob had repeatedly admonished Pete, who, of course, paid not the slightest attention. Finally, his patience exhausted, Bob decided to track Pete down. For miles he followed Pete's snowshoe prints past Mount McDonald, Macoun and even Glacier Circle. Just as he thought he was about to catch up, something unbelievable happened: Pete's fresh tracks came to a dead end and could be seen no more.

To this day the mystery is unresolved, and the question remains whether the story is true. Bob Mann was a Highland Scot. Since before Culloden, the Highlanders have never betrayed their friends — and Pete was a friend. Bob, however, had a powerful moral streak and a belief in duty inherited from his ancestors of John Knox's day and which had been intensified by his studies at Edinburgh University. Long after he retired, and years after there was no need for further coverups, Bob continued to tell the story as though it were Gospel. "I don't know what he did," Bob would say, "But Pete knew all the tricks and he made up a lot no one had ever known before."

Pete also knew river country — unlike Ed — he never had a fear of water. He was one of two men who ever successfully piloted a canoe through the Columbia's formidable Surprise Rapids — all the others drowned. He was the only man to navigate by canoe all the rapids between Golden and Revelstoke.

Even when laden, Pete could move through bush twice as fast as his nearest rival. His working hours in the forest were short, only five hours — exactly — but always productive. He would set out at ten in the morning, rain or shine, and stop at three, when he'd settle in a comfortable place, then chop half a healthy stack of firewood to keep warm the following night. Pete managed to be at ease in the forest with a minimum of work and a maximum of achievement. The forest was his home. He was a 20th Century version of Cooper's Natty Bumpo. After Pete's death, in 1971, a considerable tract of land belonging to his family, in the river bottom north of Golden, was set aside as a wild life refuge. The fundamental of his ethic was thus made clear.

The spring of 1912 was a momentous one both for the Columbia River Valley and for the Swiss guides. The winter had been unusually dry, and, with drought continuing into late spring, forest fires broke out all over the valley. By mid-June it was filled with smoke and Golden itself was threatened. In the town there were ladders and hoses everywhere, even in the hotel corridors, and the population was in fear of firebrands blowing in from the surrounding forests. For a time it looked as though the town might be destroyed. If Ed had been in residence, he would have been thinking of the fate of Grindelwald twenty years earlier. Fortunately, around mid-month a severe storm blew in from the Pacific, it rained for four days, and the flames were at last extinguished.

The Swiss guides, however, were not yet in residence. They were still en route from Switzerland, several of them getting ready to settle permanently, and Ed's chief concern during the voyage had been with a completely different kind of news. Two months earlier, off the Newfoundland Banks, a brand new, reputedly unsinkable White Star Line vessel in the same sea lane followed by Uncle Ed's Canadian Pacific ship, had struck an iceberg and gone down with heavy loss of life, including the President of the competing Grand Trunk Railroad. Ed kept reminding himself that he wasn't a strong swimmer and didn't like water.

The guides finally arrived in Golden just as the fire hoses were being put away, and it was time for another big event. Chris Haesler and Rosa Margarita Feuz got off the train and their wedding took place forthwith. To top it there were two climbers in town, Howard Palmer and Ed Holway, just arrived from Glacier, who needed guides immediately to go into the north country near the Big Bend. They had a big prize in mind, Mount Sir Sandford, the highest summit of the Interior Ranges. It was as remote as anything in Alberta or Interior British Columbia, and it was defended by rivers, glaciers, tangled forests, canyons, alder slides and vast armies of mosquitoes. It would be a difficult climb, too, because Palmer and Holway, both experienced alpinists, had tried it three times before and always failed.

Palmer had visited the area every year since 1908. He knew how to reach the mountain's base, but he could not find a good way up it. The last two times he tried, he got stuck on a steep snow and ice slope that was more than he knew how to handle. He had learned, however, that a different climber had engaged Ed and Rudolph and went into the region briefly the previous year by a roundabout overland route. They had been stopped short of the summit only by a shortage of supplies. As soon as Ed and Rudolph stepped off the train from Montreal, Palmer and Holway collared them. They were hired on the spot and given only enough time to participate in the wedding festivities and say goodby to loved ones.

"We've got a twenty foot canoe" Palmer grinned as he informed Ed, "and Pete Bergenham will give us a start by paddling us down the Columbia and up the Gold River."

"Canoe?" Ed's pipe almost fell from his mouth. "That's no way to climb a mountain!"

Palmer and Holway went into a huddle. "Tell you what we'll do," Palmer finally announced. "You guides walk down the Government trail from Donald to the Gold River. Then Pete will ferry you across the Columbia when you arrive in those flats near the Bush River. , That way you'll be on the water only ten minutes — and with a fine skipper, too."

"Well," Ed replied, "that seemed almost good enough, even for me. Pete was a friend. I figured Rudolph and I could trust him to get us over the river. But to go on up the Gold River in a canoe? That was for the fish! Rudolph and I would walk through the bush."

"That Palmer, he was a strong fellow and a good man in the forest. But he made us carry big loads, and the rules said that guides were never to carry more than thirty-five pounds. Lucky for us we had Pete, and his tough wife, Annie, and a couple others like Sam Brown for packers."

"It took five days to get out of the bush, first up Gold River, where Sam's dog, Topsy, nearly drowned, and then up Palmer Creek, the wildest place I've ever been. What a mess! I know the Columbia Valley is my home, but if that north country is part of it, then it's the outhouse. The route was marked, all right, but you couldn't find the markings, the leaves were so thick. Everything was a tangle with fallen logs, and loose boulders and that prickly Devil's Club and the alder. But the worst of all was the mosquitoes. The only person they didn't bother was Pete — he must have been part mosquito because they never went near him. But the rest of us. Why if you needed to go to the bathroom for a big job, it took two people; you, to do your business, and an assistant to stand behind and slap at the mosquitoes while you did it."

"Mr. Palmer had some right words for those creatures. He said "they were our worst tormentors. They swarm in millions and vitiate everything with their presence. They boil in the soup, they bake in the bread, they are crushed in one's notebook; they get into one's eyes, nose, mouth, ears and hair. . ."

"Those bugs were just as bad when we got to our final camp near timberline as they'd been on the Columbia — maybe worse. They even chased Rudolph and me out onto the glacier when we went off with Palmer to take a look at Sir Sandford while the others were pitching the tents."

"Rudolph and I went out on the ice some distance because we wanted to have a really good look at the big mountain, which was behind us, so we couldn't see it well from camp. When we'd gone as far as we thought we should, we turned around. And there it was, all alone, a great white banner surrounded on all sides by the blue sky. I'd never seen anything like it, even in the Oberland. I turned to Rudolph; 'Hier ist ein koenig — ein wundershoener Berg, the finest peak outside the Oberland.' 'Amen' said Rudolph."

"I took my field glasses. Palmer's route, the one he'd tried a couple of times before, was just no good. It formed a sort of hour-glass about a thousand feet high. Too steep, too long, too much step cutting in ice, no security. But over to the left I figured we could work a way through a small ice cliff. It was risky because the stuff kept falling off, but it was no worse than the Death Trap below Abbot Pass on Mount Victoria. Also, in those days Rudolph and I were young, and young people sometimes like to take chances."

"We leave at 1:00, first thing in the morning," Ed announced when he and Rudolph got back to camp. And so they did. By six-thirty the four men, after much step chopping on Rudolph's part, were across the danger zone and above the ice cliffs. Then came a long walk up snow with two delicate crevasse crossings, and finally the summit ridge. For Palmer that last part was the hardest."

"Palmer," said Ed, "was very strong. But he wasn't a good climber. We came to a corniced spot that was steep on both sides. Rudolph

Mt. Sir Sandford from Little Blackfriar; Vidette on right; Ravelin in front. Palisade Station in foreground. E ridge on left. D. Michael Jr., photograph.

The summit ridge of Mt. Sir Sandford varies in difficulty from year to year. In 1953 it was obviously a dog route, albeit a malemute. J.M. Newall photograph.

was in front and crossed over. Palmer got to the difficult place and immediately became sort of paralyzed. I said a few words to Rudolph in Swiss so Palmer couldn't understand. Then, while Rudolph pulled on the rope, I gave Palmer a push from behind. Away he went and his troubles were over. Holway came last, but I didn't worry about him; he was like a goat — almost as sure-footed as we were."

They spent an hour in the sun on the summit. Here they were at last on the apex of the Interior Ranges, on a spot which ten previous parties and at least eighteen mountaineers, guides included, had vainly tried to attain. The nearest human habitation was over forty miles away. But what they did not know was that it would be thirty-four years before another party, this time following Palmer's old route through the "hourglass", and without guides, would again reach the summit of Interior Canada's most remote and at least in that respect, most difficult mountain.

Except for apprehension as they crossed the ice cliffs and the need to vault an occasional crevasse, the descent was uneventful. They were back in camp at five in time to share Pete and Sam's afternoon pot of tea.

*On the Sir Sandford Glacier the day after the successful ascent of Mt. Sir
Sandford. E. Feuz Jr. (seated), E.W.D. Holway (rear), R. Aemmer on right. Howard
Palmer photo, 1912. Archives of the AAC.*

*Adamant Group and Gothics Group from Azimuth Ridge. D. Michael
photo, 1953.*

Two days later the four climbers were at it again. Their start, however, was delayed until 6:30 by an early morning thunderstorm. This time they headed across Azimuth Mountain in the direction of a cluster of sharp granite spires to the north which resembled Chamonix's Grepon and culminate in Mount Adamant — a scant four hundred feet lower than Sir Sandford, and at the time unclimbed. Holway and Palmer had been in these parts before: they had climbed Pioneer Peak and Mount Austerity, Adamant's lesser neighbor.

At first there was indecision. Should it be Adamant? The hour was not early. Besides, some slightly lower but magnificent peaks beckoned nearby, the Blackfriars. Ed, however, was after big game only; he thought he saw a good way up Adamant through a steep snow couloir. Ed's loud voice and strong arguments, plus a few tugs on the rope in the right direction, won the day. The climb, however, proved harder than he had expected. With thunderclouds threatening on all sides, the four reached the spacious top at the late hour of 5:00 p.m. They barely had time to look over to the northeast down the huge Granite Glacier beyond, then build a small cairn, take a few photographs, and beat a hasty retreat.

It was almost dark and with rain everywhere when they reached the spare gear they had left behind on the Adamant Glacier. It took four hours across Azimuth Mountain, down steep grass and moraine, and then a final soaking march over the Silvertip and Sir Sandford glaciers before they stumbled into camp.

Next day everyone stayed under cover as the deluge intensified with flashes of lightning and as thunder echoed from every mountainside. The great event of the day was when Sam Brown's Airedale, Topsy, the one that almost drowned, gave birth to eleven puppies. "What will become of them?" Ed wondered. Sam decided to keep seven and later named the strongest, Sir Sandford.

On June 28, just eleven days after they had started from the railroad, Holway and the guides left for the distant tracks. Bergenham accompanied them to act as ferryman across the river and then return with additional supplies for Palmer and Brown who were cleaning up details of earlier survey work.

Holway moved fast — too fast, Ed said, for a man of sixty. That same afternoon he and the guides crossed the Columbia and headed south on the excellent Government Trail. With one bivouac they covered the forty-five miles from Sir Sandford Camp to the railroad at Donald, in eighteen hours marching time. Ed had one more experience. During that bivouac, near a small lake above the Columbia, he had a dream. It was Judgement Day and all God's creatures were called before St. Peter's throne. Everyone was the same size. Here was a bear, and Ed shook his paw; down the hall was one of Chris' friends, a mountain goat, and Ed gave him a friendly hug; but there glowering at the end of the hall was a mosquito — as big as the grizzly. Ed turned to run — and woke up.

Years later, Ed commented, "That Holway. Too bad he died so

soon. He would have made a perfect match for Georgia Engelhard."

Ed always looked back on his great ascents in the north country with immense pleasure. After all, he and Rudolph had taken their clients up the two highest, most magnificent and difficult summits in one of Canada's finest alpine paradises. On top of that he'd acquired new friends, for both Holway and Palmer, even when they did not hire him or his brothers, always stopped in to see him on their later travels in Canada.

"That country was more like Switzerland than any part of Canada I know," Ed would say. "If it hadn't been for the rivers, the bush and those terrible mosquitos, I'd have talked some climbers into going in there with me every year. But nobody except people like Palmer and Holway, and, of course, Bergenham, ever wanted to go into that kind of place."

We asked Ed about Sir Sandford.

"The way we went up it was perhaps the most difficult and dangerous mountain I ever climbed. It was certainly a big one."

"What about Robson?" we inquired.

"Robson? I already told you! With Katie Gardiner it was a piece of cake. I'd already eaten the frosting on Sir Sandford. And one thing more, I'm the only guide who ever tasted both."

AJ XXVII-300, The First Ascent of Mt Sir Sandford, the Loftiest Summit of the Selkirks
GJ XXXIX-446, Austerity Mountain

CHAPTER
XIII
TO MY MOST LOYAL CLIENTS

"Come, dear old comrade, you and I
Will steal one hour from days gone by:
The shining days when life was new
And all was bright with morning dew,
The lusty days of long ago
When you were Bill and I was Joe.

Your name may flaunt a titled trail
Proud as a peacock's rainbow tail;
And mine as brief appendix wear
As Tam O'Shanter's luckless mare.
Today, old friend, remember still
That I am Joe and you are Bill."

Oliver Wendell Holmes, *Bill and Joe*

Whenever he set out climbing from somewhere along the Columbia River Valley, Uncle Ed knew he was just stepping out from his front porch. Golden was home, so was the valley, and it was therefore at home or near it that he had formed lasting friendships with people like Palmer, Holway and the McCoubreys.

Like most persons, Ed believed friends to be those people who, over the decades, regardless of distance or the fortunes of life, continue to associate with you whatever your sins may be — even when some of those sins make visitations on them. They are the ones who give you a moral boost when things go wrong, and, if they can manage it, a physical push. Friends know your faults, may try to help correct them, but, regardless of all faults, honor and defend you, anyway.

It can take years to make a friend. Two decades with a business partner may fail to create lasting ties. But a single night swinging from pitons above the abyss while thunder roars and your body chills to the bone, is more than enough to create a lifetime bond with a solid companion. There is truth to the saying that friendship among men who have been through Hell together, even briefly, is more durable than a thousand years' association in Paradise.

Guides don't make friends with casual clients. Such relationships are temporary and routine with the guide acting both as leader and protector. Back in the valley the ties formed up high are dissolved by the rope's removal. This was even truer in Ed's day than in ours. To be sure, in Switzerland clients and guides might get together after a day's sport for a drink and a chat at a local cafe, but here the relationship ended. In CPR country the caste barriers were especially rigid; it was the rare tourist who invited his guides to a pre-prandial libation. "How can a man be your friend," Ed would ask, "who will not share a drink with you?"

But there were always exceptions who not only shared drinks, meals and tents, but who also came back to climb with Ed or his team whenever they could, year after year after year — persons like Fay, Hall, Thorington and others, too, like the Frasers.

Ed first met the Frasers at Lake Louise among the ashes of the old hotel shortly after his return from the Icefields with the Harvard boys in 1924. He was walking through the smoky but undamanged lobby of the concrete wing to look up his bookings when a tall, attractive woman rushed out of the dining room; "I want to hire you to take me to Abbot Pass tomorrow," she said. Ed checked his log: he was free.

The lady and her husband, Kaspar Fraser, met with Ed that evening in the little office on the ground floor of the unburned section. The next day the three, Ed in the lead, travelled over Abbot Pass to Lake O'Hara. In the process Ed's new clients became enchanted both with the gorgeous mountain scenery and their loquacious and loud-voiced guide. It was the first of many excursions.

The Frasers were from Toronto and were both outstanding people. Lois Fraser's father had been one of Canada's outstanding physicians, a contemporary of Sir William Osler, the father of modern American medicine. Her husband, Kaspar, a former Rhodes Scholar, was an outstanding expert on Canadian corporation law. For years, almost every summer, the Frasers arranged to climb with Ed. Often they went with him on lengthy pack journeys. In 1933 they made the first ascent of Mount Smith-Dorrien and in 1935 that of Mount Hanbury. The Frasers were the kind of people Ed liked: no fancy airs — and they'd share a drink and sit with him at meals and listen, enchanted with his stories.

Kaspar and Ed had a habit in common. Both were incurable pipe smokers. On the trail, sometimes even at the top of a steep pitch they would exchange information about the quality and aroma of different tobaccos. "That Fraser" Ed would say, "he used his pipe as a tranquilizer. He was, you know, a rather fidgety fellow, never too sure of anything. When we'd get to a steep place that looked unhealthy, he'd get nervous. I'd be up on top, holding the rope, telling him to come ahead, there was nothing to worry about. But he'd stop. Then he'd call up he had to fill his pipe first. 'You smoke a pipe,' he'd say, 'you understand.' Then he would carefully look over the whole situation. He never took my word for it: he had to reach his own conclusions."

There was, however, one man, a Canadian of hardy Scots ancestry, who held the most precious place of all in Ed's heart. He was basically a teacher; he had the born teacher's propensity to push his pupils or associates to their limits; he was hopelessly stubborn, at times deeply sensitive. Like Ed, he enjoyed a good dram of whiskey after a hard day. Joseph William Andrew Hickson was born in 1873, and first met Ed in Glacier thirty-two years later. From the outset, the two got along so well they would climb together almost every year thereafter until the 1940's.

Hickson lived most of his life in Montreal. His father, Scottish born Sir Joseph Hickson, had been president of the Grand Trunk Railway. As in most Scots families that prosper, there were plenty of assets squirrelled away for various heirs, Hickson included, but the work ethic was strong and playboys were not tolerated. Intellectually inclined, Hickson joined the faculty of McGill University where, beginning in 1901, he served first as lecturer, then tutor and finally professor both of philosophy and psychology. His twin specialties were the intricate sciences of logic and metaphysics. Hickson had an unorthodox spirit. This led to frequent clashes with university administrators in consequence of which he retired from teaching in 1924. He then took up a career in civic affairs, notably in the esthetic field with the Montreal Art Association, eventually becoming President of its Museum of Fine Arts.

Hickson's favorite pastime was mountaineering. He served for two years as Editor of the Canadian Alpine Journal, was Honorary Chairman of its Montreal Section, then President of the Alpine Club of Canada, and eventually became one of that Club's rare Honorary Members. His earliest climbs were in the Alps, where he spent five seasons, most of them while in residence at various German universities studying for his doctorate. Thereafter he took to Western Canada where he specialized in exploratory mountaineering. That's how he got to know Uncle Ed.

Maybe it was his interesting observations about people and situations, maybe his original, sometimes eccentric opinions, maybe his ability, peculiar only to the best of teachers, to extract from those around him the cream of their hidden resources, or maybe it was the silver flask he often carried in his hip pocket; but for whatever reason, Ed was drawn to him and he to Ed. They were friends from the beginning and they remained friends through sunshine and storm, concord and quarrel, safety and peril until the end.

"We shared." Ed would say. "We shared everything. He wasn't like so many of the others who disappeared into their hotel room or into their private tent after a climb was over. At day's end, Dr. Hickson would pull out that silver flask and offer me a drink."

"He was the toughest, most demanding client I ever had — maybe that's why I respected him so much. I don't know how many climbs we made together, maybe two or three hundred. I know I made at least twenty-five first ascents with him — but then he also went to the north country where I wasn't supposed to visit; so he'd hire the Fuhrers or go with a strong friend like Palmer and no guides. But he always came back to me — and that flask was always there."

"If you ever saw him walk down the street, you'd never think he was a mountaineer. He could hardly walk. Years ago a horse he was riding slipped and rolled over his leg and it never healed well. Physically, he was not strong, either. But he had an iron will, and he was the most stubborn man I ever met; after all that's what gets you up mountains."

"He never learned how to cross streams either — in Canada that can be important. Many times I'd cut a tree, sometimes two or three feet thick, to make a bridge over a torrent. He'd get about half way across the log, then he'd look at the water flowing past, get dizzy and fall in. Sometimes he'd be swept downstream and I'd have to run along the bank to catch up with him and grab his belt or the seat of his pants, or whatever I could hook my ice-axe onto and drag him in. And when I laughed, he'd lose his temper."

"The very first time we went for a first ascent, back in 1907, I got a taste of what was to come. We climbed Mount McGill, which he named after his college, and which had never been attempted because it was just too far from Glacier House. There was nothing difficult, but the round trip took almost twenty hours, and my feet were sore afterwards."

McGill was just the beginning. Hickson had an uncanny ability to test people. It happened the very next year. Hickson had brought along a thirty-one year old friend, Arthur Felix Wedgwood. Wedgwood was a civil engineer. He also belonged to an interesting family. He was a direct descendent of Josiah Wedgwood, the creator of fine English china, and he was also a great-grand nephew of Charles Darwin. Together with Ed and his cousin Gottfried, they had taken a packtrain and headed for the Mount Assiniboine area.

Assiniboine by the normal route is an easy climb despite the mountain's Matterhorn-like appearance. The weather was good on the way up, though warm, windless and hazy — and rather oppressive. On the summit Hickson and Wedgwood began discussing the idea of descending on the far side. Ed was looking at some black clouds to the west when he overheard the two discussing their plan.

"Nothing doing, Doctor" he said. "There's something wrong with the weather — I don't know what yet. But I'm not going where I don't

Mt. Assiniboine. Photo by Glen Boles.

know the way when it looks stormy. We better get off this mountain as fast as we can."

They climbed down the two top ledges immediately and headed for the huge, broken rock slope with snow and ice pitches. Hardly had they reached it than there came a resounding clap of thunder. A sudden surge of electricity knocked out all four in the party. As Ed struggled to his feet, he discovered his brand new hat had been knocked away, God only knew where, by the impact. The three others, fortunately, were unharmed. They continued down, at first in a huge downpour, then, as the air cooled, in the blowing snow. Visibility was nil, the track concealed by new snow. They downclimbed a long band of cliffs far above the meadows where camp had been pitched. At long last they crawled into camp through six inches of fresh snow, still tied to the frozen climbing rope and unable with their cold fingers to undo knots which had become Gordian through the action of moisture, cold and repeated tugging. The pony boys finally managed to liberate them.

Wedgwood rejected Hickson's proffered silver flask. Instead, he pulled out a much larger bottle of whiskey from which all four took several enormous gulps. A fine meal completed the climbers' revival. Wedgwood then produced a box of precious Havana cigars. To Ed, these tasted even better than his pipe. "Hickson and his friends — they could be really civilized," he would say in later years.

"Hickson liked to travel well" Ed recalled, "a lot like Katie Gardiner. He'd pay up to $50 a day for a packtrain — a lot of money at the time — to carry all his gear. There would be pack and saddle horses, the supplies, the rental of tentage and other material, a head packer, a cook, a wrangler or two and, of course, me. Food was always first class, and we baked our own biscuits and bannock."

We inquired about Wedgwood. "I didn't climb much with him again, though I would have liked to. He fell in love with Tom Longstaff's younger sister, Katherine, at a Canadian Alpine Club camp, or maybe even before. They were married at Wimbledon in England in 1910 and had a daughter with whom I climbed a few times many years later. Poor Wedgwood, he was a fine man. Like all those English gentlemen, he volunteered at once when the war broke out in 1914. They made him a captain in the 5th North Staffordshire Regiment. One day in 1917 he got in the way of some of that stuff that was always flying around between the trenches. He never climbed again. He was killed."

With Hickson there was always adventure, such as that overnight bivouac on Quadra in 1910. When the climb itself didn't turn into adventure, it involved remote areas and was long and difficult like Mount Moloch in the Northern Selkirks.

Moloch is like Sir Sandford in that it rises in the middle of nowhere, west of the head of Tangier Creek. It is, however, considerably lower, only 10,150 feet, but it has its defenses. Various people, like Professor Sissons, had tried to climb it and failed. Ed and Hickson made two attempts, one too many, Ed always said. The first time in 1915 the weather was bad, one of the horses which they took up the new mining trail was over thirty years old and could barely walk, and the party ran out of time and supplies. Much effort was wasted in bushwhacking.

Two years later, in 1917, Hickson decided to try again with Ed and Ernest. This time, they took plenty of food and decent animals. The trail up Tangier Creek was now excellent because wartime demand for base metals had made it profitable to expand the Waverly mine at the head of the valley. However, at the junction of Tangier and Moloch Creeks, they had to leave the trail and cut one of their own. This took days, but little was lost because the weather was terrible.

"We had tried to reach the north side in 1915" Ed recalled, "but had run into a lot of ice and snow. Hickson didn't like it and now insisted we climb from the east. This meant scaling a long, long ridge where you had to be especially careful with loose rock. It took forever. Finally we got up; and just as he'd wanted to do on Assiniboine, Hickson decided we should traverse the mountain — sure enough, again, there was a thunderstorm coming up. So Ernest and I said: 'Nothing doing, Doctor — we're going home the way we know, not over those overhangs and crevasses in bad weather on some route we've never seen.' And now the Assiniboine affair was

Mt. Sir Douglas. Photo by Glen Boles.

repeated. We got caught. This time we never even made it back to camp. We spent the night in the rain. I managed to build a small, smoky fire to keep us from freezing. Fortunately the Doctor had brought along that silver flask of his to warm us in other ways. It was a long, hard excursion. Moloch has been climbed once or twice since then but nobody ever wanted to repeat our route."

There was a less demanding trip in 1919 into the French, Italian and British Military Groups and into the Royal Mountains beyond Spray Valley, past Assiniboine and Kananaskis Pass. It had its amusing moments. Ed had just returned to Louise after his dreaded duties with the Alpine Club of Canada to find Hickson nervously eager to climb Mount Sir Douglas Haig beyond Palliser Pass. The big problem this time was competition.

"Doctor," said Ed, "Mr. and Mrs. Fynn and the Eddys are already there with Rudolph. If we follow them, it will be a mess. Besides, Fynn is one of the best climbers around, and he'll have climbed everything before we can get there."

Hickson, as usual, was obstinate. "I've already hired the outfit. We go!"

Days later, arriving at Spray Lakes they inquired of the local warden about the Fynn party. He told them that instead of heading for Sir Douglas Haig, the Fynns were going first into the Royal Group.

So next morning, Ed and Hickson continued with their train to the meadows below Palliser Pass where they caught a first glimpse of Mount Sir Douglas Haig. The sight was magnificent. Ed felt an immediate, irresistible urge. "We just might be in luck" he said to himself.

They camped short of the pass in a sheltered place by a stream — a lovely spot. It had only one trouble: a large colony of porcupines got into the leather goods at night and chewed up part of Ed's saddle. Without hasty, patchwork repairs by the pony boys, Ed might have had to ride bareback, but at least the creatures had not decided to demolish his boots. Ed picked up an ice-axe after breakfast and went on a fruitless hunt for porcupines. So it was a late start — almost nine — Hickson felt it would be at best a reconnaissance.

"Let's take a walk in the woods towards the glacier on Douglas Haig," Ed suggested. He had ambitious ideas but didn't dare reveal them — not just yet anyway. In barely three hours they reached the ice and continued up it. Ed could see no difficulties above. He turned to Hickson: "Doctor, would you be willing to climb this mountain *today*? We'll be out late, we might have to spend another night the way we did on Quadra and Moloch, but the weather's good. How about it?"

"Lead off," Hickson responded.

It was peaches and cream. They were on top at five, built two huge stonemen, one on each of the twin summits, both visible from Palliser Pass. There was no sign of Aemmer, Fynn or any previous ascent.

The descent was rapid and they reached camp shortly after dark. They had only used the lantern an hour. On arrival, Curly Perillo, one of the pony boys, informed them that the Fynn party had that day pitched its tents at Palliser Pass, half an hour away. Ed turned to Hickson, took a quick swig from the proferred silver flask, then, with a malicious look in his eye, said: "Let's go pay them a visit tomorrow and show them our stoneman."

Next afternoon Ed and Hickson strolled leisurely to the other camp. Only the Eddys and Mrs. Fynn were in residence. Ed asked: "Where are Mr. Fynn and Rudolph on this lovely day?" "Oh, they're out climbing Sir Douglas Haig," said Mrs. Fynn. She pointed to a steep ridge. "They went that way" she said. Ed looked the ridge over, saying nothing. "Looks like a very difficult route" he observed as he sipped Mrs. Fynn's tea. Then he asked: "I wonder why they didn't go our way, where we went yesterday. We even had a chance to build those two big cairns on top." "What? You've already *climbed* the mountain!" "Take a good look at the cairns" Ed insisted. "But don't worry," he addded, "that ridge Rudolph and your husband are on will make a fine *second* ascent."

The ridge was harder than Ed imagined. Fynn and Rudolph never got up. They returned, weary and frustrated, late at night, only to learn about Hickson's and Ed's success. They were furious.

"On our way over the pass the next morning," Ed related, "we met the Fynn party coming down in the other direction. A funny thing happened: for some reason none of them even said 'hello'. In fact, we had to go all the way back to Lake Louise to learn about Rudolph's and Fynn's bad luck. I guess they didn't appreciate what we'd done. But it didn't last — Fynn even said good things about us in the article he wrote for the Canadian Alpine Journal."

After a visit to the French Military Group, where they made the first ascent of Mount Joffre, they returned with a camp en route under Assiniboine.

The weather was beautiful. "I'd almost like to go up there and spend the night on top," Hickson remarked. "No thank you," said Ed, "not another bivouac. But I tell you what: we can traverse the mountain, the way you wanted to." And so they now carried out the plan hatched with Wedgwood eleven years earlier.

Up they went on the north side and along the summit ridge. After an early lunch on the crest they started down the steep snow that had been the line of the first ascent back in 1901 when Sir James Outram had been up there with Haesler and Bohren. At the big ledge, Ed turned to the right and led his clients back to the col between Assiniboine and the smaller Mt. Sturdee, to the southwest. Then they crossed the high glacier to the ledges overlooking their camp by Lake Magog. Once again, Hickson produced the silver flask. "Ed, you rate a double drink for what you did today."

They had been to the North Selkirks, around Lake Louise, into the Southern Rockies and more places than Ed could count. Now Hickson wanted to go into the north country. So in 1920, the very next year, he hired Ray Legace, the Brewster packer at Lake Louise, and one helper with, of course, his guide, Ed, for a three week trip to the Mount Forbes region. Once more Hickson had a tough program. One reward, as usual, was visible as a silver bottle neck that protruded from his hip pocket.

The approach took three days. Hickson wanted to go the hard way. Instead of taking the leisurely route over Bow Pass, the party started at Emerald Lake, went across the Amiskwi, down into the Blaeberry and over Howse Pass, arriving at camp on the banks of Forbes Creek in three days rather than the normal four.

Forbes is one of the great and beautiful peaks of the Rockies. It rises to 11,852 feet in an area of its own between the Lyell and Freshfield country. It had been climbed only once, eighteen years earlier, by the Collie-Outram-Stutfield-Weed team under the guidance of Ed's pet hates, Hans and Christian Kaufmann.

"We'll take the first ascent route" Ed told Hickson, "and find out if those fellows knew anything about climbing."

Hickson and Ed started through heavy timber with overnight camping gear. They reached a deep canyon, described by Outram as a prominent feature on the first ascent route. They found a way

J.W.A. Hickson.
Archives of the Canadian Rockies.

Mt. Forbes. Photo by Glen Boles.

across it, then proceeded through progressively lighter timber, mostly larches.

"Around noon," Ed recalled, "we came to a nice alpine meadow. I poked around here and there with my ice-axe, and found a rusty tin can. 'Doctor,' I exclaimed, 'we're right where they camped — why I even see the ashes from their old fire. Why don't we spend the night here? It's a lovely spot — and we're already up quite a way.' "

"We left the next morning before light and headed for a ridge to the left where the real climbing started. At first it was pleasant with good holds and beautiful slabs. Then, suddenly, it narrowed to a knife-edge with rock that crumbled on all sides. For half an hour I tried to continue but I couldn't get anywhere. For the first time in my life I wished we had pitons. Hickson tried to help, but he just wasn't strong enough. Finally I tried a ledge to the right. It was vertical below for several thousand feet, but I went out and found a hole through the ridge but it was full of ice. I had to chop for a while, a big job, because I could only use one hand. I had to hang on with the other."

"Finally I got through. First I brought up my pack which I'd left with the Doctor. Then I threw the rope down again, and Hickson climbed up the steps I'd nicked in the ice."

"There was rotten shale rock all the rest of the way — very treacherous. But it was not steep anymore and we could walk. Soon we were on snow, and then on top. It was five o'clock, already a long day."

"I looked at the Doctor: 'If those Kaufmann boys came our way, then I have to admit they knew how to climb — but in other ways, they were real scum!' "

"I didn't want to return down that route — too dangerous. There seemed to be an easier way, on snow, to the west. But it was steep, and this late in the day, it was ready to avalanche. So for two more hours we traversed south across little rock ribs and nasty couloirs. Finally we reached the saddle with Forbes Creek way below on the south and Glacier Lake on the north."

"We went down the glacier slowly, carefully, because it was getting dark now. The slope was steep, lots of crevasses, and the snow bridges were weak. Night came. Even with the lantern I could not see well. 'Doctor,' I said, 'We've got to stop. You know what it's like — we've bivouacked before.' Hickson sat down on an ice lump, reached into his rucksack and pulled out the silver flask. 'We can at least have a nip or two to keep warm,' he suggested."

"Around midnight he thought he saw a clump of trees nearby. 'Doctor,' I said, 'You're seeing things. We're over 9,000 feet and trees don't grow that high in the Rockies. We've just got to wait on this cake of ice until light.' I pulled my cap over my ears and leaned on my axe. The Doctor did likewise."

"With daylight we could see. We were off the glacier in twenty minutes, then down a big moraine to a meadow, where I lit a fire

Cathedral Crags. Photo by J.F. Garden.

while Dr. Hickson napped. I heated him a cup of tea because we still had a long way to go through the bush. It was afternoon when we reached camp. We'd been gone almost three days."

"Ray Legace met us. 'I was getting worried,' he said, 'I was ready to go look for you.' "

" 'Never worry about me,' I replied, 'I'm double careful with just two people on those high ridges and big, crevassed glaciers. Besides, you pony boys don't know the mountains well enough. You'd get lost.' "

"Doctor Hickson was very happy, even if it hadn't been a first ascent. He loved to watch me work on long, hard climbs — I think the reason he came every year was to spend at least one night sitting with me on a ledge above nothing. He was so happy, he kept pulling out his flask and offering me a drink every meal all the way home."

Hickson was always restless. He was at the Chateau in 1923 when he learned Ed had never climbed Cathedral Crags. "Take me up," he ordered.

"I'd never been there. I'd seen it: pretty steep near the top, and others told me that last bit was very difficult. Since I'd had my share of bivouacs with the Doctor, I asked Walter to join us. Two guides would be better than one."

"We took the tramway from Louise to Laggan and caught the midnight train to Wapta where, of course, there was nothing but the track, a tiny station and a small section house. It was half past two in the morning, pitch dark, when I lit the lantern and we hit the trail."

"First thing, we had to cross a river, opposite the mountain. The water wasn't swift, but the channel was deep and maybe twenty-five feet across. While Walter held the lantern, I chopped a big tree to cross the stream. I left some branches so the Doctor could hang on. I expected any moment he'd fall in. He always did when crossing water. But this time, no, he made it. Most likely it was because in the darkness he couldn't see the water. Walter and I cheered when he stepped off on the far side."

"By dawn we were at timberline. We walked up a ridge, came to a glacier, and roped up. We had plenty of rope because Walter had brought his, too. We went up the snow quickly — it was frozen solid — then up a long, open couloir that led to the final pinnacle. We had no trouble until we reached a big needle, just one hundred feet from the top. That last bit more than made up for the rest. Walter had to give me a shove from below so I could reach the key handhold. The rest was easy. By eleven, we were on the summit of the highest pinnacle."

" 'Well, Doctor,' I announced, 'this is it.' 'What about those other pinnacles over there?' He pointed to some lower ones. 'Oh, they don't count,' I replied. 'Never mind,' said Hickson, 'we must climb them all!' Always pushing to get the most out of you, he was. So on we went along the ridge, looking straight down at the railroad, which from up here seemed like a child's toy."

"We stopped on the final pinnacle, ate lunch and started down. It was OK until we reached an overhang. I decided to rappel — it was only eighty feet, and we had plenty of rope. 'Nothing doing,' the Doctor announced, 'We must climb down!' He didn't like to rappel and once got into trouble on St. Bride with my father and me a dozen years before. 'What's wrong?' I said, 'It's just an easy rappel.' "

"I argued, I pleaded, I waited. 'If we downclimb,' I said, 'it will take forever, we'll miss the evening train and have to bivouac.' No luck. Finally, Walter offered to give him a double safety with his climbing rope — and still no luck."

"Now I lost my temper and called him names — the only time I ever did with that man. I cursed him out. I yelled, I almost had a tantrum, then I got into the rappel rope, exchanged a few words about what to do next in Swiss with Walter so Hickson wouldn't understand; and slid down the rope to the next ledge. Then I waited some more."

"Nothing happened. For a while there was silence. Then, at last, Walter shouted down in Swiss, 'He's on his way . . . Get ready!' I looked up. There he was, moving slowly, with the rope snarled around him the wrong way, all his weight on his hands, looking like he'd fall any moment and scared stiff. I grabbed his feet, placed them, and sat him down on the ledge. 'Doctor,' I said, 'You're a stubborn, stubborn man!' But he said nothing. He was so upset he wouldn't speak."

"Walter came, we coiled the ropes, then went down into the forest and marched to the stream where I'd cut the tree as a bridge. I warned Walter. 'You watch. Sure as fate, now that it's daylight, the Doctor will fall in the water.' "

"Hickson stepped onto the log, grabbing the branches for support. He got half way, looked down, tottered, and, Ka-Plunk, he was in it up to his neck. I burst out laughing — I couldn't help it. The Doctor swam ashore and crawled out and I helped pull him, laughing all the time. His face was white, he didn't even smile, but he looked at me and said: 'That was quite refreshing.' Those were his last words to Walter or me that day."

"We went with him, soaking wet, to Wapta, rode the train, which, was an hour late, to Laggan, and then took the tram to Louise. The Doctor never opened his mouth, never spoke to us. Two incidents in one day were more than enough. We had wounded his pride. I felt terribly ashamed."

"There was no silver flask that evening, no drink, no handshake, no word of thanks. Hickson disappeared to his quarters. I was sure I'd lost my friend. But in the morning, with the sunshine, I spotted him on the Chateau lawn, and he saw me. He walked over and held out his hand. I said: 'How are you? You were terribly obstinate yesterday, you know, you wouldn't do what was necessary.' 'I know,' he said. He bore no grudge. He paused for a minute, then added: 'Come to my room before dinner tonight, Ed, and we'll share a good stiff one.' "

"And so I did. He just about emptied the flask into the two glasses. I held up mine: 'To my most honored client' I said. He raised his: 'And to my true and loyal friend' was his response."

"That's how it should be among mountaineers. You get into a tight spot, and one of you loses his nerve for a moment, or quarrels with his companions about what to do next. It can be life or death, you know, so it pays to disagree momentarily. Sometimes there are hard words you don't really mean. But when it is over, you're the best of friends again. You don't go around like a peacock never speaking, and hanging up complaints in articles for all to see. Hickson understood things, he was a true mountaineer."

"We climbed together another seventeen years. We rarely had any more fights, just maybe one or two little ones. We understood each other. When he went to Switzerland one year I even found him a guide, Christian Bohren, a good man and a friend of my father. First thing, Hickson fell into a crevasse and Bohren wasn't strong enough to get him out — had to go down to the village and get help. Hickson was in the hole for quite a while and froze some fingers. When they pulled him up, he popped out just like a cork from a champagne bottle."

Time passed and every year Dr. Hickson's leg — the one the horse had fallen on — kept getting worse. His climbs became easier, there were no more long days and bivouacs, no more baptismal river crossings. But when he wanted a guide, Ed was always ready. "He always paid well," Ed said, "But I'd have climbed with him for nothing — we were buddies, you see, just like Rudolph and me in the early days."

Ed continued: "Finally the year came when he just stayed in Montreal. He died in 1956 when he was 83, very suddenly, I'm told. They named a mountain for him — and he deserved it — but it's out in the Coast Range somewhere and I've never seen it."

"I liked the Doctor, I liked him very much. He was very well educated, and sometimes I didn't know what he was talking about. He was stubborn, but I enjoy stubborn people as long, of course, as they're not like Wheeler. You know, I'm kind of stubborn myself. Also, the Doctor always treated me as he did all other men, as an equal. He didn't care whether a person was rich or poor, worked with his brains or hands, or both. What counted was how genuine you were. He was a Scot, you know, and he used to quote a Scottish poet: 'A man's a man for a' that' he would say."

It was almost evening. Uncle Ed, puffing on his pipe, had talked for four hours with only one interruption, when we had asked about Wedgwood. "We really must be going," we said.

"Wait a minute," Ed asked us. He reached into a cupboard. "You're friends, too. You can't leave without a drink." — and he pulled out a battered silver flask. "Dr. Hickson left it for me in his will," Ed said simply.

AJ XXXII-305, Around Lake Louise, Canadian Rockies, in 1918
AAJ I-1, Travel and Ascents South of Banff
CAJ III-40, Two First Ascents in the Rockies
CAJ IX-17, The Ascent of Mount Moloch
CAJ XII-26, A Visit to the Saskatchewan Valley and Mt Forbes

CHAPTER
XIV

A FEW WISE WORDS
FROM UNCLE ED

"All of us at certain moments of our lives need to take
advice and to receive help from other people."

(Alexis Carrel, *Reflections on Life*)

It was our final interview, and it was already late. The blue haze
of tobacco smoke almost hid those great antlers over the fireplace.
Only the nose, with its big, rounded nares and the shiny glass eyes
projected clearly through the fog.

"What" we asked Ed, "Is your advice to climbers?"

Ed took a deep puff. The clouds thickened. He thought a moment.

"Take a guide!" was his reply.

He paused, then went on; "The best climbers often take guides.
Colonel Amery and Katie Gardiner always did. But the guides like
me knew they could have gone anywhere without us. They hired
us because we made things easier, maybe also because we could
tell good stories and sometimes teach them a trick or two."

"It's no shame to take a guide. Even that German fellow, the best
climber of his time, who later became an American, Fritz Wiessner,
when he grew older, he always took guides when he went to the
Alps. But he was careful to choose the best because he wanted to
do hard things: Raymond Lambert, Lionel Terray, Gino Solda —
people like that. I can go one better; Hans Gmoser, one of the finest
modern guides, he always climbs with guides when he goes to
Europe — of course he already knows most of them, personally. But
he also knows they can do a lot of work for him that he'd rather
not do all the time. So take a guide!"

"What about the poor young fellows who can't afford one?"

"I'm coming to that. Nowadays guides are expensive, like
everything else, and there are more people than ever who want to
climb, but very few of the younger ones have any money. There just
aren't any Fields and Harrises around any more. One system they
use in Europe a lot is for young fellows to follow behind a guided

party. But in Canada, even now, there's just not that much climbing, and the country's a lot bigger. Still, if you can't afford a guide, you can always talk to one. We guides are always ready to talk with climbers and give advice. We have a sense of responsibility for everyone in the mountains, not just our clients."

"The best thing is to start out with a good teacher on little cliffs and mountains near home. You can often get a good teacher for almost nothing if you join one of the clubs. It costs you dues, no more. In Canada, there's the Alpine Club and a lot of smaller ones that have good reputations, and if you can't or won't join the Canadian Alpine Club, they can always steer you to a decent outfit."

"There are also professional instructors who charge money; but in the United States you have to watch out because nobody has to pass any government or other tests to call himself a climbing teacher or a guide, the way it is in Canada or Europe. And there are a lot of frauds around who may know a little about this or that, but can get you into a lot of trouble, too. Sometimes they teach you things that are just plain wrong, or stuff that's all right below timberline and near home but more like suicide when you get to the real mountains. The climbing clubs, those with a reputations, like the Alpine Club of Canada, the American Alpine Club, the Seattle outfit called the Mountaineers, and the Appalachian Mountain Club which Professor Fay belonged to, they're all more reliable. At least they've had experience and know which of their members are the best teachers and leaders."

"The main thing is to learn how to walk properly in the mountains and how to use the right techniques. After that, it's all practice."

"Mountaineering is a dangerous sport. It's very important to use good common sense, which is more valuable than any technical ability. Don't exceed your skills — more important, don't exceed the skills of your companions. Always be sure to look after your buddies as much as you would yourself."

"Be careful who you climb with. Guides like me have little choice, but other people can go with whoever they please. It's always better to have a companion who's stronger and better than you because he can teach you a lot. Be a good judge of your companions — don't try anything they're not up to even if you can do it."

"Don't climb alone — at least not unless you've had years and years of experience; and even then it's not a good idea. And always let someone know when to expect you back and what your plans are. Then stick to those plans as closely as possible. If you don't, and anything happens, people won't know where to look for you. It will be Mount Eon and Mrs. Stone all over again."

Ed paused and got ready to digress: 'You know, come to think of it, giving advice about mountain climbing is like what you tell children: most of it is *don't* this and *don't* that. Not too many *dos*. I guess that's the way it is with anything that can be dangerous."

"When you plan a climb, the first thing to do is check the weather. In the Alps, the Rockies, I guess the Coast Range and Alaska, too, you lads have been there, there's no real way of knowing exactly what things will be like twelve hours after you start, when you may be on top or on the way down. But you can get a good general idea. If you're near a radio, you can listen to weather forecasts. They may be no good for the mountain you're climbing, but as a rule, they help. In the Rockies when it's clear in Vancouver, you can be pretty sure good weather is on its way, bcause it usually moves from west to east. Still, it's no guarantee. If you wake in the morning shivering in your bag from a cold night, and the sky is crystal clear, and there's not a cloud to be seen, you can probably count on a good day — even an extra good one, like the time Colonel Amery and I were up Mount Saskatchewan. But if it's warm and humid, and there are a lot of low, long clouds and way above them another layer of streaky ones, like the time the Colonel and I climbed Mount Amery, watch out! You could be in for afternoon thunderstorms or worse."

"Some years you can pretty much predict the weather a week or more in advance. Often there's first a spell of terrible weather that lasts for weeks, and then things clear, not suddenly (that's a bad sign), but gradually, over several days. And after that it's one cloudless day after another, with maybe a thundershower or two when things get too warm; and then more good weather; and if you're an experienced climber you don't have to use the radio or the barometer — you just get a feeling which tells you things will be fine. Other years it storms four days out of five and never really clears up, and you've got to stick to short climbs and don't try the long, hard ones."

"Sooner or later every experienced climber gets caught in bad weather. It is always unpleasant, but it can also be terribly dangerous. A storm can change an easy climb into a nightmare. Those fellows who've only practiced on cliffs in the East are all fair-weather climbers until they get caught by weather somewhere in the Alps or the Rockies. It doesn't matter how well you can climb cliffs below timberline; what counts is how you get out of the mess you and your buddies are in on a mountain like Robson when real bad weather strikes. What you do then, or don't do, that's the test of a real mountaineer."

"That's one reason you must always set out with good equipment and emergency gear. Always check everything first: rope, ice-axe, footwear, everything you need for climbing. Be sure to carry spare clothes and keep them dry — an extra pair of socks, a wool shirt, a sweater, a rain parka and maybe rain pants, mittens, snow goggles if you'll be on the glacier. Don't ever forget matches — and keep them dry, too. Also a headlamp in case you're caught by darkness."

"If it's to be a long climb above timberline, you might need a small stove; and unless you know you'll always be where you can get water, which sometimes isn't easy even when you see it thirty feet away but across a chasm, you should have a canteen. Be sure there's a first-aid kit in the party. Have enough food to last the excursion and a bit left over — candy, sugar, chocolate, bouillon cubes are good. That way, if you're benighted you'll have a bit to eat, some soup and and maybe some tea, enough to fill your stomach. And if you smoke, like me, don't forget your tobacco and be sure not to drop your pipe into a crevasse the way Rudolph did that time on the Illecillewaet. What you want is to be warm, dry and comfortable as much of the time as possible."

"Carry enough equipment, but don't bring too much. Every extra pound tires you and slows you down. People have died because they didn't have enough gear, but some have also died because they had too much and couldn't move easily when they had to. In my time, everything was heavy; but nowadays there's a lot of excellent light-weight stuff around. Unless you're on a long back-packing trip, there's no need to weigh yourself down. Even if you're off on a two-week expedition and don't plan to climb anything really hard, your pack should not weigh over sixty pounds when you start out. You might even manage with less than fifty."

"Unless you've got camping gear or a decent place to hole up, go home if the weather turns bad. Don't wait for the first clap of thunder. If there's an electrical storm coming up, get off the ridges or summits, avoid taking shelter under overhangs — they're very dangerous if there's ground current. Keep as dry and warm as possible. If you're wet, keep moving to prevent getting chilled and wear all your warm clothes. Remember, some of the best moun-taineers, even guides, have been killed in thunderstorms."

"Before you set out you should get information from people who've already done the climb or who know the area, guides, for instance. Study the guidebook, if there is any. Take a large scale topographic map and get trained in how to read it."

"Learn to climb both safely and rapidly. To be safe, you may have to go slow, one man at a time; and safety is more important than speed. But speed is important too, because you may have to cross ground that's dangerous where stuff might fall on you. Also, the longer you're on a mountain, the more you're exposed to its dangers. What you need is efficiency, which combines speed and safety. The only way to be efficient is to practice, and that takes time — often several years. There's a modern Italian mountaineer, they say he's very good, named Rheinhold Messner, and he believes in a combination of speed and safety efficiency. He climbed the North Face of the Eiger, in my Oberland country, a very dangerous climb, in less than a day. Most people take three and usually get hurt, or even killed."

"Remember that a slow, steady pace with few stops will get you up a lot sooner than spurts of energy with huffing and puffing and frequent rests. So learn to keep moving."

"If possible, get an early start. Conditions are usually at their best around daybreak. An early start gets you back early, and gives you extra hours of daylight in case you run into problems. It's a lot easier to move over frozen snow at dawn than to slosh around through mush in mid-afternoon the way Henry Hall did when he tried to climb Columbia in 1924."

"When you get to a glacier you should always rope up as soon as the ice becomes covered with snow, which is called névé. That snow hides crevasses. Sometimes it's thick enough to make a solid bridge, but a lot of times it isn't. Any party on a glacier should consist of three or preferably more people roped together, and they should keep their distance from one another — maybe thirty-forty feet or more in bad places. Where there are crevasses visible, the leader should probe ahead with the ice-axe. If the axe handle goes in too easily, the place should be avoided. The leader should mark any hidden crevasses he finds by drawing a cross with the axe so his companions will know not to step in the wrong place. Every person should carry Prussic slings or something similar so that if he falls into a hole, he can make a stirrup and stand in the rope."

"On a glacier the best bet is to go where there are the fewest crevasses, keep away from the messy stuff if you can. If you have to go through an ice-fall, remember that the biggest crevasses are usually just above it, where everything gets flat again."

"When you are on glaciers, or anywhere on snow, be sure to use your snow goggles, even if the sun isn't shining. It's the ultra-violet rays that can burn your eyes and make you snow blind, and they go right through the clouds. You should use a good cream to protect your face, hands and lips from sunburn. The sun at high altitudes, with snow as a reflector, can get very powerful."

"In the mountains, there's a thing called objective dangers. One is the weather, which I've talked about, and another is crevasses. But a third, extremely dangerous one is avalanches — and yet you can usually avoid them by simply keeping out of places where they occur. There are three kinds of avalanches: rock, snow and ice — or a combination of all three, and some variations. The most likely place for rock avalanches is in gullies. You can usually tell a dangerous one if there's a big pile of rocky junk at the bottom and if any snow in the gully is streaked with dirt. If you have to go into such places, do it in the early morning when things are usually frozen solid. Later, things soften up and it all comes down. I've even seen birds knock rocks down."

"Snow avalanches can happen on almost any slope and are very difficult to predict. Any fresh snowfall should be allowed to settle for anywhere from a day to almost a week depending on the type of fall, the weather and other conditions. Snow over hard ice, especially if there is a melt layer between the two, is especially treacherous. Soft granular snow under a firm surface layer is also extremely dangerous. So is breakable crust. You only learn to judge the safety of snow slopes from experience, but most of all watch out when there has been wind and snow together; this makes very dangerous slabs."

"If you have to deal with a snow slope you are unsure of, go straight up or straight down. Do not cut across it, because that can set the whole thing in motion. Whenever you descend a snow slope, test it first by rolling a few rocks or snowballs down it. If the slope holds, it is probably safe. Or if you start a big enough slide, you may be able to sweep off the dangerous stuff and make the area safe to descend."

"In summer snow avalanches are usually small. But remember a little avalanche can kill you just as dead as a big one."

"Ice avalanches are usually from falling seracs or glacier cliffs. The avalanche that almost killed me in the Death Trap below Abbot Pass was caused by falling ice. Whenever you have to cross a place overhung by seracs or ice-cliffs you should look for places to take shelter if anything happens. One of the best places is the lee side of a big ice block that has already fallen. Better yet, be ready to scramble to high ground like a ridge or rock outcrop — but look out for the wind from the avalanche. It can knock you over a cliff."

"If you get caught try to stay on the surface and keep arms and legs clear. If you get buried, try to keep some air space in front of your face, and raise at least one arm as high as you can. That's what saved me in the Death Trap."

"When you're on skis the first thing to do, if you can, is to get rid of them, because they'll drag you under. Lots of people get killed by avalanches when they're skiing in dangerous places."

"Don't trust any ropes or pitons you find on the mountain. If you must use them, test them first."

"In the Rockies the rock is almost always bad. So keep out of couloirs that act as funnels for everything that falls. Try to stay on the ridges, even if the climbing is harder there."

"When you go on a big snowfield, like the Columbia Icefield, the Freshfields or even the Illecillewaet, carry a compass and maybe mark the way with wands so you can find your way back if it gets foggy."

"Unless you are *sure* of a descent route, go back the way you came. If you must rappel, use a safety rope for all but the last man. When descending difficult places, the best climber should be last unless there's a special reason he should be first."

"Do not glissade down a slope you've not been on before unless there's a clear run-out in snow at the bottom. Do not glissade any slope that ends in rocks or cliffs, except when belayed from above. Never go on any steep snow or ice without first learning how to do a self-arrest with your ice axe."

"If the weather is bad and you are cold and wet, stop at the first good timber on the way down and build a big fire. That's what your matches are for."

Ed stopped. He seemed to have run out of words.

"You said a mouthful, Ed," we commented.

"Yes, and that's not all. Just the general idea. The important thing is to be careful all the time. A really good climber will do things that may look reckless to people who don't know anything about mountains; but if you watch you'll see he takes all kinds of precautions and thinks out every move ahead of time. Caution, caution, caution, that's the thing."

"At least that's what I always tried to tell the young fellows who couldn't pay for guides but who came to see me anyway. We guides, as I already told you, always give advice and information free. That's the way with all real mountaineers — no secrets. I even used to worry about experienced fellows, like Ken Jones, who was also a guide, and Norman Brewster — both fine skiers and good climbers. They used to go out near Glacier in the winter and do the craziest things, like thumb their noses at avalanches and take off up the Asulkan Valley to camp in a blizzard, and then ski everywhere when the sun came out. It wasn't safe. But at least they listened to me part of the time. After all, I was their old Uncle Ed who knew more about mountains than most climbers put together; and a lot of the time they did what I told them — that's the only reason they're still alive."

We asked: "What about accidents?"

Ed puffed more blue smoke and thought a bit. Finally:

"First rule is not to have any accidents at all. But be ready. Know the distress signals and what you should do. Again, people must be able to find you, that's why you must leave a schedule behind. Also you must know first-aid, as we guides do, and you have to have a small medical kit. If someone is injured, at least one person should stay with him while others go for help. If you have to leave him alone, be sure he's tied in and can keep warm with all the clothing he has and any additional stuff you can spare. You'd be surprised how many injured climbers left to themselves have had a second fall and been killed. Be especially careful when you go for help: an accident shakes your nerves and can make you do dangerous things."

"Anything else?" we inquired.

"Yes, no matter how good you are, get in shape before the season starts. Do short, easy climbs first, then, as the days pass, more difficult and longer ones. Save your hardest climbs for the end, when you're really in shape. Even we guides, who keep fit all year round, do that. The only exception I can think of was when Rudolph and I took Palmer to Sir Sandford; we sure had hangovers from Chris' wedding the first day out. So get in shape first. It's just common sense."

Ed was now running short of tobacco. He was getting tired — after all, he was well into his nineties and had been talking almost without interruption all afternoon — but then, of course, he was as good a talker as he was a climber.

"We'd like to go on all night," we said, "but it's getting late and we should go back to the motel."

Ed stared at us briefly. Then he reached out and opened the silver flask. "Not without one for the road — and it's on Dr. Hickson, too!" he urged. We each took a swallow — and almost choked. It wasn't the usual Scotch malt; instead Ed had substituted overproof British Columbian Demerara!

As we recovered slowly and prepared to leave, Bill turned to Ed one last time:

"Look, Ed, you've told us a heap of things, but we're writing a book and I like to be brief. Is there any way you can summarize all this in a few words?"

There was a moment of silence. Then the sky-blue eyes grew maliciously small, the nose sniffed the smoky air, the narrow lips tightened, then parted:

"It's like I told you before, Bill. TAKE A GUIDE!"

CHAPTER
XV

HOME IS THE HUNTER

"Farewell to the mountains, high covered with snow,
Farewell to the straths and green valleys below;
Farewell to the forests and wild-hanging woods,
Farewell to the torrents and loud-pouring floods.
My heart's in the Highlands, my heart is not here,
My heart's in the Highlands, a-chasing the deer,
A-chasing the wild deer and following the roe —
My heart's in the Highlands wherever I go."

Robert Burns: *"My Heart's in the Highlands."*

Several dates may be used as the year of Uncle Ed's retirement. The most appropriate is 1949 when he ceased working as a Canadian Pacific employee and took a pension. But any date is misleading, for Ed continued to guide on a free lance basis until 1953, and for many years thereafter went on taking out ancient clients and special friends. He did it because he loved them, because he loved the mountains and most of all because it provided him with a chance to talk about old times with people who understood and appreciated them.

Ed came honestly by his longevity as an alpinist. One day in the summer of 1939, when war was brewing in Europe, he received a postcard from the old country which he showed all over among his friends. It was a picture of the Jungfrau, where he had made his initial big climb forty two years before. More importantly, it was from his father, who had celebrated his eightieth birthday by making yet another ascent of this beautiful mountain.

In many ways Ed never retired. Every year until his death he somehow managed to go high on the glaciers, way above timberline at least once and, more often, several times each summer season. He was over eighty-five when he made the last of a hundred-odd ascents on foot to Abbot Pass, straight through the Death Trap which had once almost cost him his life and then on to the summit of

Mount Victoria for a CBC documentary. A few years earlier he was seen with tears in his eyes at the head of Bugaboo Glacier, whither the modern leader of Canadian guiding, Hans Gmoser, had transported him by helicopter. In Ed's ninetieth year Hans also took him to a cabin high up beside the Granite Glacier where Ed could look up at the summit of Mt Adamant which he had so briefly visited sixty-five years before. At age ninety-five, the year before his death, there was time for a similar brief flight to a mountain cabin at timberline in the hitherto almost inaccessible wilderness of the legendary Battle Range. He loved every moment of it. Ed's heart, like that of all true guides, was always in the Highlands.

Like the old bull elks he was fond of hunting, mostly without success, Ed never once relinquished his grip on the herd over which he had long since established ascendency. If Hans Gmoser had become the dean of Canadian guides, Ed, with a standing ovation from all who had ever known him as a mountaineer, had been promoted to patriarch, and he relished the role. To the very end his speech was constant, his voice loud and clear, his opinions trenchant, his prejudices unwavering. The Oberland origins never faded.

His was a simple mind. There were the good guys and the bad guys — and precious little in between. Ed's petulance and obstinacy never surrendered. "Arthur Wheeler was too bossy; Edward Whymper was a drunk; the Kaufmann brothers were crooks; Albert MacCarthy, a martinet." Ed might grudgingly concede them elements of greatness but, in general, these men and certain others were the devils. A very few were in between, such as the Fuhrer brothers who "didn't know how to climb Mount Robson," or Val Fynn "who tried to steal our climbs" (forgetting, of course, that it was probably the other way around). And then there were some friends who always deserved modest criticism; Howard Palmer, the "strong explorer" who was "no mountaineer"; Norman Brewster and Ken Jones "who took too many chances, but are alive today, thanks to me"; and modern guides in general, like Hans Gmoser, Sepp Renner, Leo Grillmair and the others "who rely too much on special gear."

Finally, there were the real stalwarts, the persons who climbed well (and paid generously), people like Professors Fay and Holway, the Fields, and Colonel Amery, or those who returned year after year — Thorington, Hall, the Frasers, and above all, that Canadian man of steel, Dr Hickson.

Funny thing. Ed never uttered a word of criticism about his many women clients. He used to complain, like everyone else, that Georgia Engelhard climbed too much like the Canadian Pacific's 2-10-4s when they pulled the eastbound silk trains up the hill out of Field. But in fact the remark was a compliment. As for Kate Gardiner, she was Ed's heroine, not just because she paid big tips, but because she had spirited him into Canadian National territory, where he had taken her up Mount Robson and had at long last climbed the Rockies' highest summit himself.

When asked, Ed always indicated women could be as good mountaineers as men; "and in general they have a lot better morale and a greater respect for the guide!" he insisted. Even when they wore the long skirts, of which he disapproved and which quickly went out of fashion anyway, Ed loved to climb with women. "Some of the girls, you know," he used to say, "they've got a lot of guts."

Ed's wife, Martha, never climbed. She was an Oberland girl of the old school, and in the Oberland the role of a guide's wife was as a Hausfrau, at home, not as a mountain antelope. Martha's devotion was to her man and her children; she lived for little else. Besides, she was afraid of heights.

Once, just once, Ed persuaded her to come above the glaciers. They were stationed at Lake Louise, Ed at the guide's house, Martha at the Tea House. A German lady wanted Ed to take her up Mount Victoria. Martha agreed to join the party as far as the Abbot Pass hut. She did well both coming and going. But during the hours she spent alone at the cabin, while Ed led his client up and down Victoria, she was terrified. She never climbed again; "It's a man's job," she would say.

Martha was one year Ed's senior. She died in 1974 at the age of ninety-one. Nobody ever found out how well or badly she really adjusted to the Canadian 'wilderness'. Her loyalty to Ed and to his career precluded adverse comment. Perhaps not even Ed ever found out. In those first years at Golden she was desperately homesick, frightened of bears and other wildlife, and she yearned for the pleasant amenities of western European surroundings. Later, came adjustment, or at least, accommodation. And she loved Ed whatever his faults. Her loyalty was her strength; no matter what happened, she was, like most mountain people, a survivor.

Ed had been blessed with a staunch and honest wife. In addition, the Lord had endowed him with a loud voice and a facile tongue. It was Ed's mouth, not so much his hands and legs, that made him the leader and later patriarch of Canadian climbers, however much he merited the title in other ways. One intimate friend put it; "Ed became the leader not because he was his father's eldest son, but because he talked longer, yelled louder and complained more frequently than all the rest of the Swiss guides put together."

"Come to think of it," the same observer added, "he had a lot in common with Arthur Wheeler, whom he hated. They could both be pretty crabby and opinionated when they wanted. Maybe that's why they never got along."

Ed had another qualification for leadership, one he really earned. When he retired he had over one hundred first ascents to his credit. There is hardly any other professional guide, living or dead, in Europe, North America, or anywhere, who can match that record. The only person who may come close is Conrad Kain.

Ed never lost his petulance nor his Oberland obstinacy. But in some ways he mellowed as the years passed. For instance, after he had, by his own account, resolved the problem of winter employment, the CPR ceased being a mortal enemy. It remained, however, an antagonist until Ed started collecting his pension in 1949. After that the company slowly became a friend.

"The railroad?" he would ask himself in later years. "It tried to make slaves of us Swiss, but when I taught them that was impossible, that we'd all rather go home, things got a bit better. Of course, I always had to be on guard to make sure nobody pulled another fast one, like making us cut ice for years on end or punch time clocks as caretakers of the Chateau. But, except for stuff like that, the company wasn't all that bad."

"You have to remember that without the CPR there would have been no transportation across Canada, no hotels and no guides. All that beautiful country would have gone to waste. It took men with guts and imagination to put a track through those mountains. There was a good chance it would never be profitable, the company might go bankrupt; or the job could have been impossible, like that sea-level canal the French tried to build in Panama at about the same time. It took even more imagination to start hotels, and for railwaymen to come to understand that some people loved mountains, not just trains, and needed guides. Sure, the CPR made stupid mistakes with me and the other guides; but over the years they've run a pretty good show — solid, conservative and profitable — the way we Swiss run a bank. The CPR isn't like a lot of railroads in the United States; here today, gone tomorrow. The CPR is here to stay."

"Besides, since I retired, they've been good to me. I got a pension and a lifetime pass, and medical care, and a lot of other things. I'm not sorry I worked all those years for the company. I'd do it again if I had the chance. Of course, I'd always fight for my rights; you have to do that with all big outfits, even the government."

Ed's attitude towards the Alpine Club of Canada slowly improved, too. "Once Wheeler was gone, things were fairly good. I was retired and could watch from the sidelines. I didn't have to take those incompetents up the glaciers to teach them about climbing, and I didn't have to hold out my hat for the tips that nobody ever passed out. The Alpine Club camps have been a good way to get people interested in the mountains, and they've got good instructors now, so that beginners can learn something. They're a pretty big outfit these days, and they're getting a good hut system going in the Rockies and Selkirks. Sometimes, though, they get a bit too bureaucratic and don't treat their friends decently, I think that has cost them something over the years."

Unlike many amateur climbers, guides seldom confess to professional error. This is particularly true when an ice-axe, considered

Up to President Pass, 22 July 1952. Bert Wiebrecht, Louis Bergmann and Ed Feuz, leading. H. Bergmann photograph.

Mt. Shaughnessy — now Mt. President — and Mt. McNicoll — now Mt. Vice President — annotated photo by Edward Whymper, 1901.

a badge of authority, is involved. Armand Charlet, the greatest Chamonix guide of his generation, once tested a group of apprentices on the treacherous Whymper Couloir of the Aiguille Verte. For reasons unclear, the lead trainee dropped and lost his ice-axe. Charlet spent the next dozen minutes berating the unlucky culprit in French NCO military language, in front of everyone. "Since you are all so incompetent," he concluded, "I'll take the lead." Five minutes later the mountain dealt out poetic justice. A chunk of ice proved too tough, Charlet lost his grip, and his ice-axe flew down the mountain. At once, cool and collected, he turned to his wards; "I did that on purpose" he lied, "to teach you numbskulls a lesson. Now, I will show you how a real guide leads the Whymper Couloir, without an ice-axe". And up he went with the others incredulously tagging behind.

Ed had a somewhat similar experience, but not until 1952, when he was almost seventy. He had taken Dr. and Mrs. Bert Wiebrecht, old clients, to Stanley Mitchell Hut in the Little Yoho. There the party was joined by Dr. Louis Bergmann and his wife, Herta. Wiebrecht, a Milwaukee dentist, was not allowed 'strenuous climbs' because he presumably had a 'heart condition'.

Next morning Dr. Wiebrecht and Ed, accompanied by the Bergmanns, but leaving Mrs. Wiebrecht behind, set out to "take some movies". Ed, however, set a slow, steady pace and headed for Mount President. To everyone's surprise, except Ed's, all four reached the summit by eleven o'clock. Here, the party split. The Bergmanns set off for Vice-President while Ed and Bert, both getting their second wind, decided to descend by another route and then make the long traverse back to the hut. "It's a good place to make movies," Ed stated.

The Bergmann trip to Vice-president was rapid and successful. They returned to the hut by 2:30 to help Mrs. Wiebrecht prepare a reception meal and cocktails for everyone. The other two, one an alleged invalid, the other a superannuated guide, arrived around 5:00, both still looking fresh and healthy, but with unusually little to say about their excursion. Ed, normally so loquacious, seemed uncommonly quiet and reserved. He hardly opened his mouth except to swallow his cocktail and eat dinner.

The truth emerged next morning. Ed was outside the cabin, out of earshot, sawing wood. In deep secrecy Dr. Wiebrecht whispered to Herta Bergmann that Ed had somehow fumbled a great deal on some ledges, gotten into an awkward position, and then dropped his ice-axe to the bottom of a deep bergschrund where there was no hope of recovery. "Fifty years in the Rockies," Ed complained to Wiebrecht, as the two commiserated after the event, "and I have never, never dropped my axe. I am finished."

Ed was far from finished. He was to remain his peppery self for another twenty-eight years. True, he gave up guiding the following season, after the ice-axe incident, about which he never uttered a word. But he continued to climb with personal friends, usually on an amateur basis; and on the slopes he remained their boss. Once on Mount Odaray a member of his party dropped a lens filter, which promptly started to slide down the frozen slope gathering speed. The owner jumped to retrieve his property, only to find himself brought up short on the rope by Ed. "Let it go, doctor, let it go! It's not very important if you fall down the mountain, but it's very important for me!"

In later years Ed spent many hours each summer comfortably seated with his pipe on the Chateau Lake Louise lawn, basking in the sun, enjoying the view and watching climbing parties on Lefroy and Victoria through his telescope. On one occasion he was approached by a naive, budding young alpinist who asked him "the way up Mount Temple." Ed eyed the novice skeptically. "Go to Moraine Lake," he said. "Follow the valley behind Mount Temple to the big snow slope, then up that to the yellow rock ridge. Climb the ridge. If you don't know what to do after that, you don't belong there. My guess is that you probably don't belong there, anyway. What you need is a guide!"

Ed invariably tried to keep a watch on others climbing, especially guides. No matter how well a colleague behaved, Ed always had a word of criticism. Take the case of Bruno Engler, one of the 'post Feuz' generation. A strong, handsome, gregarious man, a good climber and a superb photographer, he never quite seemed able to meet Ed's standards and thereby qualify as a senior guide. Maybe it was because Ed disapproved of Bruno's many domestic problems, or maybe it was, simply, that Ed saw him as a newcomer. Whatever the reason, no matter how hard Bruno tried, Ed was never satisfied with his performance.

On a summer day in 1960 Bruno led a party from Abbot Pass hut up the usual route on Mount Victoria; all in full sight of Chateau Lake Louise's south lawn, where as Bruno knew, Ed would be watching each move through his telescope. Bruno determined, therefore, to do everything in absolutely perfect accord with Ed's frequently announced precepts. He cut steps quickly and efficiently, kept an eye on his clients, he moved with speed, precision, agility and safety. Belays were few, but firm and prompt. So swift was progress that the party even had time for a second breakfast on the summit where they had views of Lake O'Hara on the south and Lake Louise on the north.

Late that afternoon Bruno brought his party back to Louise. He had, he believed, performed nobly, and for once without some flaw the old man could berate him for. He strode proudly over the lawn to the easy chair where Ed still sat with pipe and telescope. There was a look of disgust on the Master's face. "No, no, NO, Bruno," Ed cried; "next time you pee down O'Hara!" Even as an armchair guide, Ed had a long reach.

Ernest Feuz. N. Morant photograph.

Rudolph Aemmer. N. Morant photograph.

When Ed was not climbing, or watching others climb, he went hunting. His aim had not improved with age, and he continued to blaze away at rocks and trees while the targets scampered out of range. His only great trophy was the giant set of antlers from the moose he had mistakenly killed with a .22 bullet many years earlier on the Chateau Lake Louise lawn. But no matter; next to climbing, hunting was the finest of sports, whatever the results. There was hardly a fall season when Ed failed to oil his rifle and take off into the highlands a'chasing the deer.

Some guides, like Ed, are immortal. But sooner or later, all of them die. Ed was to be the last survivor of his era. Among the Swiss guides in Canada, who belonged to Ed's generation, the first to go was that lover of animals, Chris Haesler, who never quite recovered from the mauling he received from the grizzly bear. Twenty years later, in 1966, aged seventy-seven, Ed's equally competent but often overlooked brother, Ernest, followed; then, back in Switzerland in 1973, Ed's teen-age buddy, Rudolph Aemmer. Brother Walter survived in body, but hardly in mind. In a sense, by the time Ed was eighty-five, they were all gone. Their places had been taken by a younger generation of European-trained guides and ski-professors with a handful of U.S. and Canadian climbers organized around Austrian-born Hans Gmoser, whose modern gear and concepts Ed found so difficult to accept. The newcomers venerated Ed, but he didn't always fully reciprocate. "Very good guides, good climbers," he'd say; "but they carry too much fancy equipment."

Other guides Ed had known also vanished. His father, whom he worshipped and emulated, died in Switzerland in 1944, and war prevented a trip home to attend the funeral. Joseph Biner, who had been Lem Harris' guide on the classic 1924 Icefield trip, went in 1932. Others followed; Bohren, Burgener, the Fuhrer brothers and many more. Christian Kaufmann died in 1930, his brother nine years later — 'and good riddance', Ed would say. Then he'd growl; "Just hope they won't be wherever I go after I'm dead."

Ed's clients and friends slowly disappeared, too. Professor Fay, with the long white beard who could speak a hundred languages, the man Ed championed against the 'wicked' Kaufmann brothers, died in 1931. Alex McCoubrey, the railway engineer who had introduced him to the Purcells, died in 1942; Howard Palmer, of Mount Sir Sandford and Adamant fame, in 1944; the crusty Arthur Wheeler, Ed's frequent antagonist, in 1945; Kaspar Fraser, the pipe-smoking attorney who shared his tobacco with Ed, in 1949; the gentle distinguished statesman, Leopold Amery, in 1955; and Professor Hickson, the hardest blow of all, in 1956. Then Basil Gardom, the innovative farmer and later CPR superintendent of construction, in 1961; Charlie Deutschman, the speleologist of Cougar valley and Ed's first real Canadian friend, in 1962; Caroline Hinman, who introduced so many affluent young ladies to the joys of alpine pack-trains, in 1966; Pete Bergenham, king of the forest and master river-

Walter Feuz. N. Morant photograph.

Edward Feuz, Jr. N. Morant photograph.

rat, in 1971; Jim Simpson, packer, trapper and raconteur extraordinary, in 1972; finally, Kate Gardiner, Ed's favorite woman alpinist, in 1974.

A few remain — at this writing. Bill Field lives in Western Massachusetts; his brother, Freddie, whose self-imposed exile in Mexico finally ended; Lillian Gest, Kate Gardiner's companion on the Mount Bryce adventure, resides near Philadelphia; Henry Hall still attends American Alpine Club and trustee meetings, and signs an occasional check; Roy Thorington sits dreaming alone of the Glittering Mountains; and Georgia Engelhard, long since married to Tony Cromwell, has exchanged the Selkirks and Rockies for more comfortable surroundings in the Oberland only a mile from where Ed was reared.

Ed's two daughters, Gertie and Hedye, long since married, live in Golden. Ernest's three children survive, and a vast brood of other nephews and nieces with their own progeny descended from brother Walter and double sister-in-law, Joanna. The name of Feuz is today almost synonymous with the social establishment of the town where Ed and his family settled with such misgivings in 1912.

By 1980, Ed had devoted close to a century to alpine activity. The great years when he guided from about 1900 to 1950 were a golden age for Canadian mountaineering, never to be repeated. Slowly, the exploits of fifty years climbing took permanent roots in the past and became a part of history.

Edward Feuz, Jr., certified Swiss guide, died quietly in his sleep at his home in Golden during the night of April 13, 1981, near the mid-point of his ninety-sixth year. His ashes were scattered over the mountains he loved. But surely the best of him is busily looking for new summits to climb, or off chasing the deer and the moose among the misty peaks and valleys of a better world than ours.

W. L. P. and A. J. K.

APPENDIX "A"
BIOGRAPHICAL

PHILIP STANLEY ABBOT (1867-1896) was a skilled climber and Harvard educated attorney in the employ of the Wisconsin Central Railroad. His death in an unexplained fall from near the summit of Mount Lefroy was, in its time, the most widely publicized mountaineering fatality in the history of North American alpinism.

RUDOLPH AEMMER (1883-1973) received his guide's license in 1907 and came to Canada in 1909, at the same time as Ernest Feuz. He returned to Interlaken the first two winters, but thereafter stayed in Canada from 1912 until his retirement in 1950 except for a brief visit home at Christmastime 1921. He and his wife, Clara, had two sons, both of whom died in 1936; Irvin, the younger, of a kidney ailment in March, and Rudi, Jr. in an automobile crash in September.

SAMUEL EVANS STOKES ALLEN (1874-1945) of Philadelphia, was a Yale graduate, an exploratory alpinist and the pioneer of nomenclature in the Lake Louise area, of which he prepared a map based on his surveys done with W. D. Wilcox in 1893, 1894 and 1895. The last forty years of his life were marred by mental instability and confinement.

LEOPOLD CHARLES MORRIS STENNET AMERY (1873-1955) wrote with erudition on matters of govertent and politics ("The Empire in the New Era" and "The Forward View"). His two volumes "Days of Fresh Air" and "In the Rain and the Sun" describe with humor and zest a series of climbing activities around the world. Amery served twice as President of the Ski Club of Great Britain, was President of the Classical Association and, in 1943 was elected President of the Alpine Club, of which he had then been a member for 44 years. In his valedictory address, when retiring from that office, he noted that "public life is very much like mountaineering. It needs determination and endurance. It needs judgement of what lies ahead and skill in dealing with each problem as you come to it. It needs, not least, a steady head on exposed summits. Above all, one enjoys it for its own sake, whether one gets to the summit or not."

COLONEL FREDERICK G. BELL, M.D. (1883-1971) of Vancouver, was a founding member of the Alpine Club of Canada and its President from 1926 to 1928. He served in various capacities as bacteriologist and hospital administrator, and was for some years surgeon of the CPR liner, "Empress of Russia".

GERTRUDE E. BENHAM (19? -1938) was the first woman to climb Kilimanjaro, solo for the upper 4000 feet. Laconic and reserved, the mountains were her life. She only became a member of the Ladies Alpine Club when elected to Honorary status in 1935. She died at sea on her return from a solo trip across Africa.

PERCY BENNETT (1905-1972) was a popular trail hand who became a rancher but finished his days as Banff Park Warden at Castle Mountain.

PETER BERGENHAM (1886-1971) trapper, riverman and versatile outdoorsman whose special area of expertise was the notorious Bush River. He was one of only two people to successfully run the Surprise Rapids. When on the trail, or in the bush, Pete was notable for his practice of moving for five hours per day, no more — no less — non-stop, rain or shine. His wife, Annie, kept up with him all the way.

JOSEPH BINER (1876-1932) was a distinguished member of an old Zermatt guiding family. He made only one visit to Canada, but had an extensive American clientele when at home in the Valais.

CHRISTIAN BOHREN (1865-1937) the son of Christian, and Elisebeth Gatthard, married a local girl in Grindelwald, Marianna Jossi, who outlived him by thirty-one years. Their son, Christian (1911-1975) was the fourth generation guide of that name. Bohren was in Canada only for the seasons of 1903, 1904, and 1905. There were several other active guides in the Grindelwald area named Christian Bohren around the turn of the century.

JAMES BOYCE (1891-1982) was a partner with Max Brooks, outfitters in Banff. They were both originally employed by Jim Simpson, as were many of the packers later hired by visiting alpinists and hunters. Boyce had business liasons with many other people, but they were never very permanent. He was "difficult to work with" but was Caroline Hinman's favorite outfitter.

JAMES IRVINE BREWSTER (1882-1947) was the most prominent of the four brothers who built the local transport system of the Canadian Rockies. Originally delivering milk, then to occasional guiding, this family came to have meaning in the visit of every tourist through their packtrains, busses and hotels. The entire operation was purchased by the Greyhound Corporation in 1965, but the name lingers on.

JAMES, LORD BRYCE (1838-1922) was a distinguished British historian, jurist and statesman. His historical works included the authoritative dissertation "The American Commonwealth". As a diplomat, he travelled extensively and climbed in many parts of the world. In his honor, in 1898, was named the prominent peak just north of Thompson Pass, first climbed by Sir James Outram in 1902. Lord Bryce was elected President of the Alpine Club in 1899. He was distinguished and loved on both sides of the Atlantic.

HEINRICH BURGENER (1876-1959) son of the famous Alexander Burgener, was born in Eisten near Zermatt and came to Canada only in the employ of Edward Whymper.

FREDERICK KING BUTTERS (1878-1945) was a botanist associated with the University of Minnesota from his entry in the Class of 1899 until his death. He participated in many exploratory ascents in Canada with Howard Palmer and E.W.D. Holway. He was an authority on ferns.

THOMAS EDWARD CHESTER started with the CPR in 1919 in Vancouver and worked his way up, becoming Assistant General Manager of the Western Hotels in 1937, a position he held until 1951. He closed his career in 1955, retiring as Manager of the Empress Hotel in Vancouver. He was "very fond of and close to the Swiss Guides and the Rockies were his favorite location."

CHARLES CLARKE (1878-1935) was one of the interesting "wild cards" of his day. British born, he resided most of his life in Switzerland but worked four years under contract to the CPR, staying over two winters in Western Canada. He applied (unsuccessfully) for a place on the 1921 Everest Reconnaissance Expedition. His father had been court physician to the King of Portugal and retired to Interlaken in 1895.

JOSEPH DANNIKEN was a native of Arolla in the Valais. He was employed as manager of the boat livery at Lake Louise, and his wife as cashier in the hotel dining room. Upon his retirement they returned to Switzerland.

CHARLES HENRY DEUTSCHMAN (1875-1962) was a native of St. Peter, Minnesota who came to Canada after a spell at Cripple Creek in Colorado and discovered Nakimu Caves while on a hunting trip. He promptly recognized their tourist potential and filed a mineral claim for the entire Cougar Valley. Though, with Park status, his claim was disallowed, thereafter he maintained a tea house near the entrance and employed Joseph Butterworth as a guide to those wishing to tour his caves. After the closing of Glacier House he became a mining superintendent in the U.S.A., and died in Connecticut.

HAROLD BAILEY DIXON (1852-1930) was a British gentleman alpinist of only moderate distinction. He gave up the study of Classics in order to enter chemical research and, in time, his professional researches led to the evolution of neon lighting.

CHARLES BROWN EDDY (1872-1951) was a descendent of a distinguished Connecticut family, though at the time of his greatest interest in the mountains of Canada, he was a member of the New York law firm of Simpson, Thatcher and resident in Plainfield, New Jersey. During World War I he was the Associate Director of the United States Railroad Administration, and after the War, Chairman of the League of Nations Greek Refugee Settlement Commission, for which work he was awarded the Grand Cross of the Order of Phoenix.

CHARLES ERNEST FAY (1846-1931) was by far the most famous name of his day in North American alpinism both as a climber and writer on alpine topics. He was a founder and four times President of the Appalachian Mountain Club and a founder and three times President of the American Alpine Club. He maintained a lifetime association with Tufts University as Professor of Modern Languages.

EDWARD FEUZ (1859-1944) was born in Lauterbrunnen, the youngest in a family of six; and in turn the father of the principal figure of this narrative. His wife, Suzanna, was a distant cousin from the Gsteigwiler branch of the Feuz family. He received his guide license in 1881 and was employed by the Canadian Pacific Railway from 1899 through 1911, stationed mostly at the Glacier House.

EDWARD FEUZ, JR. (1884-1981) of Gsteigwiler, Canton of Bern, ascended the Jungfrau at age thirteen. Took out porters license in 1901 and employed by Canadian Pacific Raiload after 1903. In 1906 he became a licensed guide, and was married in 1909 to Martha Heimann. Daughter Gertie born in 1910, and Hedye in 1912. Moved permanently to Canada in 1912. Made first ascent of Mt. Sir Sandford, 1914; first visit to Purcells with McCoubrey, 1919; ascents with Hickson in French and British Military Groups, 1922; ascents in Freshfields with Thorington, 1924; and trip to Columbia Icefield with Field brothers. In 1929 spent five weeks with Amery; in 1937 with Kate Gardiner and Lillian Gest to Trident and Bryce. In 1939 was with Haesler and Kate Gardiner on Robson. Retired from employ of CPR in 1949 and from all formal guiding in 1953. Continued until his death to give interviews and frequent the mountains of Western Canada.

ERNEST FEUZ (1889-1960) was the third son and fourth child of Edward and Suzanna. He came to Canada first in 1909 and stayed over two winters in Glacier to "learn the language". He married Elise Schmidt (1899-   ) in 1912; and lived in Golden thereafter. His family returned to visit Switzerland in 1924 and 1967. Children: Ernest, Jr. 1916; Frederick 1919; Alice (Pollard) 1922.

GOTTFRIED FEUZ (1880-1966) son of Johannes, elder brother of Edward Feuz, was employed by the CPR for six years from 1906 through 1911. After retiring from guiding he and his second wife, Rosa, ran a rooming house in Interlaken.

WALTER FEUZ (1894-1985) younger brother of Edward, Jr. and Ernest, married Joanna Heimann after coming to Glacier. Their numerous offspring have maintained the greatest "presence" in the assimilation of the Swiss guides into the mainstream of the social and economic life of Golden and vicinity.

FREDERICK VANDERBILT FIELD (1905-   ) became a specialist in Far Eastern relations, and one of the editors of "Amerasia". The editorial content of this publication placed him at odds with influential persons in the U.S. Department of State, and in 1955 he became a victim of Senator McCarthy's attentions. His refusal to turn over lists of names caused him to be cited for contempt of Congress, and he served a year in jail for his courage. Subsequently he lived several years in Mexico, and in 1983 published an autobiography "From Right to Left", detailing many of the philosophical views which placed him at odds with a number of his social peers.

WILLIAM OSGOOD FIELD (1904-   ) is a world renowned student of glacial recession and was a long time benefactor and official of the American Geographical Society of New York. He was elected to Honorary Membership in the American Alpine Club in 1976 and awarded the International Glaciological Society's "Seligman Crystal" in 1983 for his many years' study of glacial recession.

JAMES DAVID FORBES (1809-1868) Scots physicist whose most notable scientific work was in the study of the transmission of heat. As a fellow of the Royal Geographical Society he was very supportive of the Palliser Expedition (1859-1863), and in his honor was named the high, sharp peak in the headwaters forks of the North Saskatchewan River. His work in glaciology was contemporaneous with that of Louis Aggasiz.

WILLIAM KASPAR FRASER (1884-1949) was a distinguished authority on Canadian corporate law. A Rhodes scholar, he founded his own firm in 1928, now one of Toronto's most prestigious. His wife, Lois, was a strong climber and accompanied him on his mountaineering trips. His father had been a highly respected professor of modern languages at the University of Toronto.

DOUGLAS WILLIAM FRESHFIELD (1845-1934) was probably the greatest all-around alpinist of his age, and was introduced to alpinism by his mother, herself the author of three books on her tours of alpine peaks and valleys. Freshfield became editor of the Alpine Journal in 1872 and was elected President of the Alpine Club in 1893. In the Royal Geographical Society his services were no less distinguished. North of Kickinghorse Pass, a mountain group, glacial system and the prominent peak at its head were named in his honor in 1897 by J. Norman Collie. In his 75th year, Freshfield visited those mountains. The peaks of the Freshfield Group are named for a variety of prominent members of the Alpine Club. Clinton Thomas Dent (1850-1912) elected President in 1887; Frederick T. Pratt Barlow (1843-1892); John Henry Gibbs Bergne, KCB (1842-1909); Charles Pilkington (1850-1919), godfather of Katie Gardiner and President of the Alpine Club in 1896; Albert Frederick Mummery (1855-1896) who lost his life in an attempt on Nanga Parbat in the Himalaya; William Martin, Lord Conway of Allington (1856-1937) President of the Alpine Club in 1902; and Horace Walker (1838-1908) born in Canada and elected President in 1890.

HANS (1897-1957) and HEINRICH (1891-19?) FUHRER of Innert-kirchen, on the east of the Oberland, were employed as guides on Mount Rainier for a number of years before going to Jasper in the employ of "the government". They were good guides, often hired for trips in more distant areas.

VALERE ALFRED FYNN (1870-1929) was born in Russia where his father was a railroad location engineer for the Imperial government. Fynn attended the best technical schools in Switzerland where he then conducted a prosperous electrical manufacturing business. In 1908 he moved to the United States and was employed as a consulting engineer in St. Louis. Here, he invented alternating current motors and achieved international repute. His climbing career in Switzerland included a number of outstanding ascents and was continued with distinction from 1909 through 1924 in Canada.

KATHERINE MAUD GARDINER (1885-1974) was the daughter of Frederick Gardiner (1850-1919) a distinguished alpinist, the first man to reach the highest point of Mount Elbruz in the Caucasus. He took her each season to the Alps, and after his death she continued to climb, not only in the Alps, but extensively in Canada and New Zealand.

BASIL GARDOM (1875-1961) came to Canada at age 17 and commenced homesteading in the Okanagan Valley. After returning from the Boer War he held various jobs in the vicinity of Enderby until 1914 when he bought a farm near Dewdney. When his champion herd of Holsteins was condemned as tubercular, he went to work for the CPR and for twelve years, from 1916, was superintendent of construction for the hotels in the Western Division. He returned to the farm at Dewdney in 1928 and began his dairy business again with Jersey cattle.

LILLIAN GEST (1897-1986) first came to the Rockies in company with Caroline Hinman. She became a regular visitor to these peaks and an official of the American Alpine Club. Her literary emphasis was understandably on Canadian alpinism, and she wrote histories of Lake O'Hara, Moraine Lake and Mount Assiniboine.

ALEXANDER MACLENNAN GORDON (1875-1965) was a native Canadian and persistent climber who studied for the ministry in Europe. He served Presbyterian flocks in several provinces and was a chaplain in both World Wars.

WILLIAM SPOTSWOOD GREEN (1847-1919) ordained in 1872, was incumbent of Carrigaline in Cork during the 1880s and then served as Commissioner of the Irish Fisheries until 1915. He is best known for his mountainering accomplishments in New Zealand in 1882 and his explorations of the Selkirks in 1888 under commission from the Royal Geographical Society.

CHRISTIAN HAESLER (1857-1924) was born in Gsteigwiler and first came to Canada in 1899 with the senior Feuz. He worked for the

CPR during the summers thereafter until 1911. However, after his wife, Emma, died in 1918, he returned to Canada and stayed thereafter with his only son in Golden. His death was by suicide after an argument with his son.

CHRISTIAN HAESLER, JR. (1889-1942) was born in Gsteigwiler and received his guide's license in Meiringen in 1911 in the same class as Hans Fuhrer. He married Rosa Margaritha Feuz (daughter of Rudolph Feuz, whose sister, Suzanna, was the wife of Edward Feuz, Sr.) in 1912 and thereafter lived in Golden. The Haesler family was afflicted with many tragedies. Rosa became dangerously insane and died while in confinement. Their two sons both died in accidents, William Albert (1920-1937) while making a Hallowe'en bomb, and Christian Walter (1915-19?) after a car accident in Kimberly, B. C.

SIR DOUGLAS HAIG (1861-1928) commanded British forces in the Sudan conflict, the Boer War and in India. He was Commander-in-Chief of the British Expeditionary Force during most of the Great War.

HENRY SNOW HALL, JR. (1895-   ) a tireless supporter of alpinism and the world's foremost patron of the sport and its organizations. He served over fifty years as director or officer of the American Alpine Club prior to becoming its Honorary President in 1974.

ROY HARGREAVE and others of his family were highly respected guides and outfitters of the Jasper area and later Mount Robson, Berg Lake and Kinney Lake.

LEMENT UPHAM HARRIS (1904-   ) the second president of the Harvard Mountaineering Club, was business manager of the Harvard Lampoon. He was a frequent climber in the Oberland and Valais until giving up the sport in 1931. A specialist in agricultural land values, he became concerned with rural economic issues, a world traveller and an avowed Communist.

GEORGE M. HARRISON was originally in the employ of the Brewsters, but after 1918 offered a business card inscribed "guide and outfitter; Glacier, B.C. and Banff, Alberta". His younger brother, Bill, was similarly employed participating in countless mountaineering pack trips, and was routinely, as late as 1984, employed as the chief packer for the annual ACC camps.

WILLIAM RANDOLPH HEARST (1863-1951) was born in California and achieved some fame (though others called it notoriety) as editor of the San Francisco Examiner where he perfected the technique later known as 'yellow journalism'. From 1903 to 1907 he served as a member of the U. S. Congress from New York. After 1919 he devoted his principal efforts to the construction of a "castle" at San Simeon, California, later a state park.

HEIMANN sisters of Grindelwald, all emigrated to Canada. MARTHA (1883-1974) married Edward, Jr in 1909 and bore him two daughters, GERTIE (1910-   ), Mrs George Marrs, and HEDYE

(1912-   ), Mrs G. R. Longlands, both of Golden. CLARA, the middle sister, married Peter Gattiker and lived briefly in Golden before settling in Seattle. JOANNA (1892-   ) married Walter Feuz and bore him nine children several of whom remain active in the business and social life of Golden.

JAMES CHALMERS HERDMAN (1855-1910) was a native of Pictou County, Nova Scotia, and came to Alberta in 1885. For nearly twenty years he was pastor of Knox Church in Calgary, in 1903 assuming the position of Superintendent of Presbyterian Missions for the Province of Alberta and Eastern B. C. He was one of the organizers of the Alpine Club of Canada and its first Western Vice-President.

JOSEPH WILLIAM ANDREW HICKSON (1873-1956) was born and lived most of his life in Montreal. He was one of the most persistent patrons of Edward Feuz, making some thirty first ascents with him over a twenty-five year period. He served at various times as President of the Alpine Club of Canada, Honorary Chairman of the Montreal Section, Editor of the Canadian Alpine Journal, and in 1945 was elected an Honorary Member.

CAROLINE BORDEN HINMAN (1884-1966) was a Smith College graduate and occasional school official of Summit, New Jersey. She was an inveterate mountain traveller and led camping and climbing trips to many areas. From 1917 to 1960 her visits to the Canadian Rockies were almost annual affairs, arranged with various outfitters, mostly Jim Boyce.

EDWARD WILLETT DORLAND HOLWAY (1853-1923) was for many years a banker in the Norwegian settlement of Decorah, Iowa. He retired in 1904 to take up his hobby of botany and became Assistant Professor at the University of Minnesota. Though he also climbed elsewhere, his finest mountaineering accomplishments were in Western Canada where he was introduced to alpine techniques by the guide, Jacob Mueller. [The Winneshiek County State Bank, like so many others, closed its doors in 1932, but the banking premises remain in use today by the Decorah State Bank.]

MORITZ INDERBINEN (1856-1926) visited Canada in his early years to "seek his fortune", but soon returned to his home near Zermatt where he became a guide. Having also spent time in England, he had a good command of that language. During his visits to Canada in 1909, 1910, 1911, 1913 and 1920 he was in the employ of such distinguished alpinists as Collie, Freshfield and Mumm, participating in a variety of first ascents and extended alpine explorations.

RICHARD KENNETH JONES (1910-   ) remains western Canada's foremost native-born alpinist. Born on a 'stump farm' near Golden, his education as a doctor was cut short by the Great Depression. Finding employment where he could, in mining, construction, and as a guide, the mountains became his life. At this writing he is not quite a legend, but is well on the way.

CHRISTIAN JORIMANN (1872-1948) was a native of Graubunden and employed as a guide by the CPR intermittently from 1903 for ten years. His wife, Anna, was a cousin of Rosa Haesler. He was not a participant in any noteworthy climbs, and died in Vancouver.

CONRAD KAIN (1883-1934) of Nasswald in the Austrian Tyrol, came to Canada in 1909 with employment at Alpine Club of Canada camps for many years thereafter. He made a number of notable ascents in New Zealand, but was best known for his leading the first ascent of Mount Robson in 1913. A fine and touching semiautobiography of Kain, "Where the Clouds Can Go", was compiled in 1935 by Dr. J. M. Thorington. Kain was widely felt to be the finest alpinist to appear on the Canadian scene. He was a philosopher, friend and companion, loved by all who knew him.

CHRISTIAN KAUFMANN (1872-1939) was born in Grindelwald of a famous guiding family. He received his official guide's license in 1892, and in 1894 was second guide to Winston Churchill on the Wetterhorn. He spent seven weeks in the employ of Tom Longstaff in 1899 and went with Whymper to Canada in 1901. He was with Outram on Mount Bryce and Columbia in 1902, returning each summer thereafter in the employ of the CPR until 1906.

HANS KAUFMANN (1874-1930) first came to Canada with Collie, Stutfield, Woolley and Weed in 1900 and was in Whymper's retinue in 1901. He and Christian were sons of Peter Kaufmann (1850-1929) a distinguished Oberland guide who was in Canada in 1903. The Kaufmann brothers were highly respected by many of the better British and American climbers. They had an excellent command of English, which served them well in their profession. They guided Hudson Stuck, Archdeacon of Alaska, on Mount Victoria in 1904. Their nephew, Peter, also a guide, was party to a number of Canadian climbs in 1930.

CHRISTIAN KLUCKER (1853-1928) a native of Fex, in the Engadine, was the dean of active Swiss guides at the time of his death. He was, among other things, notable for never wearing an overcoat, and made 44 first ascents and 88 new routes in the Alps. He was with Whymper in the Rockies in 1901. Klucker expressed a low opinion of the mountaineering potential near Banff.

RAYMOND LEGACE (1892-1975) was employed in Banff in 1917 by the Brewster Company, and started his own business in 1930. He was an entrepreneur of consequence, having been involved in Skoki Lodge and the Post Hotel. His father was on the CPR survey and is in the picture of the completion of the railway at Craigellachie.

WALLIS WALTER LEFEAUX (1881-1972) came to Canada from London at the age of twenty. He was a land agent and fur trader in Revelstoke for several years, then settled in Vancouver. He became a lawyer and socialist political leader, touring Russia in 1920, thereafter taking an active part in provincial political as well as business affairs.

TOM GEORGE LONGSTAFF (1875-1964) was a medical doctor and alpinist of very great distinction who made twenty visits to the Alps, six to the Himalaya, one to the Caucasus, five to the Arctic and two to Western Canada. He served in various capacities with the Alpine Club and was elected its president in 1947 and an Honorary Member in 1956. He played a very prominent part in the early British attempts on Mount Everest. His younger sister, Katherine Wedgewood, was president of the Ladies Alpine Club in 1929. His younger brother, Frederick Victor Longstaff, (1879-1961) was a Victoria architect, a naval historian, an active participant in Canadian mountaineering, and a devoted patron and chronicler of the Glacier House.

ALBERT HENRY MACCARTHY (1876-1955) was a native of Ames, Iowa, who graduated from the U.S. Naval Academy and, in World War I attained the rank of Captain. He had an extensive business career after his resignation from the active naval service in 1897, and climbed often in the Purcells when he was the proprietor of a ranch near Windermere. He was best known as the leader of the 1925 Mount Logan Expedition, following which he was elected an Honorary Member of the Alpine Club of Canada.

ALEXANDER ADDISON MCCOUBREY (1885-1942) spent his entire adult life in the employ of the Canadian Pacific Railway. As draughtsman and assistant engineer he was largely responsible for locating and building the Kootenay Central branch. He served the Alpine Club of Canada as Vice-President, President and Editor of its Journal. As an alpinist he made numerous first ascents, mostly in the Purcell Range. He was instrumental in the construction of the Stanley Mitchell Hut in the Little Yoho valley.

DAVID MCNICOLL (1852-1916) worked five years for the North British Railway, then in 1883 entered the employ of the Canadian Pacific, becoming General Manager in 1900. He served as Vice-President and on its Board of Directors from 1907 until his death.

HENRI MARTIN (1879-1959) "The Swiss consul in Montreal" from 1912 until 1917, was a native of Geneva who served in foreign relations posts from Berlin (1905) to minister plenipotentiary in Lisbon (1940). He enjoyed a wide respect among his peers and was minister in several countries following his departure from Montreal.

BRIAN MEREDITH a native of Ottawa and diligent skier was at Mount Assiniboine in the spring of 1936 and at Skoki Lodge in 1937. Author of "Escape on Skis" (London, 1938) he was only occasionally employed as a 'flack' by the CPR but was an editor for the Ski Club of Great Britain and the Ski Club of Canada.

FRIEDRICH MICHEL of Meiringen, across the Grosse Scheidegg (Great Divide) from Grindelwald, was only one season in Canada at Glacier House. He did not participate in any noteworthy climbs and was sent back in mid-season because of homesickness.

JACOB MUELLER (1860-1951) was a competent mountaineer as attested by Professor Holway. He was a native of Lauterbrunnen, the son of Jacob, and married Carolina Gaumann but never held a full guide's license and was only two years in Canada at Lake Louise.

SIR RODERICK IMPEY MURCHISON (1792-1871) was a prominent British geologist who identified the Silurian System and became Director General of the Geological Survey of Great Britain. In his capacity as President of the Royal Geographical Society he was a patron of the Palliser Expedition of 1857 to 1860. In his honor was named that peak which the Stony Indians believed to be the highest of all the Rocky Mountains.

SIR JAMES OUTRAM (1864-1925) a graduate of Pembroke College at Cambridge, served as Vicar of St. Peter's Church in Ipswich until 1900 and thereafter lived largely in Canada. He made a number of outstanding first ascents, including that of Mount Assiniboine, but after 1902 made few climbs of note.

HOWARD PALMER (1883-1944) was a graduate of Yale and the Harvard Law School who practiced law in Boston until 1918, following which he devoted his full attentions to the Palmer Brothers Company of New London, bedding manufacturers. After Professor Fay, he, more than any other American, personified mountaineering in all its phases from the tedious drudgery of exploring wrong valleys to the glory of first ascents, the staunch support of its primary organizations and the contemplation of the spiritual aspects of alpinism. A tireless scholar, his classic volume "Mountaineering and Exploration in the Selkirks" remains, to this day, one of the finest examples of alpine literature. It was no coincidence that in the 1945 issue of the American Alpine Journal he contributed an article "More About Mountain Mysticism" as well as the obituary of one of his predecessors as President of the American Alpine Club, while his own obituary was written in three parts by Thorington, Hall and Hickson.

DEAN PEABODY, JR (1888-1951) led the Appalachian Mountain Club members to the Canadian Rockies in 1923 as his first venture in large group leadership. This trip was so successful that a number of similar ones followed. He held a variety of offices in the AMC and the American Alpine Club and was professor of structural engineering at MIT and later professor of architecture at Harvard. He was one of the early proponents of pre-stressed concrete as a building material and achieved wide recognition for his pioneering work in this field.

HARRY ALLISON PERLEY (1849-1933) was a native of New Brunswick who entered the hotel business in Manitoba in 1880. He was the first manager of the Glacier House, opening its doors in October 1887 and serving in that capacity until March 1897. He continued in the hotel business in Calgary and elsewhere, but spent most of his last thirty years in southern California, where he and his wife are buried.

DONALD (CURLY) PHILLIPS (1884-1938) was a guide, packer and mountaineer who became the leading authority on the mountains near Jasper. According to Ed Feuz, Phillips' 1909 attempt on Mount Robson with the Reverend George Kinney was in fact the first ascent, and that of Conrad Kain was only a new route. He was a master of whitewater and died in an avalanche on Mount Elysium.

JOSEPH POLLINGER (1873-1943) was a native of St. Niklaus. His father, Alois, and his son, Adolph, were also guides. He came to Canada with Whymper in 1901, but did not return subsequently. In the Alps he climbed with Amery, Mummery, Collie and Henry L. Stimson, among others. According to Klucker, he was a trencherman.

WILLIAM POTTS was not a prime mover in packing or guiding. He finished his days as chief park warden in Banff. His younger brother, Wattie, was a famous camp cook with an unfortunately insurmountable fondness for John Barleycorn.

RALPH RINK (1885-19?) immigrated from Sweden while quite young. He was a guide and outfitter in the Banff area between the World Wars, and was associated with Wheeler's walking tours to the Assiniboine and Sunshine areas. He retired to White Rock, B.C. about 1940.

PETER SARBACH (1844-1930) of St. Niklaus in the Valais, was in Canada in 1897 with Professor Dixon, Norman Collie and others. He was also guide to Phillip Abbot in Switzerland in 1892.

WALTER SCHAUFFELBERGER (1881-1915) was a native of Zurich who sought unsuccessfully to become employed by the CPR in 1913; but was engaged by the Alpine Club of Canada for that season, and again in 1914. While highly regarded he did not want to settle in Canada and thus did not fit in the CPR plan. He was killed in an avalanche in the Bernina and his body never found.

ALBERT KARL SCHLUNEGGAR (1854-1920) of Wengen, was a large, strong man who came from a long heritage of mountain people, and whose descendents for three subsequent generations have been noteworthy Oberland guides. His son, Johan, died on the Lobhoerner in 1939. His grandson, Karl, (1920-1983) and wife Henriette Arnmann also ran the Cafe Oberland in Wengen.

SIR THOMAS GEORGE SHAUGHNESSY (1853-1923) saw a doubling of the system during his nineteen years as the third president of the Canadian Pacific Railway. He was American by birth and came to the CPR with Van Horne. Under his leadership the mountain hotels and associated amenities were greatly expanded.

JAMES JUSTIN MCCARTHY SIMPSON (1877-1972) the "grand old man of the Rockies", came to these mountains in 1896 from Stamford in Lincolnshire. He became an explorer, trapper, packer and raconteur without peer whose overall knowledge of these mountains was unsurpassed. He worked briefly for the CPR and thereafter largely for himself. Jimmy's camp at Bow Lake (Num-ti-jah) was named for the marten, on whose hide he did quite well. From this spot pack trains accommodated alpinists visiting Canada from 1898 until this tradition faded in the 1940s.

CHARLES BRUCE SISSONS (1879-1965) was a classicist of long Canadian lineage and first principal of Revelstoke High School, serving through the spring of 1908. Thereafter he was noteworthy as a professor of classics at Victoria College. He received his first introduction to the mountains during summers spent as an assistant to the Dominion Topographical Survey crew under Arthur Wheeler.

HARRY SLABODIAN (18? -1959) was of Ukrainian ancestry and came to Alberta in his youth. After a number of years in logging, some of it under contract with the Banff Park, he retired to the plains of eastern Alberta.

ALONZO CECIL (SOAPY) SMITH (1867-1948) was a native of Vermont (like Simon Fraser) and migrated to the mountains of Canada in 1904. He worked intermittently for the Brewster Company and thereafter variously as a camp cook and guide, raising horses on his own in later years.

JOSHUA HARRISON STALLARD (1821-1899) served in various field hospitals during the Crimean War and graduated in 1857 from the Royal College of Physicians and Surgeons. In 1870, he emigrated to San Francisco and established a flourishing practice in Menlo Park.

JAMES ERNEST STENTON (1904-1966) was one of the few natives of Banff to be prominent on the mountain scene. He was a keen conservationist and had served as park warden at Minnewanka for twenty-nine years at the time of his death.

WINTHROP ELLSWORTH STONE (1862-1921) was a native of Chesterfield, N.H. and a graduate of Massachusetts Agricultural College. After considerable postgraduate study, mostly in Europe, he became professor of Chemistry at Purdue, later Vice-President and was President of that University from 1900 until his death. He was introduced to alpinism in 1906 but never became truly expert and lost his life on July 16, 1921 making the first ascent of Mount Eon, near Assiniboine, in one of the more publicized rescue operations of the period. U.S. Chief Justice Harlan Fiske Stone was his younger brother.

SIR FREDERICK CHARLES DOVETON STURDEE (1859-1925) was a distinguished naval officer who commanded the British squadron at the Battle of the Falkland Islands in 1914 and became Admiral of the Fleet in 1921.

CHARLES SPROULL THOMPSON (1869-1921) a native of Maine, was freight and commercial agent for the Illinois Central Railroad in a variety of important communities. He climbed exclusively in western Canada for over a decade, being the first person to ascend the Alexandra River in 1900 and reach the pass which now bears his name.

JAMES MONROE THORINGTON (1895-   ) a doctor of ophthalmology, native of Philadelphia, and tireless scholar of alpinism, "Roy" served the American Alpine Club as the first editor of its Canadian guidebook series and as editor of its noteworthy Journal. He was elected its President in 1941, and to Honorary membership in 1949.

WILLIAM CORNELIUS VAN HORNE (1843-1915) was a railroad executive without peer. Engaged at the recommendation of James Jerome Hill, he pushed construction of the Canadian Pacific with enormous vigor. His poker playing became as legendary as his managerial ability. Upon his retirement from the presidency of the CPR in 1899 he undertook the construction of railroads in Cuba.

VAUX FAMILY: MARY (1870-1940), GEORGE, JR (1863-1927), & WILLIAM, JR (1872-1909) were amateur scientists of distinction. Collectively, they studied the glaciers of western Canada with emphasis on the Illecillewaet. Their studies became the foundation for much of the modern science of glaciology. Mary became the second wife of Charles Doolittle Walcott, director of the Smithsonian Institute and American member of the International Boundary Commission. The brothers both served as Treasurer of the American Alpine Club. George, outliving his younger brother, used his legal training in the cause of penal reform in Pennsylvania, an activity in which his grandfather had been a pioneer.

ARTHUR FELIX WEDGWOOD (1877-1917) fifth generation descendant of Josiah, the potter (and great grand nephew of Charles Darwin) was a civil engineer killed in action as Captain in the 5th North Staffordshire Regiment at Bucquoy in France. His wife, Katherine (1880-1976) whom he married in 1910, was the sister of the Longstaff brothers and an alpinist of distinction in her own right. She was among the party that made the first ascent of Mount Wedgwood.

ARTHUR OLIVER WHEELER (1860-1945) was a native of Kilkenny, Ireland, who took up topographical surveying upon his arrival in Canada in 1876. He had a varied career in government and private service of which his best known accomplishment was the precise triangulation of the Interprovincial Boundary between Alberta and British Columbia. He was instrumental in the organization of the Alpine Club of Canada in 1906 and served first as its president, then its director and later its Honorary President. A prominent peak south of Glacier bears his name.

EDWARD WHYMPER (1840-1911) an artist by heritage and training was commissioned in 1861 to illustrate the second series of "Peaks, Passes and Glaciers". This started him on a career of alpine ascents, explorations and writings that made his name the greatest in the field. The events on the Matterhorn of 14 July 1865 ("The Day the Rope Broke" — R. W. Clark, London, 1965) made him controversial and withdrawn, even if innocent and maligned. He climbed little in the Alps thereafter, but turned his attentions to Greenland, the Andes and the Rockies of Canada. He became a geographer, honored but irascible.

SIR WILLIAM WHYTE (1843-1914) was in 1906 Vice-President of the Western Division of the Canadian Pacific. The highest summits climbed from the first ACC Camp were named for the then current officers of the CPR and later renamed for the titles they bore.

WALTER DWIGHT WILCOX (1869-1949) was a seasoned hiker and the first American writer of importance to visit the "Canadian Alps". A graduate of Yale, who came to these mountains with S. E. S. Allen, he later became Secretary of the American Alpine Club and was an Honorary Member of the Alpine Club of Canada.

HENRIETTA TUZO WILSON (1880-1955) made climbs near Glacier in 1904 and in 1906 made the first ascent of the seventh of the Ten Peaks. The daughter of a Victoria physician, she became less interested in vigorous alpinism after her marriage in 1907. Her son became a world renowned geophysicist, responsible for much of the modern concept of continental drift and related phenomena.

TOM WILSON (1859-1933) assisted Major Rogers in the CPR mountain surveys. After completion of the railroad, he became a guide and outfitter in Banff. His later horse breeding activities at Kootenay Plains were unsuccessful and marred his declining years.

JOSEPH WOOD, JR. (1890-1958) was a well-to-do gentleman farmer of western Pennsylvania, whose father had been a high executive of the Pennsylvania Railroad. He climbed only one season in western Canada, and thereafter principally in the Alps where he owned a home in Gstaad.

JULIA MARY YOUNG (1853-1925) was the daughter of Freedom Hill, a cousin of the famous James Jerome Hill, an early stockholder in the CPR and later the "Empire Builder" who dominated the Great Northern and Burlington Railroads. She was born in Quebec and worked in several of the mountain hotels, training as assistant manager at Field in 1898 and moving up to Glacier House late in 1899. She managed that hotel for twenty years, beloved by both employees and patrons, during which time it became the focal point of North American alpinism. She retired in 1920 and died in Victoria.

APPENDIX "B"
GENEALOGICAL

The following chronology is derived from various sources. Initially, many hours were spent in the Genealogical Library of the Church of Jesus Christ of the Latter Day Saints in Salt Lake City. The major source here was a compilation by Julius Billeter, a professional genealogist who researched several family names in Lauterbrunnen. From this work we were able to reconstruct segments of several family trees, following only the male line (except when female cousins married back into the family). Despite its exhaustive nature, however, this research failed to connect forward effectively into the generations that became famous guides in Canada.

Further efforts by correspondence having produced little, in October 1981, Erica Broman and one of the authors, armed with the segments deduced from Billeter, spent three days in the Zivilstandsamt records of Interlaken, Lauterbrunnen, Grindelwald and Gsteigwiler. Our work in this area was greatly assisted by conversations with Miss Ida Feuz, Ed's next younger sister, who still lives in her father's house and was able to give us the first and family names of all her grandparents. She also affirmed that the maternal line (also named Feuz) were long time residents of Gsteigwiler. From the data thus adduced we were eventually able to pursue the civil records (which coopted the religious ones) in Lauterbrunnen to the point of substantiating considerable confusion in the paternal line, about which more below.

Our research on the maternal line, through Ed's mother, Suzanna, took us to a cousin Emil, a resident of Gsteigwiler, a cousin Hans, who still lives in the home of Ed's stone-mason grandfather, and Johan Ernst Haesler, the village historian and custodian of civil records. Here we were able to carry the common ancestry of Suzanna and her brother, Emil (father of our informant), back through six further generations to one Heinrich Feuz, who married Maria Jossi on 6 November, 1716.

Coincidentally, our Emil's father married a Marianna Feuz, and so we traced her line back through five generations to where it coincided with a line deduced from the Billeter papers. This effort brought us back a total of ten generations, from our informant to Martin Feuz, born in 1606, who married a Christina Rubi, born in 1608. A complete family tree would be an enormous undertaking as each set of parents produced an average of six children, some of whom died in infancy (though the given names were sometimes reused on subsequent issue).

We were less fortunate in researching the paternal line of Edward Feuz, for the civil records of Lauterbrunnen reflect a disorderly condition. Most such records list an individual (generally masculine) and follow it with the names of a wife, or wives, including where known, dates of birth, marriage and death. Then follows a listing of the children of each union in the order of primogeniture. These names are also cross-referenced to where they may appear in records further along, or back, as they relate to other family units. The Billeter research was entirely based on church records which often used the date of baptism rather than of birth, a fact which causes confusion by a matter of weeks, often months, and results in many birth dates being entered as of the first of January.

However, the record relative to Johannes Feuz, born 27 July, 1794, is more than a trifle confusing. It indicates an early liason with one Magdalena Haesler, from which union resulted a son, also Johannes, born 13 April, 1817. Considerably later, on 8 March, 1838, it appears that the elder Johannes married Elizabeth Beuggert, from which union resulted five children, in order: Elizabeth, Friedrich, Margaritha, Johannes, and Peter, listed in that order in the church records, as indicated on the accompanying chart. The civil records, however, list first a Gottfried, born in December 1854, who lived only a few days, and then Edward, born 20 December 1859. After that come the other five children, born on various dates from 19 August, 1838 to 18 December, 1850, but numbered as the third through seventh children of this union. Given this anomaly, or discrepancy, between church and civil records, and given the social practices of that and other times, while it is not biologically impossible for a father to be aged 64, or for a mother to be producing children over a twenty-one year span, it is, however, socially improbable that this record is likely.

A more likely explanation was provided by Fraulein Staeger, daughter of the proprietor of the Hotel Staubbach. She suggested, upon studying the raw data we had accumulated, that the true oldest child of this official union (who later married Josef Abereg and moved out of town), may well have given birth to an illegitimate child that was taken in and brought up by her parents as one of their own. This was, and remains, a common social practice under such conditions. A further possibility is that some confusion may have crept in to do with the son of Magdalena Haesler. He would have been twenty-one at the time Elizabeth Beuggert married, a more likely age than forty-four, to marry a woman capable of bearing children until 1859. In any case, both the civil and church records indicate no ancestral track back beyond Christian Feuz, born in 1765 and Suzanna Buehlmann, born in 1768, the parents of Johannes, and according to the official record, the paternal grandparents of Edward "chief guide of Interlaken" in 1898.

MATERNAL LINE

Martin Feuz 1606 — ?
Christina Rubi 1608 — ?
[+]
Peter Feuz 29/10/1632 — ?
Anna Geiser 1640 — ?
[+]
Heinrich 27/11/1672 — 15/11/1754
Heinrich
Anna Rubi 1675

Maria Jossi
[+]

[+]
Christian 1/1/1708 — 13/7/1766
Christian 15/9/1720 — 2/8/1756
Maria Michel

Margaretha Brunner 9/1723 — 15/12/1762
[+]

[+]
Christian 21/4/1729 — ?

Hans 21/11/1751 — 2/8/1820
Irma Rubin 18/9/1739 — 18/1/1810
Maria Seiler 29/2/1759 — 29/5/1833
[+]

[+]
Christian 2/12/1764 — 3/1/1833
Hans 8/7/1781 — 2/2/1843
Elisabetha Michel 7/4/1771 — 10/2/1843
Margaritha Michel 2/3/1783 — 18/11/1833
[+]

[+]
Christian 4/10/1795 — 10/4/1838
Johannes 4/3/1804 — 17/4/1886

Irma Toni 21/2/1790 — 1/1/1830
Irma Haesler 11/10/1804 — 18/11/1869
[+]

[+]
Johannes 8/6/1826 — 3/6/1900
Johannes 17/2/1826 — 29/8/1904
Anna Abegglen 22/4/1832 — 16/4/1879
Marianna Soltermann 27/8/1826 — 8/1/1897
[+]

[+]
Marianna 12/7/1865 — 7/5/1933
Susanna 15/10/1857 — 28/12/1948**
Emil Feuz 6/2/1871 — 22/3/1962**
Edward Feuz 20/12/1859 — 12/6/1944
[+]

[+]
Emil 14/2/1906

Edward, Jr 27/11/1884 — 13/4/1981

** Siblings

PATERNAL LINE

Christian 1765 — ?
Susanna Buhlmann 1769 — ?
[+]
Johannes 27/7/1794 — ?
 Magdalena Haesler
Elizabetha Beuggert (m 8/3/1838)
[+]
[+]
Johannes 13/4/1817 — ?
Elizabetha 19/3/1838 — 27/2/1862
Josef Aberegg

Friedrich 14/11/1841 — ?
Josephine Weller (m 15/2/1868)

Margaritha 17/7/1844 — ?
Rudolph Isler (m 28/4/69)

Johannes 26/4/1847 — ?
Elizabetha Aemmer (m 27/1/73)

Peter 18/12/1850 — ?

Gottfried 1854 (died young)

Edward 20/12/1859 — 28/12/1948
Susanna Feuz (m 17/10/1884)
[+]

Edward, Jr. 27/11/1884 — 13/4/1981

Martha Heimann

Emil 17/1/1886 — 1960

Ida 1887 (died young)

Ernest 1889 — 1966

Elise Schmidt

Ida Emma 16/10/1890

Frieda 12/9/1892 — ?

Walter 8/1/1894 — 25/1/1985

Johanna Heimann

Alfred Werner 1895 (died young)

Clara 30/3/1897

Max Georg Thomen

Werner 18/7/1898 — 16/10/1918

APPENDIX "C"
A BOHREN STORY
(From the Glacier House Scrapbook)
A Novice on Cheops

Only two persons have been known to climb that mountain, and my informant turned away with a shrug of his shoulders. What better incentive could a youngster have to try it? My previous experience had been to climb Eagle Peak on the day before, of which my chief memories were bruised shins and sore fingers, smoke from forest fires having spoiled the view usually obtainable. This, and climbing Observatory Hill in Greenwich Park, comprised my experience of this fascinating pastime. The pyramid of rock which forms the summit of Cheops had an attraction for me that I seemed incapable of resisting. Stiff? Yes, I was rather, but that I thought would soon wear off.

It was 9:30 on Saturday morning when I saluted the grave and sedate guide, Christian Bohren (who seems to have his full share of the "Peace of the Mountains"), with "Will you take me up Cheops today, Bohren?" He opened his eyes and ejaculated "Why, sure!" In ten minutes we were off up the track in the direction of Rogers Pass at a gait which evidently meant business. At the eastern end of No. 14 shed (about two miles from Glacier House) we struck into the bush and made good time for nearly five minutes.

Then my troubles began, even Scotch knitted stockings will not stay in position when various thorns, broken boughs, etc. are doing their best at every step to pull them off. Here, my guide, who seemed to be prepared for all emergenices, produced a pair of puttees from the depths of his pack and proceeded to bind my stockings on in a way which defied both bush and rock. Have you ever tried scrambling and climbing through bush in a timbered country, over and under fallen trees, through clumps of stout bushes and raspberry canes, slipping over dead branches and stepping into mud holes? If not, I would make bold to suggest that you try, say a few hundred yards.

My pacemaker was sauntering along with an easy swing, logs and rocks apparently not disturbing his equanimity in the slightest degree, while the perspiration was dropping from me in a way that promised to run me dry in a very short time. About half way through this tangled mass I had the pleasure of adding a, to me, new experience to my list, in the shape of the enmity of a tribe of wasps. I wonder what I did to cause such a commotion, or did they consider that I was getting too far behind my guide and proceed to hasten me as much as they could? However that may be, they commenced operations on a scale that caused me to bolt over logs and through bushes as if I were mad. What is a wasp sting like? I should think that red hot pins applied to one's face and neck would give some idea. With a yell, I made off after Christian who looked at me with surprise written all over his countenance, apparently thinking I had gone mad. By this time I had killed about a dozen of the attacking force and the remainder retired in good order, evidently considering they had done their duty and driven me from their castle. Mopping my face, I excitedly exclaimed, "Wasps!". To which the man whom I'd bought for the day, leisurely replied, "Vaspen? Ya. Vaspen vairy bad dis year."

He is a cool man, this Christian Bohren, his English is certainly weak, but he had my body hanging at the end of his rope several times that day, and I would not hesitate to trust it there again. Nothing in the shape of a precipice or wall of ice or snow seemed to disturb him in the least. He would stand and chop holes in the ice at the top of a five hundred foot precipice, with nothing but a few inches of ice between him and the next life, looking as if nothing were at all out of the ordinary, even with a novice at the end of his rope liable to slip and give him a send-off over the Styz at any minute. I used to think these men earned their money easily, but I have changed my mind entirely. However, I am drifting from my story and must get back to the bush.

We soon reached a creek bed which ran up to the first bench and I was very glad to get my feet onto the rocks and do an hour up this irregular stairway. There were loose rocks and I got wet, but what did that matter; it was far preferable to wasps and fallen trees. At the top of this creek we reached a small plain strewn with boulders and sparsely covered with grass. Here, my guide informed me, goats grazed. At least, I presume that was what he meant when he pointed to the grass and said "Goats." It was hot and Christian Bohren reminded me of the motto I had often seen on a furniture mover's van at home, short and concise, but very full of meaning, "Keep Moving."

At this point we rested for fully four or five minutes and then started off for that pyramid which looked farther off than it had an hour and a half before. We walked up for a few hundred feet on a nice, hard bed of snow and then got onto a stretch of loose rock that would have had a very trying effect on my temper if it had not been for the absolute serenity of that guide. Rocks did not seem to turn under his feet, the snow beneath did not let him through and the heat seemed to suit him admirably.

In this way we proceeded for about half an hour when suddenly I heard a slight rumbling and my guide, shouting "ROCKS!", did a sprint for a hundred yards that would have done credit to a mountain goat. I followed at a more clumsy gait, but kept well out of the track of those rocks which thundered down like a waterfall in the spring. Bohren just glanced up, as if he had been dodging rocks all his life, and said, "this way", pointing to a mass of solid rock and snow that bordered the rock slide. We negotiated this in about an hour of climbing and then reached a small snow field which ended in a solid wall of ice and frozen snow that seemed to me to effectually bar all further progress.

We were nearly at the base of the pyramid, and our position I will try to describe as well as I can remember it. We had reached what might roughly be described as the apex of a triangular field of snow. To our right a few rocks edged a precipice which, on inquiry, my guide informed me, was about 500 feet deep and sheer drop, too, which would not have troubled us had we slipped over. A few yards higher up and we walked along a ridge of snow, with this accomodating precipice on one side and a fissure in the glacier on the other. This ridge widened to the before-mentioned wall of ice.

I planted my feet firmly in the snow and stuck my ice axe in as far as possible and said to myself, for the second or third time, "Well, you are an idiot." I looked over at my guide, who appeared to be sizing me up and who greeted my look with the cool remark, "Preeety steep!" To which I replied, "Yes, a bit," feigning an unconcern which I did not feel. He had not been up Cheops before, and if he had suggested giving it up, I would have easily forgiven him, but this thought apparently did not enter his mind.

Taking his axe, he proceeded to cut steps in the wall (which had a decidedly outward slope) and would have puzzled a cat. Two steps convinced him that even he could not hope to succeed in tackling it at that spot, so he gave it up. After a few minutes search he found a place about twenty feet high with a suspicion of a slope in our favor and which looked, to a green hand like myself, about as good as to climb the wall of a jerry built house. Here Christian commenced to cut holes for our feet and he went up, step by step, with the worser following. We must have looked like flies on a wall. Strange to say, I did not feel at all doubtful as to our safety, although the least slip, as far as I could see, would have shot us down that precipice in double quick time. I saw only the humorous side of it, like a criminal going to execution, a rope around my neck and with the pieces of ice my guide was cutting running down my back in a stream that would have cooled the hottest fire-eater on record.

At last, we reached the top of that wall, the guide keeping a strain on the rope all the way. The next little trouble was a wall of solid rock which formed one side of the base of that pyramid. I had, by now, such faith in the powers of my guide that I half expected to see him swarm up that, too. But he did not try it, a glance showed him a ledge of rock about three or four inches wide which ran around one corner of the pyramid. Away he went, I following the end of that rope feeling it was not worse than the snow wall. Around this corner we got onto a mass of loose rock through which we climbed to the top. Here my guide astonished me by giving vent to a shout, while I selected a soft rock to lie on in the sun and demolish my share of the fruit in our luncheon bag.

The summit commands a splendid view of the local scenery, but long distance views were spoiled by the smoke from forest fires which covered the country with an atmosphere as dense as that of London. We stayed on the summit for 3/4 of an hour; it seemed to me like fifteen minutes. We had taken four hours and thirty minutes to ascend the northerly face, and descended the side facing Ross Peak in two hours and thirty minutes to the railway track at the Ross Peak water tank. Another hour saw us at Glacier House, which I was truly thankful to reach, my feet sore and my body aching all over; but Christain Bohren looked good for the same trip all over again.

The descent on the Ross Peak face was uneventful, principally a grass and rock slope for two thirds of the way, and then bush which I need not describe. We struck several goat tracks which materially assisted us. I found the bush as hard descending as in ascending, it being very slippery. The first sight of the steelway, I hailed with a sigh of relief, but my guide coolly commenced to unwind his puttees as if a climb over Cheops were a walk to give him an appetite. I am trying to solve the problem as to why people (myself in particular) climb mountains.

August 24th 1904

W.W. LeFeaux
Revelstoke   &   London
British Columbia   England

APPENDIX "D"
BIBLIOGRAPHICAL

Further Reading that touches on this narrative

"The Queen's Highway Stuart Cumberland London 1887

"Among the Selkirk Glaciers" William S. Green London 1890

"On the Cars and Off" Douglas Sladen London 1895

"Camping in the Canadian Rockies" Walter D. Wilcox New York 1896

"Climbs and Exploration in the Canadian Rockies" H. E. M. Stutfield & J. Norman Collie London 1903

"In the Heart of the Canadian Rockies" James Outram London 1905

"The Selkirk Range" (2 vols) Arthur O. Wheeler Ottawa 1905

"The Canadian Rockies" Arthur P. Coleman London 1911

"Old Indian Trails" Mary T. S. Schaeffer New York 1911

"Among the Canadian Alps" Lawrence J. Burpee New York 1914

"Mountaineering and Exploration in the Selkirks" Howard Palmer New York 1914

"Campfires in the Canadian Rockies" William T. Hornaday New York 1916

"Sunset Canada" Archie Bell Boston 1918

"Western Avernus" Morley Roberts London 1924

"The Glittering Mountains of Canada" J. Monroe Thorington Philadelphia 1925

"Edward W. D. Holway" Howard Palmer Minneapolis 1931

The Purcell Range of British Columbia" J. Monroe Thorington New York 1946

"In the Rain and the Sun" L. S. Amery London 1946

"The Unknown Mountain" W. A. D. Munday London 1948

"Nil Alienum — Memoirs of C. B. Sissons" Toronto 1964

"Great Days in the Rockies" Carole Harmon Toronto 1978

"Wheeler" Esther Fraser Banff 1978

"Diamond Hitch" Edward J. Hart Banff 1979

"The Mountaineers" Phil Dowling Edmonton 1979

"The Brewster Story" Edward J. Hart Banff 1981

"The Great Glacier and Its House" William L. Putnam New York 1982

"The Selkirks — Nelson's Mountains" J. F. Garden Revelstoke, B.C. 1984

"Climbers Guide to the Rocky Mountains of Canada" — American Alpine Club; 1921, 1930, 1940, 1943, 1953, 1966, 1973, 1974, 1979, 1985.

"Climbers Guide to the Interior Ranges of British Columbia" — American Alpine Club; 1937, 1947, 1955, 1963, 1969, 19071, 1974, 1977, 1985.

APPENDIX "E"
DISCREPANCIES

There are always alternative versions of events; and often the truth is made up of portions of each variant in due proportion. So it is with the story of the Swiss guides in Canada. Some of those variants are very significant and are offered below, not that they change the basic flavor of the narrative we have offered through the words of Edward Feuz, Jr., but because they amplify and explain the main course of the story.

[1 — Chapter I] While possibly untrue, the following story was widely believed to be true, particularly among those who sympathized with France during World War I. It could well have been a fabrication disseminated by French intelligence authorities, and might merit further research by an interested scholar.

Before World War I, the Maggi firm was German-owned. Around 1910, Maggi began placing advertising billboard signs at various crossroads, mostly in Belgium and northern France [the Schlieffen Plan itinerary]. Allegedly these billboards contained coded graphic information which could indicate, to persons in possession of the proper ciphers, certain vital military information, such as the proximity of major intersections, defense points, communications positions, railway bridges, drinking water supplies, etc. The appropriate code books were, of course, believed to be in the possession of German commanders during the fateful days of late summer, 1914. While Maggi's role is unproven, there is considerable evidence to suggest that German forces benefited from substantial intelligence preparations during the first month of their advance into France.

*   *   *   *

[2 — Chapter I] In September, 1896, Dr. Joshua Stallard, an expatriate British medical doctor then living in San Francisco, wrote to then CPR Passenger Traffic Manager, David McNicoll. "I have just returned from a six week holiday spent chiefly in the Rocky and Selkirk Mountains. For the purpose of this letter it is necessary to introduce myself. I am an English physician, a graduate in honors of the London University and one of the oldest members of the Royal College of Physicians......In consequence of serious pecuniary reverses, largely sustained in California, I came to San Francisco where I have resided for 24 years, being for some time President of the San Francisco Polyclinic and one of the Professors in the Post-Graduate Department of the University of California. I have now relinquished my more arduous duties and reside near Stanford University, where I enjoy the friendship of the President, David Starr Jordan, and many of the Faculty."

"During my residence in London, I spent nearly all my holidays in Switzerland and my first visit dates from 1852......I have crossed over nearly all of the snow-clad passes of the Alps, and I have made ascents to the summits of the Breithorn, Monte Rosa, and Mt. Blanc......I have visited all the principal points of interest at Banff, Laggan, Field and Glacier......."

"The scenery of these excursions, in my opinion, equals if it does not exceed any to be found in Switzerland......It seems to me a thousand pities, however, that the attractions of these mountains are so little known......Passengers on your road are compelled to see the Gorge of the Fraser River and the wonders of the Kicking Horse Pass, if forest fires permit it, but not one in a thousand ever hears of the sublimity of Mt. Temple or the glorious panorama of Mt. Abbott, to pass which without a visit is an artistic sin."

"I have no desire to complain of the annotated time table published by the Company, except that it is exclusively taken up by the notice of scenes visible from the observation car, and this is almost the only source of information. The writings of Green and Wilcox were not to be found at Banff, Laggan or Field. Amongst the majority of Hotel Managers there is a remarkable apathy or ignorance. Few of them have personally visited the most interesting points. Mr. Perley is only a partial exception, and it was at my strong invitation that he made his first visit to Asulkan Pass......"

"A great defect of the district is the almost complete absence of well qualified guides......I spent the day with the Fay party before their unfortunate attempt to ascend Mt. Lefroy. I examined the route they proposed to take. I expressed my opinion as to the difficulties to be encountered. Mr. Abbot had done excellent work and was a more experienced mountaineer than any to be found in your district, and yet his inexperience was the cause of his disaster. A true cragsman is reared from childhood, and gets his knowledge as a goat boy, and if the party had been conducted by a competent Swiss guide, the death of Mr. Abbot would not have occurred......"

".....The best Swiss guides earn IN THE SEASON from 8 to 10 francs a day and there are scores who would jump at a contract for constant employment at much less. I would, therefore suggest the importation of a good Swiss guide from Chamounix or Zermatt to conduct visitors to the more difficult points of view, and in the

off season to supervise the construction and repair of trails. . . . . ."
Dr. Stallard's letter went on for several more pages with other suggestions, some of which were later implemented.

In transmitting the letter up to then CPR Vice-president T. G. Shaughnessy, McNicoll noted, "Enclosed is copy of a letter received from a Doctor in California who had visited the Canadian Rockies and Selkirks. It speaks for itself. As you know I have all along been of the opinion that we must provide increased accomodations and facilities in the mountains if we expect people to visit them and stay among them, and I understand a little has been done at Louise, but I think a great deal more needs to be done. The same applies to the different points of interest in the neighborhood of Glacier Station."

On September 26th Shaughnessy passed the message on up to President W. C. Van Horne, adding, "The attached is well worth reading, please return when you are through with it."

This exchange throughout the CPR hierarchy did not bear fruit immediately, but the seed was well planted and when followed up a year later by an exposition on the merits of this thought during a personal visit on the part of the distinguished amateur scientist family of Vaux, from Philadelphia, results were forthcoming.

*   *   *   *

[3 — Chapter I] Mr. O. Eaton Cromwell, a noted American alpinist, and resident of Interlaken, whose wife, Georgia Engelhard, was a regular patron of the Feuz brothers, recounted to one of these authors and Erica Broman a somewhat different version for the willingness of the senior Feuz to make the wrenching annual pilgrimage to Canada.

It seems that Edward Feuz and Christian Haesler were on the Schreckhorn in the late summer of 1896, with a climbing party. The conditions were normal, but on the descent the party was involved in a minor avalanche. The patrons were completely uninvolved, but both guides were swept a few meters down the slope. Haesler extricated himself easily and suffered no ill effects. However, the senior Feuz injured his leg in the slide. The injury was not so serious as to require rescue but it did cause him to be laid up for some weeks upon his return, and in later years cost him considerable loss of mobility in his knee.

The fallout, though, was more serious than the physical disability, for the word spread rapidly throughout the fraternity of guides in the Oberland. Suffering a minor and non-tragic accident was not then, nor is it today, a serious economic misfortune, but it doesn't help. In the competitive arena, where clients are valued as much by their regularity of patronage as by the size of their tips and the tone of their comment in the fuhrerbuch, the "disgrace" associated with the minor accident was enough to give any guide a feeling that some other locality might offer a better economic opportunity.

Thus, Feuz was quick to recognize the favor being done him by the Cook Agency through the good offices of his friend, Clarke, and equally quick to coopt his partner, Haesler, in the Canadian opportunity. It was a chancy venture on their parts, but not unduly so, for Swiss guides had already been to that country and to more remote and dangerous mountains around the world. But it was an adventure, nevertheless, for a family man with strong native ties.

Once the success of the Canadian venture became known, however, Feuz and Haesler were widely regarded as smart men, who had expanded the opportunity for employment of their countrymen, and were hailed as farsighted men of wisdom......all this from a minor snow slide.

The Clarke home, 'Choisee', remains on Alpenstrasse, though now a rooming house and bereft of its once fine view of the Jungfrau. Young Ed Feuz walked by it several times daily on his way to and from school. The schoolhouse itself was replaced by a modern complex in 1970. The Clarke estate included a private chapel (for Catholic worship in a predominantly Protestant environment) and a special 'tower' for viewing the mountains. After Charlie's death, the premises were owned by Margrit Biendl who later joked about all the whiskey bottles she found buried in the garden "so Charlie's sister wouldn't see them."

There was, in fact, no 'chief Guide' in Interlaken. Grindelwald was the headquarters of the Oberland Guides Association.

*　　*　　*　　*

[4 — Chapter VII] Colonel Amery had another son, John, as unlike his much younger brother, Julian, as night is to day. Both were raised by loving and erudite parents, perhaps too loving in the case of John, but certainly not in any sense that harmed the admirable development of Julian. John was from the outset, the bad seed; colorful, bright, a superb linguist, but always getting into trouble from the day he entered school. He was never evil, rather, a born rebel. Long before adulthood he loved expensive and fast automobiles, as well as similar women, including a famous Picadilly prostitute. While this, of itself, could be passed off as the sowing of wild oats, it led to the fringes of embezzlement and then, in 1936, to personal bankruptcy. Ever defiant of convention and of a family that continued to support him despite his faults, he went actively to work on the side of Franco in the Spanish Civil War, served briefly on the front lines, then helped smuggle arms from the French Cagoulards into Spain.

When World War II broke out he was in France. There he consorted with pro-Fascist extremists such as Marcel Deat and Jacques Doriot, continued his riotous living and eventually married a French girl who later died in Berlin under mysterious circumstances. In 1942, in opposition to his native land, not content with a neutral role in the war, and despite the growing likelihood of a

German defeat, he travelled to Berlin and went to work for Hitler's government as a propagandist in both radio and cinema. The Germans used him, but hated his eccentricity. He even visited a British internment camp in Saint Denis, outside Paris, where he tried to persuade his erstwhile countrymen to form a 'free corps' to fight against the Soviets on the Eastern Front. At the end of the war he was captured in Italy and brought back to Britain for trial on charges of high treason.

John, however, had a potentially strong defense; he had taken out Spanish citizenship in early 1939. His ever devoted brother Julian went to Spain and returned with a mountain of corroborating evidence and a battery of Spanish attorneys. In view of the accused's social prominence and an apparently air-tight defense, most observers thought he would be acquitted, or at the most, let off with a suitable judicial spanking.

The courtroom was crowded on the day of the trial. Among the spectators were Julian, and John's still loving mother. But there was no judge, no counsel, no accused. After long delay they appeared, counsel for the Crown, then John with his attorneys; finally came the judge, a very old man, Sir Travers Humphreys, who in Dame Rebecca West's words . . . "presided over his trials with a merciless, humorous, savage, solemn kind of common sense, often shocking everybody in court except the prisoner, who, out on a limb where at last he knew what was what, could see what the old man was driving at . . ."

The charges were read to John, and he was asked to answer.

To the consternation and horror of everyone present, John replied without hesitating; "I plead guilty to all the charges."

Justice Humphreys reminded him of the seriousness of his plea. The prisoner repeated his statement. Again and again Humphreys asked John if he wished to make a statement on his own behalf, and John just as repeatedly refused. His trial lasted eight minutes.

There was no choice, for at that time in Britain the penalty for treason was death. Besides, the spirit of the times demanded vengeance and there was no possibility of commutation. Justice Humphreys, himself more than a passing acquaintance of the Amery family, dropped the black handkerchief. John Amery was hanged. More on this topic may be found in "The Meaning of Treason" by Dame Rebecca West, New York and London, 1947.

*　　　*　　　*

[5 — Chapter IX] The economic rivalry between the Banff oriented CPR, and the 'government' was very real and long lived. The Canadian Northern and Grand Trunk Pacific Railroads both used the Yellowhead Pass after 1910, and thus had a stake in the promotion of the Jasper Park area and its climbing potential. With their final bankruptcies and amalgamation in 1920 into the Canadian National, it all became 'the government', and an ongoing national burden, reaching, for example in 1980, approximately two hundred million dollars; almost exactly the sum paid by the CPR in Federal taxes.

The first Swiss guides were employed at Jasper for the summer season of 1924.

*   *   *

[6 — Chapter X] Fred Field became what is known as "a man of conscience". The scion of a fabulously wealthy family, he, too, became a rebel. Traitor he was not, except, perhaps, to his class. Rather, he followed the dictates of his conscience that privilege and hereditary wealth did not serve the best interests of society and in fact, as manifested throughout history, were simply unfair and the ancillary results, generally unwise.

Turning his back on an upbringing of leisure and the finest schools, he joined first the Socialist Party of the United States, and subsequently, admitted to supporting the Communist Party. Though he never openly advocated the forcible overthrow of the United States government, he became a well known 'fellow traveller', in the days of post-World War II anti-Communist hysteria in America. This brought him to the forefront of attack by the then prominent Senator Joseph McCarthy. His position as the first American Secretary of the Institute for Pacific Relations and then as a functionary of several related enterprises resulted in associations with sympathizers for foreign policies that differed from those then in vogue, and thus brought him into conflict with the right wing and conservative forces in the Legislative branch.

After serving nine months in jail for contempt of Congress (for refusing to turn over a list of names of those providing support for the Civil Rights Bail Fund) in 1953 he left the United States to take up voluntary exile in Mexico; where he stayed for almost thirty years. While there he took up the study of pre-Hispanic Aztec culture and became an authority on the burial 'stamps' which had previously been largely neglected by archeologists.

Having lost, through his political views, the possibility of a considerable inheritance from his great uncle, Frederick Vanderbilt (grandson of the Commodore), who died in 1934 leaving a fortune of seventy-eight million dollars, Fred nevertheless lived in considerable comfort throughout these years of tribulation; though his later years have been marred by economic problems resulting mostly from unwise investments.

The whole saga of Frederick Vanderbilt Field; his evolution of a social conscience, his gradual conversion to support of Communism as what he believed to be the essential step in the economic evolution of mankind, his tribulations at the hands of political shysters such as Senator McCarthy (aided no small bit by the supposedly professional FBI), and his courage under the subsequent adversities; none of it is part of this narrative. But the interested reader can find it all in a volume entitled "From Right to Left", an autobiography published in 1983 by Laurence Hill &

Company of Westport, Connecticut. His political life, however, remains controversial to this day, and there are many who differ with Field's viewpoint.

Lement Upham Harris became a translator and followed a path very similar to his friend, Freddy Field. Theirs was a generation that produced many sincere and able people of conscience, whose outlook caused alarm to their peers, and who, through their idealism, became embroiled in causes with seemingly altruistic goals, but whose methods and manipulators were considerably less idealistic. His brother, John, became an Episcopal clergyman, while Lem sought to ease the plight of Depression-ridden farmers through land ownership changes in the American upper mid-West. He, too, consciously rejected most of an economic heritage of considerable extent. The investment firm whose full name is Smith Barney, Harris Upham & Company was managed by two other brothers, Henry and George.

Harris also paid another price for having the courage of his convictions. During one rural organizing trip in the Depression years, his car was edged off the road into a ditch and barbed wire fence. The resulting crash and injuries left him permanently scarred. His great familiarity with agricultural land usage has provided him, in his later years, with a modest livelihood as a tour guide and travel advisor to those with a global interest in these issues of growing urgency.

*   *   *

APPENDIX "F"
UNCLE ED'S RECORDS ON MOUNTAINS AND FIRST ASCENTS IN THE CANADIAN PACIFIC TERRITORY FROM 1885 UNTIL 1950

NOTE BY THE AUTHORS: In certain respects the records kept by Ed Feuz, Jr., are a bit arbitrary. He also makes certain exceptions to his own rule, but though not grave, the anomalies deserve mention.

Ed's "territory" comprises the Canadian Rockies from the United States border to the northern edge of the Columbia Icefield, where by tacit consent, the mountains then become the "turf" of the Canadian National (formerly the Grand Trunk Pacific and Canadian Northern Railroads). In his list Ed included a few north of that line, but in the following text, such peaks are indicated with asterisks. Ed's territory also includes the entire Purcell Range and the Selkirks with the exception of certain areas, such as the Battle Range, which were inaccessible in his day, or which, like the Templeman Group, were either unknown, extremely distant, or simply not of particular importance or interest. It does not include the Cariboos, into which profesional guides never ventured during this period; nor, with the exception of Mount Begbie, the Monashees.

A very few of the first ascents listed by Ed were actually made after 1949, mostly by his brother, Ernest, who remained active for a few years after Ed formally retired from the CPR.

The most likely points of error involved first ascents by amateur climbers. In some cases Ed did not have the details; and in others the data has been reconstructed by the authors from existing sources, some of which have a few errors.

We have carefully checked Ed's material and believe that, in substance, his data is highly reliable, even though other compilers might come up with slightly different figures. In some cases arguable discrepancy can come about because some mountains have various high points, as Mount Murchison in the Rockies and Mount Dawson in the Selkirks. In other cases, especially those involving the Dominion Topographical Survey, the records are difficult to interpret. In general a few summits under 9000 feet above sea level have been omitted, and more than a few that are under 7000. Like most guides, Ed had a tendency to treat low or unimportant summits in a cavalier fashion. A final point of difference comes in because some parties engaged more than one guide.

Number of guides making first ascents	35
Total number of peaks in the area	1166
First ascents of peaks 1885 through 1949	638
Number of unclimbed summits in 1950	528
Number of peaks where guide led first ascent	396
Peak first ascents with women in the party	159
Number of different men making first ascents	356*
Number of different women making first ascents	76*

*Includes both persons climbing with or without guides

All new routes below are marked with [brackets].

FIRST ASCENTS BY EDWARD FEUZ, JR. (102 total, 78 of peaks)

1903	[Macdonald]
1906	Amgadamo, Tupper, Terminal
1907	Begbie, McGill
1909	Pinnacle, [Victoria Traverse], [Goodsir Traverse], Ptarmigan
1910	Quadra, Cyclone, St. Bride
1911	Richardson, Pika #2, [Ptarmigan]
1912	Sir Sandford, Adamant
1914	[Uto Traverse], Tomatin, Findhorn, Delphine, Slade
1916	Camels
1917	[Whyte Traverse], Moloch
1919	Joffre, [Beatty], Sir Douglas Haig
1920	[Athabaska W Ridge]
1921	French, Fifi
1922	Gilgit, Solitaire, Nanga Parbat, Trutch, Barnard, [Coronation E Ridge]
1923	Rhondda, Spring Rice
1924	Patterson, Epaulette, Outram, 10800 (Columbia Icefield), [Columbia S Ridge], 9800-(Hamill Gl)
	South Twin, Snow Dome, Hamill, Lady Grey
1925	Devil's Head
1926	[Castle SE Ridge], [Collie E Ridge], [Forbes, W Ridge], Lyell I, [Lyell II], Lyell III, Lyell IV, Lyell V
1928	Nivelle, Mangin, Robertson, [Farnham], Maye, Unnamed 10050
1929	Amery, Llysyfran*, Unnamed *, Unnamed *
1930	[Louis N Face], Pulsatilla, Little Cataract, 10300 Pipestone Gp, Cataract, 10100 Drummond Gl
1931	Klahowya, St. Mary
1933	Smith-Dorrien, [Vaux W Face]

1935	Hanbury
1937	Chephren, Gest Tower, Three Brothers (3),10400 (Pipestone), Queant, [Bryce SW Ridge] Trident
1938	Engelhard Tower, Cromwell Tower, [Andromeda], [Athabaska NW]
1939	[Howse W Gl], White Pyramid, [Prior] [Pilkington]
1940	Hall Tower
1941	Feuz Tower, [Nanga Parbat, W Face], Niverville, Bison Tower
1944	Aries, Stairway

FIRST ASCENTS BY CONRAD KAIN (62 total, 50 of Peaks)

1909	[President N Ridge]
1910	Quintet
1911	Resplendent*
1913	Nasswald*, Robson*
1914	Farnham Tower, Farnham
1915	Terrapin, Birthday, Peter, [Delphine], Spearhead, McCoubrey, Jumbo
1916	Louis, Bugaboo, Howser Spire, Howser Pk, Ethelbert, Black Diamond, Monument, Unnamed N of Monument (3), Karnak, 9850 (Blockhead), Blockhead, Cauldron, Truce
1919	[Jumbo (solo)]
1922	[Castleguard E Ridge], Cleaver
1923	Terrace, Saskatchewan, North Twin
1924	King Edward, Little Alberta, Hooker, Kain, [McDowell NW Ridge], Simon, [Edith Cavell E Ridge]*, [Robson SSW Ridge]*
1928	Commander, [Cleaver], [Cleaver], [Jumbo], Pharaoh Pks, Earl Grey, Christine, [Toby], Katherine, Griswold
1930	Marmolate, Findlay
1933	[Yoho], Trapper, Peyto, Mistaya, Conrad Barbette, Crescent

FIRST ASCENTS BY CHRISTIAN KAUFMANN (45 total, 42 of peaks)

1900	Michel
1901	Stanley, Whymper, Little, Mitre, Whyte, Kern, Vice President, President, Marpole, Collie, Kiwetinok, Isolated, Des Poilus, Trolltinder
1902	Neptuak, Pollinger, Freshfield, Forbes, Mons, Lyell II, Alexandra, Fresnoy, 10025, Wilson, Bryce, Columbia
1903	[Assiniboine N Ridge], Deltaform, Collier, Pope's, Huber, Hungabee, Biddle, Goodsir, Sheol
1904	Ball, 10000 (near Quadra), Fay, Allen, Stephen, [Gordon], [Balfour W Ridge]
1906	Yuzo, Mummery

FIRST ASCENTS BY ERNEST FEUZ (40 total, 19 of peaks)

1910	Green
1911	[Uto]
1913	Duncan, Beaver
1915	[Bonney]
1916	[McGill], Copper Pks
1917	Moloch, [Ursus Minor]
1920	[The Marshall]
1922	King Albert
1925	[Hermit]
1927	Kaufmann, Recondite, Augusta, Lyell IV
1931	[Chancellor W Ridge], [Rogers Traverse], [Bagheera], [Sir Donald], [Terminal], [Bonney]
1933	[Grizzly], [Wheeler], [Huber N Ridge]
1934	[Quadra N Ridge]
1936	[Glacier N Ridge]
1937	[Macoun]
1939	SE Murchison Tower, 10784, [Hanbury W Face], NW Peak, West Pk, Center Pk, NE Pk, North Pk, East Pk, Eastpost
1951	[Victoria NW Ridge], [Narao Traverse]

FIRST ASCENTS BY RUDOLPH AEMMER (33 total, 22 of peaks)

1909	Pinnacle, [Victoria Traverse]
1910	[Assiniboine NW Face], Sunburst
1911	[Richardson E Ridge], Pika, Ptarmigan
1912	Adamant, Sir Sandford
1913	[Lefroy NW Buttress]
1915	[Biddle W Ridge]
1917	[Temple SE Cirque]
1918	[Glacier E Couloir]
1919	King George, Tipperary, The Marshall
1920	[Freshfield S. Ridge]
1922	Prince Albert, Queen Mary, Maude, Birdwood, [Victoria NE Face]
1923	Baker
1925	[Hungabee W Face]
1926	Smuts
1927	Cline, [Wilson NE Slope]
1928	Princess Mary
1934	Byng, Aye, Haiduk, Garth, Valenciennes

FIRST ASCENTS BY WALTER FEUZ (23 total, 20 of peaks)

1928	[Farnham], Maye, [Commander], [Guardsman-W Ridge], 9800 (Starbird Gl)
1929	Abruzzi, Cardona, Prince Edward, Prince Henry

1930   Foch, Sarrail, Petain, Cordonnier, Warrior, Lyautey,
          Bogart, Galatea, Brussilov, Alcantara
1933   Teepee, 10210 (Ottertail Gp), Foster, 9650
1935   9900 (Bugaboo Gl)

FIRST ASCENTS BY CHRIS HAESLER, JR (23 total, 14 of peaks)

1913   Beaver, Duncan
1914   [Uto traverse], Tomatin, Findhorn
1916   [Fox]
1923   Wenkchemna
1924   Iconoclast, [Fox]
1926   [Pope's E Face]
1931   [Neptuak N Face]
1933   [Ennis traverse], Unnamed
1935   [Glacier NW Face]
1936   Weed, Rostrum
1937   Gest Tower, Queant, 10100, [Bryce W Face] Trident
1940   Christian

FIRST ASCENTS BY PETER KAUFMANN (19 total, 15 of peaks)

1930   [Park E Ridge], Ayesha, [Olive N Ridge], St. Nicholas,
          Dolomite, Barlow, Lowe, Conway Skene, 9570 (Freshfield
          Gl), [Forbes N Ridge], Pigeon, Marmolata, Flattop,
          Thimble, Saffron, [Howser Pk], Trikootenay, Findlay

FIRST ASCENTS BY EDWARD FEUZ (18 total, 12 of peaks)

1899   [Sir Donald], Haesler, [Avalanche], [Eagle], [Eagle]
1900   Sifton, Swanzy
1902   Macoun
1903   [Macdonald], [Sir Donald]
1904   Hermit, Fleming, Grant
1907   Douglas
1908   [Sir Donald]
1909   Goodsir
1910   Cyclone, St Bride

FIRST ASCENTS BY JOSEPH POLLINGER (14 total, 13 of peaks)

1901   Stanley, Whymper, Mitre, Whyte, President, Vice
          President, Marpole, Kiwetinok, Kerr, Isolated,
          Des Poilus, Trolltinder, Collie, [Micheal]

FIRST ASCENTS BY HANS KAUFMANN (13 total, 13 of peaks)

1901   Bowlen, Eiffel
1902   Howse, Murchison NW, Freshfield, Forbes,
1903   Bident, Biddle, Hungabee, Stephen, Deltaform
1904   Crowsnest, Ball

FIRST ASCENTS BY CHRISTIAN HAESLER (11 total, 10 of peaks)

1899	Haesler, [Sir Donald]
1900	Mollison, Cathedral Crags
1901	Lunette, Assiniboine, Chancellor, Vaux
1903	Goodsir South, Daly, [Assiniboine N Ridge]

FIRST ASCENTS BY GOTTFRIED FEUZ (11 total, 6 of peaks)

1906	Tupper, Mummery, Amgadamo
1907	[Fay N Glacier], Douglas
1908	Aberdeen, [Cathedral Crags], [President traverse]
1909	[Biddle SW Face]
1910	Quadra
1911	Smart

FIRST ASCENTS BY CHRISTIAN KLUCKER (10 total, 10 of peaks)

1901	Stanley, Whymper, Whyte, Cathedral, Marpole, Isolated, Des Poilus, Trolltinder, Collie, Kerr

FIRST ASCENTS BY CHRISTIAN BOHREN (10 total, 7 of peaks)

1901	Lunette, Assiniboine, Wapta
1903	Haddo, [Mitre], Huber, Daly
1904	[Sir Donald, [Clark Pk], [Bonney]

FIRST ASCENTS BY PETER SARBACH (7 total, 7 of peaks)

1897	Lefroy, Victoria, Gordon, 9750 (Peyto Gl), Sarbach, Dome, Pollux

AMATEURS WHO MADE MORE THAN 10 FIRST ASCENTS — through 1949

O. Eaton Cromwell	54
J. Monroe Thorington	52
Howard Palmer	34
Katherine Gardiner	33
Georgia Engelhard	32
Albert H. MacCarthy	30 (ex Robson)
Sir James Outram	28
Professor J. W. A. Hickson	28
Elizabeth Larned MacCarthy	26
Professor E. W. D. Holway	25
Margaret Stone	23
Professor F. K. Butters	20
Dr. Winthrop E. Stone	18
Alexander McCoubrey	18
Dr. Sterling Hendricks	18
J. Norman Collie	16
Professor Charles Ernest Fay	14

Ed Feuz and wife of New York's Fire Chief on Saddleback ca. 1910.
Archives of the Canadian Rockies.

INDEX